John Dowden

The Celtic Church in Scotland

Being an Introduction to the History of the Christian Church in Scotland down to

the Death of Saint Margaret

John Dowden

The Celtic Church in Scotland
Being an Introduction to the History of the Christian Church in Scotland down to the Death of Saint Margaret

ISBN/EAN: 9783337131135

Printed in Europe, USA, Canada, Australia, Japan

Cover: Foto ©ninafisch / pixelio.de

More available books at **www.hansebooks.com**

THE CELTIC CHURCH IN SCOTLAND;

BEING AN INTRODUCTION TO THE HISTORY OF THE CHRISTIAN CHURCH IN SCOTLAND DOWN TO THE DEATH OF SAINT MARGARET.

BY

JOHN DOWDEN, D.D.,
BISHOP OF EDINBURGH.

PUBLISHED UNDER THE DIRECTION OF THE TRACT COMMITTEE.

LONDON:
SOCIETY FOR PROMOTING CHRISTIAN KNOWLEDGE,
NORTHUMBERLAND AVENUE, CHARING CROSS, W.C.;
43, QUEEN VICTORIA STREET, E.C.
BRIGHTON: 135, NORTH STREET.
NEW YORK: E. & J. B. YOUNG & CO.
1894.

Richard Clay & Sons, Limited,
London & Bungay.

PREFACE.

THE following pages, some of which were read in a series of Lectures delivered in the Chapter House of St. Mary's Cathedral, Edinburgh, are intended chiefly for those who, while possessing such general information in regard to the history of Scotland as may be reasonably looked for in persons of education, have not made any special acquaintance with the early history of the Church in this country. I have also, however, had in view the interests of Theological Students, and those of the Clergy and others, who may be induced to investigate the subject more minutely for themselves; and I have accordingly treated with some fullness the original sources of our knowledge in respect to the Celtic Church in Scotland, and have attempted to estimate their value.

For the sake of both classes of readers, I have in many places thought it an advantage to allow the original records to tell their own story. A modern rehandling of the contents of the ancient documents is, no doubt, to a very large extent inevitable, but it is not unattended with loss; and as far as it is feasible there is a real gain in coming, so far as may be, into direct contact with our historical sources.

The true character of the episcopate in the Celtic Church, having been long the subject of an animated controversy, not yet wholly extinct, has been dealt with at a greater length in Chapter XIV. than could otherwise be reasonably claimed for it.

It is hoped that the chapter on the archæology of the Celtic Church may serve to interest some who may be impatient of the treatment of merely documentary evidence.

The fact that the early chapters were delivered as Lectures may be offered as some excuse for the somewhat colloquial style in which they are cast.

I have to express my thanks to Rev. H. J. Lawlor, B.D., Senior Chaplain of Edinburgh Cathedral, for the care he has bestowed upon the revision of the proofs, and for many valuable suggestions; but it would be unfair to him to hold him in any degree responsible for the statements of fact and opinion in the following pages. My thanks are also due to the Rev. Edmund McClure for the valuable Appendix IV. on the epigraph of one of the Kirkmadrine stones.

CONTENTS.

CHAPTER I.
The Roman Possession of Scotland—The Christian Monumental Sculptures at Kirkmadrine, Wigtonshire—The Native Peoples—Their Religion—The Labours of St. Ninian ... ... *p.* 11

CHAPTER II.
St. Patrick a Child of the British Church in Scotland
p. 33

CHAPTER III.
St. Palladius, and his Disciples, St. Ternan and St. Serf—The Origin of the Myth of a non-Episcopal Church in Ancient Scotland ... ... *p.* 40

CHAPTER IV.
St. Mungo (or Kentigern) ... ... *p.* 49

CHAPTER V.
The Historical Character of the Documentary Authorities for the Lives of St. Ninian and St. Mungo *p.* 59

CHAPTER VI.
St. Columba ... ... *p.* 80

CHAPTER VII.
Iona: its Physical Features—The Constitution of the Columban "Family"—Life in the Brotherhood at Iona ... ... *p.* 122

CHAPTER VIII.
The Historical Character of Adamnan's *Life of St. Columba:* The Miraculous Element ... *p.* 135

CHAPTER IX.

St. Adamnan—Iona in the Eighth and Ninth Centuries   p. 144

CHAPTER X.

Influence of Iona in the South: St. Cuthbert in Lothian ... ... p. 157

CHAPTER XI.

The End of the Columban Episcopate in Northumbria—The Diocese of Lindisfarne north of the Tweed—Melrose—Coldingham—Abercorn—The See of Candida Casa as an English Foundation ... p. 177

CHAPTER XII.

The Church in Scotland in the Ninth, Tenth, and Eleventh Centuries—The Culdees ... p. 193

CHAPTER XIII.

The Faith and Ritual of the Celtic Church—The Tonsure and Easter Computation ... ... p. 208

CHAPTER XIV.

The Episcopate in the Celtic Church ... ... p. 250

CHAPTER XV.

St. Margaret of Scotland ... ... p. 267

CHAPTER XVI.

The Archæology of the Celtic Church in Scotland in its Historical Relations ... ... p. 292

APPENDICES.

I. The *Altus* of St. Columba ... ... p. 321
II. The Legend of St. Regulus 329
III. St. Margaret's Gospel Book 331
IV. The Kirkmadrine Epigraph 333

Index 335

LIST OF ILLUSTRATIONS.

1. Representation of St. Luke from the *Book of Deer*. The square ornament on the breast of the figure has been supposed to represent a case, containing the Gospel, suspended from the neck ... *Frontispiece*

2. Sculptured Stone at Kirkmadrine, Wigtonshire   *p.* 17

3. Remains of the ancient Celtic Church on Eilean-na-Naoimh, from a photograph in the possession of Dr. J. Anderson, Keeper of the National Museum of the Antiquaries of Scotland   ...   . *p.* 113

4. Double Bee-hive Cell on Eilean-na-Naoimh, from a photograph in the possession of Dr. J. Anderson   *p.* 293

5. (*a*) The Bell of St. Ninian (hammered iron). (*b*) The Bell of St. Fillan (cast bronze)   ...   ... *p.* 309

6. The " Bachul More." The metal covering has almost disappeared, many rivets are still visible   ... *p.* 313

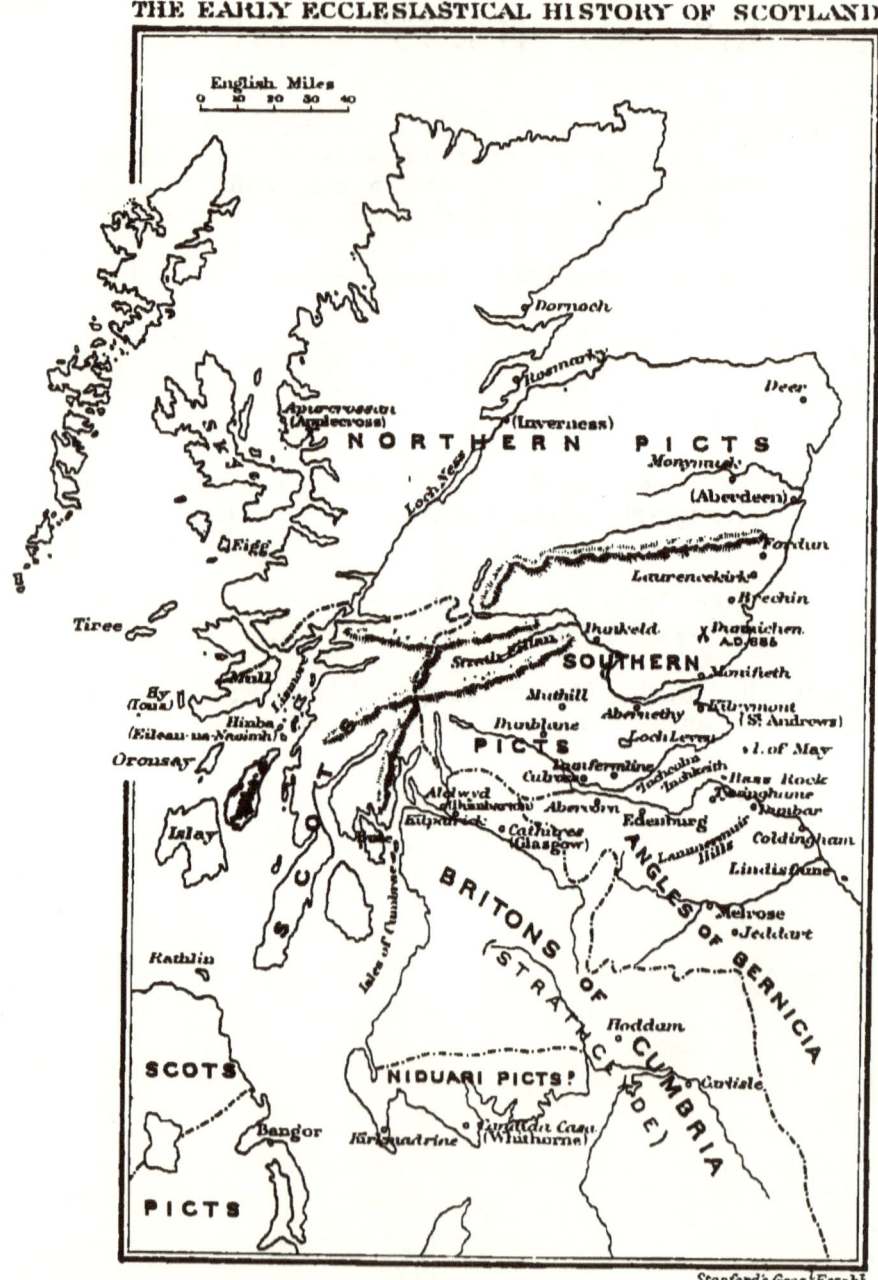

THE CELTIC CHURCH IN SCOTLAND.

CHAPTER I.

THE ROMAN POSSESSION OF SCOTLAND—THE CHRISTIAN MONUMENTAL SCULPTURES AT KIRKMADRINE, WIGTONSHIRE—THE LABOURS OF ST. NINIAN.

WITH a view to our understanding aright the early history of Christianity in Scotland, it is well to recall to mind that the present boundary line between Scotland and England had no existence in the days of the Roman occupation of Britain, nor indeed for many centuries after the last of the Roman legions had quitted the country for ever. The whole island as far as the line between the Firths of Forth and Clyde was known as Britain: north of that line was the region known as Caledonia, or Alban.

The Roman conquest of the island, so fruitful in the beneficent results of civilization, was not permanently effective in the most northern part. In Edinburgh we are close by the furthest outposts of the Empire. The line of forts originally constructed by Agricola, and strengthened in the reign of Antoninus Pius, some fifty years later, by the great rampart stretching from Borrowstowness on the Forth to Kilpatrick on the Clyde, marked for a time the practical limits of the Roman occupation. Occasional military demonstrations, partial and temporary conquests, marchings, counter-marchings, the construction of roads, and encampments of troops in the regions north of the wall might overawe, but could not civilize, the barbarian tribes. In Scotland, north of the wall, there are to be found only some few scanty indications of the existence of Roman civilization.

The rampart of Antonine was not continuously, or for any very lengthened period, maintained as a complete barrier against the barbarian warriors of the north. The northern boundary of the Roman occupation shifted backwards and forwards. We have no reason to suppose that the part of Scotland south of the line that joins the Firths of Forth and Clyde was for any great length of time continuously subjected to Roman control and the beneficent influence of Roman civilization. For long stretches of time the northern boundary was drawn back from the wall of Antonine to the defences of the far greater work— far greater in every sense—the wall of Hadrian, extending between Tynemouth and the Solway, whose massive remains still fill the visitor with wonder, and convey to him a sense not otherwise to be gained in this country of the vast resources and vast power of the Roman Empire. It is south of this southern wall we must look for such remains of civilized life as need for their growth a long-sustained feeling of security.

It was not till approaching the time of the final withdrawal of the Roman troops from Britain that by a great effort of an able commander the debatable land between the two walls—the scene of many contests between the barbarians and the soldiers of the Empire—was again subdued, and formed (A.D. 368) into the fifth Province of Roman Britain, Valentia by name. Unhappily, at longest, only some forty years were now to pass before the urgent necessities of the Empire nearer her centre and capital demanded, for her own protection, the recall of the Roman troops from Britain. In that interval there was little time for doing anything considerable toward the civilizing or Christianizing of the half-subjugated and ever-turbulent British tribes between the walls. South of the southern wall, the wall of Hadrian, when subsequently the Saxons and Angles ravaged the land, it was the invasion of a Christian country by a heathen foe. During the Roman occupation, Roman Britain, speaking generally, had been Christianized. But, in default of positive evidence, it would be hazardous to venture on any large inferences from this fact as to the spread of Christianity, even in that part of Scotland where Roman influence was most felt. It is, however, surely not unreasonable to conjecture that the Roman Christians in the northern settlements, when opportunities offered from time to time, would not have been so entirely deficient in missionary zeal as to make no effort to win to Christ the natives with whom they were brought in contact.

The researches of archæologists have not discovered any Roman remains in Scotland that can with absolute confidence be assigned to the Christianity of the Roman occupation; but there exist some two or three that may possibly belong to that early period. The most ancient Christian memorials in Scotland (indeed perhaps we may say in Great Britain)[1] are certain monumental stones in Wigtonshire. Their characteristics are such as place it beyond question that, if they do not actually belong to the period of the Roman occupation, they can be removed from it only by a short interval, and really represent Romano-British Christianity. The forms of the incised letters of the inscriptions, and the peculiar symbol that combines the sacred monogram with the penal cross, which is well known to students of Christian archæology, and is supposed to have been introduced about the time of Constantine,[2] are most certainly of a

---

[1] "Nowhere in Great Britain is there a Christian record so ancient as the grey, weather-beaten column that now serves as the gatepost of the deserted churchyard of Kirk Madrine . . . . Long may it stand as the first authentic trace of Christian civilization in these islands."—Dean Stanley's *Lectures on the History of the Church of Scotland*, p. 85. Uncertainty still attaches to the ecclesiastical character of the so-called "Church" at the Roman town of Silchester. The Kirkmadrine stones have, since Dean Stanley wrote, been placed under shelter from the weather.

[2] See Mr. R. St. John Tyrwhitt's article "Monogram" in Smith and Cheetham's *Dictionary of Christian Antiquities*. Mr. Tyrwhitt notices that this ⳨ is the only form of monogram found in the Vatican and Sinaitic MSS. of the Bible.

totally different type from the familiar Celtic crosses and Celtic inscriptions so numerous in Ireland and the highlands of Scotland where Irish influence afterwards prevailed. Indeed, the sacred monogram is said not to occur even once among the many hundred early Christian monuments in which Ireland is so rich.[1]

On the monuments at Kirkmadrine in Wigtonshire, to which I refer, the monogram is surrounded by a circle, which, though it may have been merely decorative, more probably possessed a symbolical significance. The circle was taken in early Christian times to suggest the idea of Eternity as being without beginning and without end; and in this connection it is very interesting to observe that the Kirkmadrine stones bear also the familiar symbols A and ω, expressing, in a different way, a similar thought. A monumental inscription at Milan, in which a circle similarly surrounds the sacred monogram, expresses in a Latin couplet the thought suggested by this combination. I may sufficiently render the verses by the two lines—

> "Endless, beginningless, this mystic ring
> Circles the names of the Most Highest King."[2]

Such was the faith of the Christian Church in Scotland as declared in its earliest Christian monuments:—Christ—Christ crucified—was the first and

---

[1] Anderson's *Scotland in Early Christian Times*, second series, p. 253.
[2] Circulus hic summi comprendit nomina regis
Quem sine principio, et sine fine vides.
Cited by Anderson, *ut supra*.

the last, the Alpha and the Omega, the beginning and the end.

But there is another fact borne testimony to by these, the oldest Christian monuments of Scotland. The inscription on one of them shows it to be a monument marking the graves of two priests. " Here lie," so runs the epigraph, " holy and eminent priests, namely, Viventius and Mavorius."[1]

<pre>
HICIACENT
SCIETPRAE
CIPVISACER
DOTESIDES[T]
VIVENTIVS
ETMAVORIVS
</pre>

"Sacerdotes" is the term used, a word that came early into use, and was sometimes employed with reference to both of the highest orders of the ministry —those of Bishops and Presbyters.[2]

These sculptured stones of Kirkmadrine carry us back, without doubt, far beyond the days of St. Columba and the Irish mission, up even to the days of the Roman, or Romano-British, Church. Perhaps we shall not be astray if we attribute these monuments to the Church of St. Ninian, and to a date before the

---

[1] The inscription is thus given in Stuart's *Sculptured Stones of Scotland*.

[2] It was found necessary, when it was sought to be precise, to use, when referring to Presbyters, such forms as *secundi sacerdotes*, or *secundi ordinis sacerdotes* (St. Leo), or *minoris ordinis sacerdotes* (St. Gregory the Great). Hence the *præcipui sacerdotes* of the inscription may conceivably have been bishops. *Summus sacerdos*, as is well known, was used in that sense. *Id est* is so unusual in epigraphs of this kind that I am tempted to conjecture that IDES is the whole or part of a proper name. See App. IV.

B

departure of the Roman legions from the island. These stones, and another ancient cross at Whithorn, possessing some of the same characteristic features, belong to the region Christianized or presided over by the first Bishop whose name has a place in the authentic history of Scotland. They belong to the region where St. Ninian, himself a child of the Romano-British Church, laboured a century and a half before Columba landed on Iona.

Before dealing with the history of St. Ninian, it is desirable to say something of the native population of Scotland at the time of his missionary labours. It is now very generally admitted that the whole native population of the island was made up of various nations or tribes, differing from one another, and it might be differing very widely, in dialect, but all of the one great Celtic stock. The subject of the origin, the race, and the language of the Picts presented in former days a wider battle-ground for the speculations of antiquarians than it does at present. If it be true that controversy upon the subject is not absolutely at rest, it is certain that it would be no longer possible to balance the names of eminent authorities against one another on this side and on that, as was done upon a memorable evening, vivid I am sure in the minds of many of my readers, when the tempers of Sir Arthur Wardour and worthy Mr. Jonathan Oldbuck were so severely tried over the great Pictish question at the dinner-table at Monkbarns.[1] There is at the present

---

[1] In *The Antiquary* of Sir Walter Scott.

day a substantial consensus among the most distinguished specialists that the Picts were a Celtic people, and the prevailing belief seems to be that the heathen and barbarous Pictish tribes north of the wall of Antonine were of essentially the same race as the Britons, who, south of the wall, had received some tincture of the civilization and of the new faith of their Roman conquerors.[1]

The Picts, or tribes north of the Firths of Forth and Clyde, were divided into two great clans or kingdoms, distinguished as the Northern and Southern Picts, and separated from one another by the great mountain range that crosses Scotland from the south-west to the north-east, and terminates in the Grampians. The Northern Picts may be regarded as occupying the country corresponding to the modern counties of Caithness, Sutherland, Ross, Inverness, Nairn, Elgin, Banff, and Aberdeen; while Kincardine, Forfar, Perth, Fife, and the other counties north of the Forth, were in the possession of the Southern Picts. But beside these two larger sections of the Picts, at the time of St. Ninian there may have already existed a smaller settlement of this people in the out-of-the-way corner of Galloway, corresponding to the present county of Wigton and part of Kirkcudbright. They certainly occupied this region at a later date. If any of the Scots from Ireland had at this early period possessed themselves of any part of this country, their occupancy was confined for the most part to the

[1] It is more open to question whether the Picts belonged to the Cymric or the Gaelic branch of the race.

islands and highlands of the western coast, where, at a later time, we find them in large numbers.

This may not be an unsuitable place for stating the fact, and emphasizing it, that the names *Scots* and *Scotia* were in very early times used *exclusively* of the Irish and of Ireland. Indeed, for six or seven centuries after the time of Ninian, by the word *Scots* was meant the Irish of Ireland, or the Irish settlers on the west coast of what is now called Scotland. "It is not safe," writes Dr. Hill Burton, "to count that the word Scot must mean a native of present Scotland, when the period dealt with is earlier than the middle of the twelfth century."[1] This fact, now universally acknowledged, passed out of sight after the name Scotia or Scotland had been transferred to the country that is now so called; and much confusion of thought was thereby caused to several of the earlier historians of Scotland, whose ignorance of this truth made their interpretation of the early documents extremely perplexing, and, indeed, involved them in many absurdities. We shall have occasion later on to refer again to the confusion thus caused.

It is strange that among the many lives of missionary saints in Scotland we can obtain so very little information as to the character of the heathenism which prevailed among the early inhabitants of the northern parts of Britain. Cæsar's account of the religion of the inhabitants of Gaul and of Britain, so constantly appealed to, seems to me to import into the beliefs of

---

[1] Hill Burton's *History of Scotland*, vol. i., p. 207. For ample proof, see Skene's *Celtic Scotland*, vol. i., pp. 137, 398.

the people a developed mythology which is not to be gathered from subsequent documents. Skene (*Celtic Scotland*, vol. ii., p. 109 *sq.*) investigates the question with his usual carefulness, and he comes to the conclusion that the principal objects of popular belief were "the personified powers of nature." "Mysterious beings, who were supposed to dwell in the heavens or the earth, the sea, the river, the mountain or the valley, were to be dreaded and conciliated. These they worshipped and invoked, as well as the natural objects themselves in which they were supposed to dwell." The *Sidhe*, which in later days degenerated into "fairies," were, according to some of the ancient writers, demons, sometimes appearing in the form of men and offering to show "secrets and places of happiness."

Recent travels in Africa present us with forms of heathenism which seem to me to bear some considerable resemblance to the heathenism of Ireland and northern Britain at the time of the conversion of the people to Christianity. For example, in Uganda we are told that the real objects of such worship as prevails are the *lubari*, demons, or spirits of thunder, storm, rain, etc., and especially the great *lubari* of the lake, the Nyanza. In Uganda, as in many other of the surrounding districts, there does not appear to be any idolatry proper. And among the Celtic people of Britain and Ireland, though there are occasional notices that show us that idols were not wholly unknown, they seem to play a comparatively unimportant part in the religious life of the people. The Druids again figure much more as diviners, sorcerers, or medicine-men than as priests. They could do strange things by spells and incantations. "They could bring snow on the plain, ... they could cover the land with sudden darkness, ... they could, with the charm called the 'Fluttering Wisp,' strike their unhappy victim with lunacy, and would even promise to make the earth swallow him up."[1] Savage and bloody rites to propitiate the evil powers were not unknown. The religion of our forefathers was indeed a religion of darkness and fear.

I have not come across any certain notice of the existence of idolatry (using the word in the sense of the religious worship of *images*) among the heathen of Scotland, but it would be rash to deny its existence, as we can scarcely doubt that, beside other glimpses, there is some foundation for the story, related in the *Tripartite Life*, that St. Patrick saw "the chief idol of Ireland, Cenn Cruaich, covered with gold and silver, and twelve other idols about it, covered with brass."[2]

And in the certainly genuine *Confession* of St. Patrick we find him speak of the existence of idols (*immunda idola*) in Ireland. Nor do I feel entirely certain that the rude naked female figure in wood, nearly five feet in height, with eyes of quartz pebbles, discovered (1881) in a peat-moss at Ballachulish, in Argyllshire,

---

[1] Bishop Healy, *Insula Sanctorum et Doctorum*, p. 4.
[2] See the discussion in Rhys' *Lectures on the Origin and Growth of Religion as illustrated by Celtic Heathendom* (*Hibbert Lectures*, 1886), p. 200 *sq*.

may not be really an idol deity of the early Celtic inhabitants.[1]

We may now return to relate what is known of the history of St. Ninian.

The earliest and most trustworthy authority for any facts relating to the life of Ninian is Venerable Bede,[2] whose incidental notice, though limited to a few lines, will be reasonably reckoned far more valuable than the more elaborate work of Ninian's professed biographer, Aelred, a monk of Rievaulx, in Yorkshire, writing some seven hundred years after the events he professes to relate. Aelred, it is true, claims to have made use of an earlier life of his hero; but, though this were so, the character of his narrative is such as to make it impossible to accept much of it as historical. If Aelred is not primarily responsible for all the absurdities it contains, the earlier biographer must bear his share of the discredit that now attaches to such a work. It was doubtless regarded as a precious record in its day. We, of this age, would much prefer even a very few commonplace particulars, such, for instance, as would tell us something about the books St. Ninian read or the journeys he made, or, indeed, about the food he ate and the clothes he wore,

---

[1] This figure is now placed in the National Museum of Antiquities of Scotland, Edinburgh. (KL. 53, in the Catalogue.) Sir Robert Christison discusses the nature of this figure in the *Proceedings of the Society of Scottish Antiquaries* (1880-81), and shows reasons for thinking that the image may rather be a Scandinavian idol. The Norsemen were known in the neighbourhood of Ballachulish, and figures not unlike it, and believed to be idols, have been found in Scandinavia.

[2] *Eccl. Hist.*, lib. iii. 4.

to the most brilliant firework display of his miracles. Aelred's *Life of St. Ninian* was a deliberately constructed *éloge*, written at the desire of the ecclesiastics of Candida Casa in honour of its founder. Now at any period an *éloge* must be taken with caution; but an *éloge* written in a credulous age upon a saint who died many centuries before, and whose fame it was of much practical importance and pecuniary value to maintain and extend, deserves a special scrutiny.

If Aelred did not invent, it is only too likely that he accepted with open mouth and in perfect good faith the stories told by the earlier writer. Some of the legends related possess a certain poetic prettiness, and some of them may be construed as having a moral attached to them, and thus prove attractive to people who are not over-scrupulous as to whether a tale is true, provided it be what they call "edifying." But for myself I shall confess at once that I am impatient of the prodigious and fabulous, and demand a large accumulation of evidence before I can give it another designation, or feel myself spiritually benefited by it.

The main facts of the life of St. Ninian, as they have been derived from these two sources—Bede and Aelred—and have been commonly accepted after the sifting processes of modern historical criticism, are the following. Ninian was a Briton, born, as is conjectured, about the year 350. He belonged to a district on the shores of the Solway; whether on the northern or southern side is uncertain. His father, who appears to have been a man of rank and authority—perhaps a *regulus* or tribal chieftain—was a Christian; and Ninian early received Christian baptism. He was from his youth a diligent student of Holy Scriptures, and as he grew up he expressed the strongest desire to visit Rome with a view to gaining a fuller knowledge of Divine truth. We may remark in passing that at that time, while the Empire was as yet unbroken by the invasions of the barbarians, a journey from the home of Ninian by the Solway, along the great military and postal roads, through Britain and Gaul to Rome, could have been performed with perfect orderliness, ease, and safety. He seems to have reached the capital during the episcopate of Damasus, who held the see of Rome from the year 366 to the year 384. We possess copious materials derived from the writings of his contemporary, Jerome, and other sources that would enable us to reconstruct for ourselves the surroundings, ecclesiastical and secular, of the young Briton during his stay in the great capital of the West. But confining ourselves to the outline of the facts of his history, we learn from Bede that at Rome he was regularly instructed in the faith and the mysteries of religion. The wish felt by Ninian to receive his training at Rome was as natural as would be the desire of some intelligent and eager Kaffir youth from our South African mission field, to gain the advantages of the theological training that might be had at Oxford or Cambridge, or some other of the centres of Anglican church-life at home. And we can also readily credit the statements of his biographer that he spent in Rome many years, and was, in the end, consecrated to the episcopal office by the Bishop of Rome himself, and sent back to carry on the work of missionary and pastor in his native land. On his return journey through Gaul, it is related that he was attracted by the fame of St. Martin of Tours—that from him, on leaving, he procured masons whom he might take with him to build a church, after the approved ecclesiastical style, in the district where he was about to labour. On his return home he fixed his place of abode, or, rather, his centre of missionary work, at Leukophibia, a place at or near what is now the little town and royal burgh of Whithorn in Wigtonshire. Here he built his church of stone; and in a style to which the Britons were unaccustomed. This building subsequently gave its name of Candida Casa, or White House, to the bishopric.[1]

Where chronological guides are so very few, we eagerly seize on the statement that while building this church Ninian heard of the death of his friend Martin, bishop of Tours, and that under his name he dedicated the structure to the glory of God. The death of the great bishop of Tours is now generally assigned to the end of the year 397.[2] Beside labouring in the district of Galloway and, not improbably, in

---

[1] Bede says nothing about procuring masons from St. Martin, but only that the church was built of stone, in a manner unusual with the Britons.

[2] Nov. 11th. Well known in Scotland as the term-day "Martinmas." As a help to memory, it may be recalled that 200 years later, in 597, another Roman missionary, Augustine of Canterbury, landed in the south of England.

the district that includes what is now Cumberland and Westmoreland, Ninian carried on his missionary work among the great body of the southern Picts inhabiting the middle parts of Scotland south of the Grampians. His labours were attended with success; the heathen renounced their superstition, and accepted the religion of Christ. It is further told us that he ordained presbyters, consecrated bishops, organized the Church, and divided the country into ecclesiastical districts.[1] There is, to my mind, nothing in itself improbable in this statement of Aelred's. Ninian's training was in Roman ways of thought, and the ecclesiastical organization of settled churches, like those of Italy, with which he was familiar, may well have suggested the attempt to effect something similar at home. And that the diocesan system, if established, did not long maintain itself if it were, instead of being gradually extended as success might warrant, given rather a nominal than a real existence, is no more than might be expected, when we consider the wild turbulence of the age and people, and the too speedy relapsing into heathenism of their main body.

While Ninian was absent from Britain, the withdrawal of the Roman troops by the usurper Maximus left the country exposed to one of the most formidable of the incursions of the Picts, who were now joined by the Scots from Ireland. It was not till the year after Ninian's return that the northern wall was

[1] *Vita Niniani*, cap. vi. Whether the word *parochia* is here used in the sense of bishopric, or in its more modern sense, is uncertain.

recovered, and a legion sent to Britain to protect it. It would need a greater knowledge of the circumstances than we possess to enable us to feel entirely confident that Ninian's difficulties were enhanced by this state of things when he entered on his missionary labours among the Picts. But one can hardly imagine that the Picts would not, more especially at that moment, have looked with keen suspicion on one who was so thoroughly associated with the religion of the hostile power of Rome.

In the central and south-western parts of what is modern Scotland, and in the west of northern England, Ninian laboured for many years. He died and was buried at Whithorn; but the exact date (16th Sept., 432) commonly assigned for his death has no certain basis of authority.

It is in a very high degree probable that the monastic system was introduced into northern Britain by St. Ninian, and that to him the great monastery which afterwards flourished at Whithorn owed its foundation. To this monastery, till destroyed by Saxon invaders, both Welsh and Irish students resorted in great numbers.

There has been among some historians in this country a foolish exhibition of rooted prejudice in the dislike shown by them to acknowledge the indebtedness of the British Church to Rome. A wider knowledge of ecclesiastical history and ecclesiastical literature would have shown that there was perhaps no Church in Christendom more free from doctrinal corruptions than the Church of Rome at the period of which we are speaking. As a friend of mine has sometimes put it, paradoxically, to audiences who were not likely to misunderstand him, *the Pope was then a Protestant;* or, to express oneself with more accuracy, though more diffusely, the Bishops of Rome had not then put forward the monstrous pretensions to universal jurisdiction that appear in later days, nor had the doctrines which they inculcated yet taken the unscriptural and uncatholic shapes that some of them assumed in mediæval times. There is certainly everything to be grateful for, and nothing to resent, in the interest shown by the Bishop of Rome in the Church of the Roman settlements in Britain, and in missionary effort among the heathen on the borders of what were, or had recently been, Roman possessions.

The varying fortunes of Ninian's foundation may here be briefly sketched. After the death of the founder (though of the *Monastery* we get occasional glimpses), the history of the *See* is enveloped in mist and darkness for the long space of three hundred years. On the conquest of the British kingdom of Strathclyde by the Angles, Candida Casa again emerges into light; and what is apparently an entirely new succession of bishops takes its origin in A.D. 731. But after some seven or eight occupants of the bishopric, whose names have come down to us, we again lose hold of the record amid the violence and bloodshed of that turbulent and unhappy period. At the instance of King David I., aided by the Lord of Galloway, the bishopric was (1126) once more erected, and with the king's sanction made one of the suffragan sees of York. The ecclesiastical distribution of the country, though, for the sake of convenience, tending to follow the lines of change in civil government, in this as in other instances afforded by Scottish history, exhibited an adhesion to ancient boundaries that only slowly gave way.[1] When St. Andrews was erected (1472) into a metropolitical see by Pope Sixtus IV., the bishopric of Candida Casa was, in spite of the protests of the Archbishop of York, finally removed from English authority, and remained a suffragan see of St. Andrews until it was, in 1491, subjected to the see of Glasgow, on the latter being raised to the archiepiscopal dignity.

We know, on the authority of Bede, that the body of St. Ninian was interred in his own church at Candida Casa. The possession of such venerable and highly-valued relics in the course of years brought crowds of pilgrims, of different countries, and of all ranks, to the remote corner where was situated the shrine of the saint. Even in days of war, the English or Irish pilgrim was sometimes officially secured protection during a visit prompted by so excellent a motive as devotion to St. Ninian. If Whithorn were not earlier visited by royal personages (as the Scottish historian, Boece, would have us believe), certainly the good Queen Margaret, wife of

---

[1] "In 1214 the Bishop of Candida Casa received pay from the *custodes* of the see of York for taking charge of the spiritualities during the vacancy of the see."—Bp. Forbes, *Historians of Scotland*, vol. v., p. xlix.

James III., made a solemn pilgrimage to the place in 1473; while the gallant James IV., who fell at Flodden, moved perhaps by a just remorse for the deeds of earlier years, made repeated journeys to the holy shrine.

The memory of Ninian was a power in Scotland; and dedications under his name of churches and altarages were common; nor were they confined to the principal scenes of his labours, but were to be found in every quarter of the kingdom. Holy wells bearing his name probably mark the Christianity of a date [1] earlier than the dedications.

The name "Ninian," undergoing in the language of the people a phonetic change, sometimes appears as "Ringan." Thus in the poem of Sir David Lindsay (? 1490—? 1567) entitled "Ane dialog betwixt Experience and ane Courtier," we find among "the imageis usit amang Christian men"—

> "Sanct Roche, weill seisit, men may see,
> Ane byill new broken on his thye,
> Sanct Eloye he doth staitly stand
> Ane new horse-shoe intyll his hand,
> Sanct Ringan of a rottin stoke,
> Sanct Duthow [2] boird out of ane bloke." [3]

While an ancient bell of the early Celtic type, made of iron coated with bronze, known as "Clog-Rinny,"

---

[1] See Bishop Forbes, *Historians of Scotland*, vol. v., pp. xiii—xvii. In the present century many churches have been dedicated under the name of St. Ninian, among which we may particularize the cathedral at Perth, built after a fine design of Mr. Butterfield.

[2] *I. e.* Duthac of Tain in Ross-shire.

[3] See Bishop Forbes' Introduction to the *Historians of Scotland*, vol. v., p. xxvi.

or Ringan's Bell, has come down to us, and may now be seen in the National Museum of Antiquities in Edinburgh (see p. 309). I fancy it may be through an adhesion of the final "t" of "Saint" or "Sanct" to the first letter of "Ringan," that we approach the form "St. Trinian" in the old English ballad of Flodden Field. Similarly I conjecture that by a reverse process St. Thenew became St. Enoch (see p. 54).

It has already been stated that there is no reason to doubt that Ninian founded a monastery at Candida Casa. This monastery afterwards attained much distinction as a school of learning. And it has of late been accepted by careful inquirers that this monastery, easily reached from the north of Ireland and frequented by Irish students, was one of the channels through which the monastic system reached the sister island.[1]

---

[1] Skene, *Celtic Scotland*, vol. ii., pp. 46-9. This view is also accepted by Bishop Healy (*Insula Sanctorum et Doctorum*, p. 166). These writers identify the "House of Martin" and the monastery of "Rosnat" (which word has been conjecturally interpreted as the "Promontory of Learning") occurring in Irish records with the monastery of Whithorn. If it is true that St. Finnian of Moville had been a student at Candida Casa, it is interesting to trace through him the influence of the school of St. Ninian upon his more famous pupil, St. Columba.

CHAPTER II.

ST. PATRICK, A CHILD OF THE BRITISH CHURCH IN SCOTLAND.

THE next historic name of note that meets us as we trace the story of the Christian Church in Scotland is that of Patrick, the Apostle of Ireland.

The narrative of St. Patrick's missionary labours belongs properly to the ecclesiastical history of the sister island, and I do not purpose to relate it here. But as St. Patrick may be claimed, and claimed with good reason, as a native of North Britain, and a spiritual child of the British Church in this part of the country, it will not be unsuitable to say a few words with reference to his early history; and this we are the more encouraged to do because there are two or three particulars connected with his life that happily throw some few rays of light into the mist of obscurity that envelops the condition of the Christian Church in Scotland at that remote period.

It is not now doubted by the best critical authorities that we have in our possession at least two genuine writings of St. Patrick. One of these is what is known as his *Confession*, written towards the close of his life, and giving some account of its chief incidents. The other is an epistle commonly known as the *Epistle to Coroticus*, whom some would identify with the Welsh prince Caredig ; while others—more recent scholars, among whom are Mr. Skene and Mr. Whitley Stokes—contend that this Coroticus was a prince of Strathclyde, Cerétic by name, who had his capital at Alclwyd (*i. e.* Dumbarton), from the neighbourhood of which St. Patrick had been carried captive. The epistle to the subjects of Coroticus (whoever he was) was suggested by the cruelties perpetrated by that chieftain in his ravaging the Irish coast, and carrying captive great numbers of St. Patrick's Christian converts. Both these writings seem to me to possess very many of the characteristic marks of genuineness, and, as I have just said, they have been accepted by those who are best versed in the science of historical criticism. Both these writings contain notices (though of the briefest kind) of Patrick's early life.

It has been generally believed that the birthplace of St. Patrick was at, or close by, Dumbarton on the Clyde ; and though claims to this distinction have been made on behalf of other places,[1] no sufficient reason has as yet been shown for departing from the commonly received account. He tells us himself that he was of gentle blood (*ingenuus secundum carnem*), that his paternal grandfather had been a priest, and that his father was a deacon in the Church. His father possessed a little country house attached to a

---

[1] *E. g.* Glastonbury, Bristol, Carlisle, Boulogne, Tours, Carleon, and Ireland itself.

farm, close by the town of Bannavem of Tabernia. The identification of this name has given rise to animated dispute, but I have followed the general belief in supposing the place to be what is now called Dumbarton. In this town the father of Patrick, as well as being a deacon of the Church, held the responsible post of a "decurion," an office which originated in the municipal system of the Roman Empire, and to which the office of town-councillor, or bailie, in our modern Scottish municipalities bears some considerable resemblance.[1]

You will note then, in the first place, that the celibacy of the clergy was not at this time insisted on in the Church in Northern Britain. In some later ages it would have been considered a disgrace to be the child of an ecclesiastic, but I think we can detect that, as St. Patrick states the fact, he puts it forward rather as a mark of his respectability. "I had," he writes in the opening of the account of his life, "for my father, Calpornius, a Deacon, who had been son of Potitus, a Presbyter." And if, as has been suggested by Roman Catholic controversialists, in both cases the children may have been born before the assumption of holy orders by the fathers, St. Patrick certainly

---

[1] Decurions "were found all over the Roman Empire to its extremest bounds by the end of the fourth century. Some discoveries in Spain about ten years ago (*i.e.* about 1877) showed that Decurions were established by the Romans in every little mining village, and were charged with the care of the games, the water-supply, sanitary arrangements, education, and the local fortifications."—Professor George T. Stokes, in Smith and Wace's *Dictionary of Christian Biography*.

never thought it necessary for the credit of his father and grandfather to mention the fact. The truth is that at this period both the practice and sentiment of the Church varied in different places. A belief in the superior sanctity of celibacy had manifested itself long before the time of St. Patrick in many parts of Christendom. The monastic system was an outcome of it; but the attempt, when made, to compel the clergy ministering to the general body of the faithful to live unmarried was as yet but very partially successful in the West; while in the East, where the monastic system originated and flourished in full vigour, the celibacy of the secular clergy has never even to this day been enforced, and is, as a matter of fact, quite the exception.

From St. Patrick's mention of his father as a deacon, who was also a decurion, and possibly engaged in farming operations, it may be plausibly inferred that there may have been in that age in North Britain something like what is found in the Greek Church, and what some of our bishops are disposed now to revive among ourselves, a permanent diaconate—not so rigorously debarred from secular employments as were the higher grades of the clergy. If this were so, it must be acknowledged to be an exception to the general spirit of ecclesiastical legislation elsewhere, which tended wholly in the direction of severing those in holy orders from worldly business.

While Patrick was not yet sixteen, a body of marauding freebooters from Ireland, sailing, as we may suppose, up the Firth of Clyde, seized upon him at his father's farm, and he was swept with a crowd of other captives—"many thousands" in number, he says himself (though this may be an unintentional exaggeration)—into the ships of the Irish barbarians, and carried across the sea to serve in slavery. In Antrim he was occupied for six years as a herd, and it was during this unhappy period of his life that he gained that knowledge of the Irish tongue which he afterwards used so effectively as a missionary, preacher, and bishop. But better than gaining a knowledge of Irish was his gaining during those tedious years a knowledge of himself, and of the infinite love of his Heavenly Father. The lessons of his childhood, which, if we may believe his own depreciatory remarks upon his history, had not secured in his boyhood submission to the law of God, nor, as he says in his own words, "obedience to our priests who used to warn us to the end that we might be saved"—these lessons now came back to his memory, and the truth was made known to his heart. He tells us how the fear and love of God increased within him, and how earnestly and constantly he devoted himself to prayer. There is a genuine touch of the age in which he lived when he recounts that often in a single day he would say a hundred prayers,[1] and in the night-time almost as many, and that he often rose before daybreak and offered his prayers in the woods or upon the mountain side, and this—in snow, or frost, or rain. And not only did he pray, he also fasted, and he declares of himself there was "no

---

[1] Or short devotions after the manner of collects (*orationes*).

laziness" in him, because, as he came afterwards to see, "the spirit burned within him."

After six years' captivity Patrick made his escape, and after some years, during which his history is obscure, we find him in Britain with his parents. But in his dreams he is moved to return to the land of his captivity. A messenger appears to bring him a letter from Ireland, entreating his return. He hears a cry —"the voice of the Irish"—asking him to come back and stay with them, and he cannot but respond to the call. Here his connection with Scotland ceases, and his after-career as a missionary and bishop, full of interest as it is, falls outside our province.

A few words, however, may be said on the personal character of St. Patrick. The acknowledged writings of the saint supply materials out of which a picture may be constructed, which, though slight, is no mere fancy sketch, but possesses qualities of a true moral portraiture. He is seen in these writings as a man of great determination and force of character, of earnest devotion, of deep humility. He is sensitive to the accusations of conscience; sins of his youth come back with sorrow to his memory. He is sensitive, too, like many good men, to charges made against him by others, though he knows those charges to be ill-founded. His warmth of sympathy and affection for the Irish, among whom he had served as a slave, is portrayed by some very natural touches in the *Confession*. His well-known hymn in the Irish tongue has been often translated into English, and for its glow of imagination and fervour of devotion to

God it will always challenge a high place in the history of Christian hymnology.

The chronology of the life of St. Patrick is involved in much obscurity. His capture as a youth by the Irish must be placed towards the close of the fourth or the beginning of the fifth century. It seems impossible to be more precise with any reasonable confidence. The year 432 is the date commonly accepted for St. Patrick's landing as a missionary in Ireland; but even this important and well-marked event has been placed somewhat later by some able scholars. On the other hand, one of the most distinguished of the Celtic scholars of our time, Mr. Whitley Stokes, places this event as early as 397.[2] His death at the age of 120 (A.D. 493) is still more questionable, more especially when we find the fondness of the ancient hagiologists for assigning extraordinary longevity to their heroes. Instances of this will be noticed later on.[3]

---

[1] I have accepted the prevailing opinion as to this hymn, known as the "Lorica," or "Breastplate." Tradition is strongly in favour of its being the work of St. Patrick; and its contents are not only consistent with, but confirmatory of this belief.

[2] *The Tripartite Life of St. Patrick*, vol. ii. p. 273.

[3] See p. 69.

CHAPTER III.

ST. PALLADIUS, AND HIS DISCIPLES, ST. TERNAN AND ST. SERF—THE ORIGIN OF THE MYTH OF A NON-EPISCOPAL CHURCH IN ANCIENT SCOTLAND.

THE name of a contemporary of St. Patrick, of whom we know something from a distinctly authentic source, has been long associated by tradition, and in the writings of the mediæval historians, with Christian missionary effort in the north-eastern part of Scotland. At Fordun, in Kincardineshire, a church was dedicated to St. Palladius, and was believed to contain his relics. The place was visited by pilgrims; a well situated there is known as "Paldy's Well"; and in recent times, if it be not still continued, a fair held on the festival of the saint (July 6) was known as "Paldy" or "Pady's fair."[1] John of Fordun, a "chaplain," as it would seem, or chantry-priest "of the church of Aberdeen," and the earliest systematic historian of Scotland, writing in the latter half of the fourteenth century (*circ.* 1385), would have us believe that St. Palladius was sent to Scotland by Pope

[1] "Paldy" is locally pronounced "Pauldy" or "Paudy."

Celestinus in 429 or 430, and with him he associates as disciples and fellow-labourers St. Ternan and St. Serf (Servanus), who were ordained bishops by him.

The same story is repeated by subsequent historians with more or less of modification. Nor should we have reason to question it, but for the fact that we now know the exact source of Fordun's information so far as the mission from Celestine is concerned, and we know too that he has certainly misinterpreted the authority on which he founds. The value of Fordun's authority for the labours of Palladius in Scotland, and for his converting Ternan and Serf, we are less able to estimate; and the latest critical investigator of the question, Dr. W. F. Skene, has with much learning and ingenuity maintained that Palladius was martyred in Ireland, and never laboured in the north of Scotland—attributing the Scottish tradition and the Scottish cultus of St. Palladius to Ternan having brought the *relics* of Palladius from Ireland and deposited them at some place in the north-east of Scotland.[1] A thorough investigation of the evidence would occupy more space than can be afforded to it in these pages; but I may venture to say that, after weighing what has been said on both sides, I am disposed to think that we are not entitled to reject with entire confidence the hitherto prevailing belief that a missionary named Palladius laboured for the spread of Christianity in Scotland. But, as I have said, that Fordun misinterpreted his authority for the statement that Pope Celestine sent Palladius

[1] *Celtic Scotland*, vol. ii., pp. 26—31.

to Scotland in A.D. 429 or 430, there can be no doubt whatever. His words are substantially a quotation from the *Chronica* of Prosper of Aquitaine (a contemporary of Palladius), who has, under the year 431, the words, "Palladius is ordained by Pope Celestine, and sent as first bishop to the Scots believing in Christ." It is now, I suppose, universally admitted that at the date of Prosper's writing, and indeed for several centuries after, the word *Scotia* meant "Ireland," and *Scoti* "Irishmen." But by the time of Fordun the words had changed their meaning, and hence his error, which has since been again and again repeated.[1]

The question as to the labours of Palladius in the country we know as Scotland is for us of really but little importance, for even in the fullest accounts he is little more than a name.[2]

If the Palladius of Scottish story is to be identified

---

[1] In another work of Prosper, entitled *Contra Collatorem*, a controversial treatise against John Cassian, who had written a work entitled *Conferences* (Collationes) *of the Fathers dwelling in the Scithic Desert*, we find a passage referring to Palladius— "Whilst the Pope laboured to keep the Roman island Catholic, he made the barbarous island Christian by ordaining a bishop for the Scots" (cap. xxi.).

[2] To Roman Catholics in Scotland the subject is of more interest. The Roman Catholic historian, Dr. Bellesheim (*History of the Catholic Church of Scotland*, in Hunter Blair's edition, vol. i., pp. 18—24), is evidently inclined to accept Dr. Skene's solution, but thinks it dutiful to say, "It is not in fact possible to arrive at the truth of the matter with perfect certainty; and since an ancient and venerable tradition points to St. Palladius as an Apostle of Scotland, Leo XIII. was fully justified, in his Bull restoring the Scottish hierarchy in 1878, in accepting the tradition in question." This is an instructive passage.

with the Palladius sent to Ireland by Pope Celestine, we know that it was through his instrumentality that St. Germanus, Bishop of Auxerre, was commissioned by Celestine to proceed to Britain to combat Pelagianism, which had spread widely in that country. This happened in 429, two years before the mission of Palladius to Ireland. Palladius was a "deacon of the Roman Church"—that is, as I take it, he occupied a place of prominence and dignity as one of the seven deacons of the city of Rome. It has been conjectured that he was a Gaul by birth, as the Palladian family occupied an important place in that country.

The chapter of Fordun's *Chronicle* in which he gives us his account of Palladius, came curiously enough to play a very important part in the creation of the myth—which was so long generally accepted in Scotland, and is perhaps not yet quite defunct—that there existed in Scotland in early times a church constructed, as regards ecclesiastical government, on the Presbyterian model. It is only fair to Presbyterian writers of former days to acknowledge that it was most natural for them to seize and make much of a testimony coming from a source so little likely to be prejudiced in favour of their views as an ecclesiastic of the Roman obedience in mediæval times. Now that we know that Fordun's error originated in a misunderstanding of the word "Scots," as used by Prosper, it is worth our while to quote the passage of Fordun, and observe the growth of the myth. After first recounting how Pope Celestine had introduced into the celebration of the Mass the Psalm, "Judge me, O Lord," before the Introit, and enjoined that the introit, gradalia, and allelulia should be taken from the Psalms, and that the offertoria and collects during the Communion should be sung with musical inflexions (*modulatione*)—the importance of noting these ritual ordinances will be seen by and by—he goes on to say that in the year 429 or 430 St. Palladius was ordained by the same pope and "sent as first bishop to the Scots believing in Christ." A few lines lower down, after repeating that Pope Celestine sent Palladius as first bishop in Scotia, it is added, " Whence it is fitting for the Scots diligently to celebrate the feasts and ecclesiastical commemorations (*festa simul et memorias ecclesiasticas*), since he carefully and thoroughly instructed their nation, namely the Scots, both by word and example in the orthodox faith, before whose coming the Scots used to have as teachers of the faith and ministers of the sacraments only Presbyters or monks, following the rite of the early Church." Dr. Skene's comment on this passage is so admirably lucid and cogent, that I cannot do better than give it in his own words. "There were, of course, no Scots in Scotland at that time. But, by thus appropriating Palladius, Fordun brought himself into a dilemma. According to his fictitious and artificial scheme of the early history of his country, the Scots had colonized Scotland several centuries before Christ, and had been converted to Christianity by Pope Victor I. in the year 203. But if Palladius was their first bishop in 430, what sort of Church had they between these dates? He is therefore driven to the conclusion that it must have been a Church governed by presbyters or monks only. Hector Boece[1] gave the name of Culdees to the clergy of this supposed early Church; and thus arose the belief that there had been an early Church of Presbyterian Culdees."[2]

In connection with this passage of Fordun, I cannot but think that it has been too hastily assumed that Fordun regarded the want of bishops as characteristic of the "primitive Church." There seems to me good reason for believing that the phrase, "following the rite of the primitive Church," has reference, not to the absence of bishops, but to the simplicity of ceremonial and ecclesiastical observance, which was supposed, with good reason, to mark the earlier Scottish Church. This view of Fordun's meaning is supported by the Lessons for the Feast of St. Palladius in the Aberdeen Breviary. There we read that Palladius appointed "festivals and their solemn observance," and the becoming mode of celebrating and receiving the Sacraments. He consecrates churches; he gives ordinances with respect to ecclesiastical vestments; he orders the "canonical hours" to be said after the Roman manner.[3] We saw that Fordun thought it worth while recording that Celes-

---

[1] In Latinized form, Boethius: born at Dundee about 1465; Professor of Philosophy in Paris, 1497; published his *Scotorum Historiæ* (folio, Paris), 1526; died, 1536.
[2] *Celtic Scotland*, vol. ii., p. 30. See also *Historians of Scotland*, vol. iv., p. 395. Some account of the Culdees will be found in chapter xii. of this book.
[3] *Brev. Aberdon.* Julii V.

tine, who sent Palladius "as first bishop to the Scots believing in Christ," had made several ritual and liturgical changes in the celebration of the Mass. With this in his mind he thinks of the probable want of elaboration in the liturgical ordinances of the earlier Scottish Church; and the emphasis he places, in connection with Palladius, on the duty of the Scots observing "ecclesiastical festivals and commemorations," confirms the view I have here suggested as the true interpretation of the words "following the rite of the primitive Church." If the view I have put forward is correct, we find Fordun making two quite distinct statements about the Christian Scots before the coming of Palladius. He states, what he believed to be a fact, that they were without bishops, and he adds that their "rite"—*i. e.* their liturgical observances—were different from those introduced by Palladius. The whole context must be studied that we may obtain the true sense of the passage.

The names of St. Ternan and St. Serf are constantly associated in legendary history with that of St. Palladius. Ternan is said to have been instructed and baptized by Palladius, and consecrated a bishop among the Picts. In the mediæval times, Ternan occupied, beyond question, a place of considerable importance in the local religious conceptions of the north-east of Scotland. A bell—"the Ronecht"—said to have been given to him by the Pope (who, through a formidable anachronism of some 200 years, is made Gregory the Great), and to have followed him miraculously all the way to Scotland, was preserved till the

Reformation at Banchory-Ternan, and was dignified by being placed in the custody of an hereditary keeper, as was not uncommon in the case of other sacred relics (see p. 310). At Banchory, too, were preserved his head and the St. Matthew volume of his four Books of the Gospels, which were enclosed in metal cases adorned with gold and silver. In the treasury of the Church of Aberdeen was a monstrance containing his relics. The Aberdeen Breviary honours him with six lections, chiefly devoted to his miracles. Three or four churches bore his name in their dedications.[1] In default of any secure footing for reasonable conjecture as to his labours, we must content ourselves with these indications that he had, in the region where he laboured, made a deep impression upon the popular mind.

St. Serf presents a yet more embarrassing problem to the critical inquirer. Chronological statements in the various legends are so diverse, that some will have it that there were two saints bearing this name—one in the fifth and the other in the seventh century. For our purpose it must suffice to say that, while the name of Ternan is chiefly associated with the northeast of Scotland, that of Serf or, in the popular language, Sair, is connected with Fife and the valley of the Forth. His body was believed to be deposited at Culross,[2] a village on the northern shore of the Firth of Forth, some eight or ten miles higher up than Queensferry, where the stupendous railway-

---

[1] See Bishop Forbes, *Kalendars of Scottish Saints*, p. 450.
[2] The name is commonly pronounced Coó-ross.

bridge now spans the channel. At Culross, the Festival of the Saint was kept yearly on the 1st July, "when the inhabitants marched in procession, carrying green boughs"; and, at least as late as 1839, the custom had not altogether disappeared, though by common consent the ceremonial was transferred, we are told, by a strange transmutation of sentiment, to the 4th of June, in honour of the birthday of King George III.[1] The fame of the saint certainly extended to Aberdeenshire, for a yearly fair, called "St. Sair's Fair," was formerly held at Monkege (Keithhall), and more lately at Culsamond. He was patron-saint of Creich and Dysart in Fife, at which latter place there is a cave, to which he is said to have occasionally retired.[2]

[1] *New Statistical Account*, Perth, p. 600. For a Papal parallel, see p. 291.
[2] *Kalendars of Scottish Saints*, p. 447. See also below, p. 303. Skene (*Celtic Scotland*, vol. ii., p. 32) refuses to acknowledge any claim of St. Serf's belonging to the period of St. Palladius.

CHAPTER IV.

ST. MUNGO (OR KENTIGERN).

In the early legendary records, three great figures stand out from the crowd of lesser men, all engaged in the great work of Christianizing Scotland—St. Ninian, St. Mungo, and St. Columba. Of the second of these we now come to speak. Roughly calculated, something like a century—a century enveloped for us in darkness—intervenes between the labours of Palladius and the labours of Mungo.

There is sufficient evidence to show that the Southern Picts, who had been converted to the Christian faith by Ninian about the beginning of the fifth century, relapsed in large numbers into heathenism between the date of the death of their great teacher, and the middle of the sixth century. There is also reason to believe that the Britons of the Roman province of Valentia—that is, of the country between the two great military walls—had fallen into degenerate ways and into grave errors in faith, if they did not, as a body, actually apostatize from the religion of Christ. The withdrawal of the Romans from Britain was the withdrawal of an influence that was protective of the faith. We may be helped to realize the danger to which the British Church was then exposed if we will try to conceive how it would fare at the present time with the native churches in Kaffraria, or Zululand, had the English to retire from South Africa.

It was the work of St. Mungo to restore the lapsed and to strengthen the weak in regions that included the field of St. Ninian's labours. The scene of the chief labours of St. Mungo was the British kingdom of Strathclyde, or Cumbria, which reached from a little to the north of its capital and seat of government, Dumbarton (then known as Alclwyd), down to the river Derwent in Cumberland, and extended across the island till it was met by the boundary, shifting and ill-defined, of Bernicia, the kingdom of the Angles. Of the origin of this kingdom of Cumbria we really know nothing for certain. When thrown wholly on their own resources by the entire withdrawal of the Romans, the Britons of the west learned a lesson from their eastern brethren, who found, too late, that the help afforded by their Saxon allies was a highly doubtful gain. I may mention that it has been supposed that the name of the islands of Cumbrae, in the Clyde, is the linguistic relic of the name of the ancient kingdom. The island of Bute was in the hands of the Scots from Ireland. The two islands I have named were in the hands of the Britons of Cumbria. A few miles of sea divided them. But Mungo is represented as also labouring, for at least a short time, among the Southern Picts, who inhabited the region between the Forth and the Grampians, as well as in the district of Galloway, the special scenes of the services of St. Ninian on behalf of Christ.

When we attempt to gain a knowledge of the true history of St. Mungo, we are met by many difficulties. If we are unfortunate in Ninian's biographer, Aelred of Rievaulx, we are, it must be acknowledged, even yet more unfortunate in the romancer who has given us the principal life of St. Kentigern.[1] Here, again, in the *Life* by Jocelyn, we have a life written "to order" many hundred years after the death of its subject. The facts are, that Jocelyn, who was Bishop of Glasgow between the years 1174 and 1199, commissioned a monk of the great Cistercian Abbey of Furness, in Lancashire, who was also Jocelyn by name, to write a life of the famous Scottish saint. Bishop Jocelyn commenced the building of the noble cathedral of Glasgow, and it was natural that he should desire to possess a history of his famous predecessor, whose relics were to form the chief glory and treasure of the splendid structure he designed to raise, and under whose name it was to be dedicated.

[1] There is a fragment of a somewhat earlier *Life* in the British Museum. But it, like that of Jocelyn, belongs to the twelfth century. It professes to be the work of an ecclesiastic, who styles himself "a clerk of St. Kentigern," and was written on the suggestion of Bishop Herbert of Glasgow, who died in 1164. It contains only what Bishop Forbes styles "the weird legend" (though I would prefer to speak of it as the gross story grossly told) of the saint's parentage and birth. It is printed in the *Historians of Scotland*, vol. v., p. 243, and in the *Registrum Episcopatus Glasguensis*, vol. i., lxxviii, *sq.*

Some materials, it is true, existed for this biography, but they were scanty; and if deficiencies had to be supplied, the monk of Furness, as the issue proved, possessed an imaginative inventiveness that was luxuriant in its fertility and quite adapted to the ecclesiastical taste of the day. From the tissue of monstrous absurdities, some of them being, we may say with scarcely a doubt, deliberate falsifications with an interested purpose, whether invented by Jocelyn or by an earlier writer, it is very far from easy to disentangle the threads of truth.

There has been too ready a disposition on the part of even sober investigators to follow the very easy course of merely rejecting the miraculous and accepting the residuum as truth. But a narrative is not necessarily true because it is not palpably absurd. There is needed by the critical historian in such cases an extensive general knowledge of the conditions of society at the period with which he is concerned. It is also highly important that he should possess a familiarity with other examples of a like kind of literature; for there is a remarkable proneness towards the recurrence of legendary types. A story that has proved entertaining about one saint is pretty sure to be engrafted upon the life of some other. In this way only can the inquirer secure in any degree a discriminating tact for separating, with some measure of confidence, the true from the fictitious, and gain a due perception of that which is so often, in these narrations, written between the lines. I do not myself pretend to the possession of this subtle sensibility and painfully acquired skill; but I will relate in outline what the most competent historians of our day are disposed, perhaps with too much readiness, to accept as the true account of St. Mungo.

The mother of the saint is represented as the daughter of a king in a Pictish district of the Lothians, for the Picts, after the withdrawal of the Romans, had settled themselves in several parts of southern Scotland. This king is represented as a Pagan, or, as the earlier fragmentary life has it, a "semi-Pagan." When the time drew near for the birth of the child, the princess, Thenew, or Thenog, by name, and a Christian by profession, on account of charges made, rightly or wrongly, against her chastity, was, after previous dangers and sufferings, put alone into a frail coracle on the shore at Aberlady,[1] and pushed out to sea, that thus she might perish. The winds and tides bore her boat first outside the Isle of May, and then up the Firth of Forth, past Inchkeith and the island which has since come to be known as Inchcolm, through the narrowing channel of what was afterwards called Queensferry, where now the vast structure of the Forth Bridge spans the estuary, until it was finally stranded on the shore of Culross. Here, on landing, she gave birth to a son; and, according to the legend (which would seem to be here guilty of an anachronism), St. Serf, whose residence and monastic school were situated at this place, came to the help

[1] On the coast of Haddingtonshire.

of both mother and child.[1] By Serf the child was given at his baptism the name "Kentigern" (which has been interpreted as "Chief Lord"), and afterwards the pet-name of "Munghu," or "Mungo," which is variously explained as "Dearest Friend," or "Dear and lovable."[2] By Serf the boy is brought up and educated. When he reaches man's estate, he leaves his master, and, after some wildly fabulous adventures, he reaches Cathures, now called Glasgow, where in a former age St. Ninian had, according to the story, consecrated a burial-ground. Here he took up his abode. The fame of his piety and virtues spreads, and at the early age of twenty-five years he is chosen as bishop by the Prince of Strathclyde, with his clergy and people. For his consecration, it was found easiest to bring a bishop from Ireland, and by a single bishop he was advanced to the episcopate. Consecration by a single bishop is said to have been at this time the custom of the Britons and Irish. In passing, I may say that consecration by a single bishop, though irregular, has not been accounted by the Church as invalid; and examples of such exceptional acts are to be found

---

[1] A church in Glasgow was dedicated to the mother of Mungo. It is not difficult to perceive how "Saint Thenog" became as pronounced, "Saint Henog" or "Saint Enoch," and the name is still perpetuated amid the bustle and busy life of the nineteenth century in "St. Enoch's Railway Station," and "St. Enoch's Hotel."

[2] Skene (*Celtic Scotland*, vol. ii., p. 183) says, "Cyndeyrn and Munghu are pure Welsh—Cyndeyrn from *Cyn*, chief; *teyrn*, lord. Mwyngu, from *Mwyn*, amiable; *cu*, dear."

elsewhere. A further consideration of this question will be found at a subsequent page.[1]

We may notice that the name "Mungo," suggested by affection, holds its ground through Scotland at this day in preference to the more dignified "Kentigern." If the tourist in Glasgow in search of the noble cathedral were to ask in the streets to be directed to "St. Kentigern's Cathedral," the chances are twenty to one he would get no satisfactory reply, but "Where is St. Mungo's?" would be at once understood. Indeed, it is worthy of observation that not a single church in Scotland is dedicated to the saint under the name of Kentigern, while we have St. Mungo's parish in Dumfries, St. Mungo's Chapel in Perthshire, and churches of St. Mungo at Polwarth, Penicuik, Lanark, and other places.

At Glasgow Mungo established a monastery, and there he continued to reside until he somehow incurred the animosity of a new king of Strathclyde, Morken by name, by whom he was driven from his home. He resolved to seek refuge among the Christian Britons of Wales; and, on his journey southwards, he is represented as preaching in the district around Carlisle, where it is interesting to find at this day no less than nine churches dedicated under his name. Among them is one often visited by the tourist to the English Lakes, the Church of Crossthwaite[2] at Keswick.

[1] See p. 89.
[2] Where the fine recumbent monumental effigy of the poet Southey is to be seen.

: Having passed into Wales, Mungo resided for a time at Menevia, as the guest of the Bishop David (Dewi), afterwards known as the patron-saint of Wales, and founder of the see that bears his name. Leaving St. David, he founded a monastery at Llanelwy, in Wales, on the banks of another Clyde. This monastery became rapidly the resort of great numbers of men of all classes, rich and poor, high and low, educated and ignorant.

Another change in the occupancy of the throne of Strathclyde brought Mungo back to Scotland. Roderick (Rydderch), surnamed "the Bountiful," succeeded Morken. The new king had been baptized and instructed in Ireland, and his sympathies were thoroughly with the Church. He sent a message to Mungo requesting his return, and the saint set forth for the north with many of the brethren from the convent at Llanelwy.[1] Before leaving Llanelwy Mungo placed in charge his friend and disciple, Asaph, whose name has been given to the place, and to the bishopric of St. Asaph.

Mungo was met on his journey north at Hoddam, in Dumfriesshire, by Roderick, amid a scene of wonderful rejoicing, and at Hoddam he remained for some years before finally settling in his former residence at Glasgow. If one can give credence to the speech which Jocelyn puts into the mouth of St. Mungo on the occasion of his meeting King Roderick, it would

---

[1] The return of Mungo is placed by Skene in or near the year 573.

seem that the mythology of the neighbouring Angles was beginning to mingle with the native superstitions of the Britons of these parts, and thus contributed to further impede the labours of the Christian ministry. Without accepting literally Jocelyn's account of Roderick's voluntary subjection of himself and his authority to the Church (which seems to bear the colour of twelfth century controversies), we can well believe that Mungo's influence with the king might be practically boundless.

After Mungo's return to Glasgow, and in the far advanced years of his life, must be placed his famous meeting with Columba.

The fame of the missionary labours of each of these good men must have been well known to the other; and nothing could be more natural than the desire of Columba to visit the bishop, and see, face to face, so eminent and successful a servant of his Lord. Columba is represented as approaching Glasgow with a great company of monks in three ordered bands. He sends to inform Mungo of his coming. The bishop, also accompanied by a crowd of ecclesiastics and others similarly disposed in three bands, comes out to meet him. They draw near, both parties chanting aloud as they come psalms and spiritual songs. When they meet on the bank of the Molindinar burn, the two servants of the Lord embrace and kiss one another. The bishop receives his visitors with hospitality, and when they are about to depart, Mungo and Columba exchange staves in token of their mutual love in Christ.

It was commonly believed in after time (and there is no reason to question the fact) that the staff given by Columba to the bishop found its way to the Church of St. Wilfrid (now the Cathedral) at Ripon, where it was an object of veneration down to the time of the Reformation.

CHAPTER V.

THE HISTORICAL CHARACTER OF THE DOCUMENTARY AUTHORITIES FOR THE LIVES OF ST. NINIAN AND ST. MUNGO.

THE histories of St. Ninian and St. Mungo, as they are commonly accepted by our modern historians, have now been related. But I have already hinted that perhaps more has been told than is really warranted by historical evidence. I am dissatisfied with that method of dealing with the old lives of the saints, which consists of little more than omitting the miraculous element of the stories. And of this dissatisfaction I am more particularly sensible when the stories, as in the case of Aelred's *Life of St. Ninian* and Jocelyn's *Life of St. Kentigern*, come to us in their present form from writers who lived many hundred years after the events recorded, and who were plainly little disposed to, and little qualified for, a critical investigation of the material upon which they worked. Indeed, I must confess that I am not at all satisfied that a good part of the stories told were not deliberate inventions of these two writers.

Some forty or fifty years ago it was the prevailing

vogue with religious writers of a certain school to express, and, I doubt not, to cultivate a deeply reverential feeling for everything mediæval. These writers seem to me to have foolishly shrunk from a free and rational criticism of anything that bore the stamp of what was euphemistically called "the ages of faith." The late Mr. J. H. (since Cardinal) Newman's writings on "ecclesiastical miracles" exercised an influence upon many who did not follow the author in his change of creed; and, in my opinion, that influence was distinctly injurious to the scientific treatment of the early religious history of Britain. It may indeed be admitted that it is not a sufficient reason to refuse credence to an alleged miracle only because it seems to us trivial, grotesque, or disproportionate to the occasion. But, lacking positive testimony of real and substantial weight on their behalf, I do not think it is any indication of an irreverent spirit to smile at what is ludicrous in these stories, and to be sceptical of what is, at least *prima facie*, absurd.

It is well, perhaps, that at this point we should make acquaintance with some specimens of the histories from which we have derived the particulars that have been recorded. And it is right to add that the prodigious is not a mere occasional and passing feature, but gives a general colour to the whole.

And first, to consider Aelred's *Life of St. Ninian*. The three opening chapters are little more than an enlargement of the passage from Bede which is cited by our author in his preface, and which, though consisting of only a few lines, may be regarded as of more value than all the subsequent marvels.[1] It is introduced after a mention of Columba's mission to the Northern Picts, and as cited by Aelred, runs as follows: " The Southern Picts who dwell among the same mountains had long before abandoned the error of idolatry, and received the true faith on the preaching of the word to them by Bishop Nynia, a most reverend and most holy man, a Briton by race, who at Rome had been regularly instructed in the faith and mysteries of the truth; the seat of whose episcopate, dedicated under the name of St. Martin, Bishop, and a famous church (where he rests in the body with many saints), the nation of the Angles at the present time possesseth. This place is commonly called *Candida Casa*, because there he built a church of stone in a manner unusual among the Britons (*insolito Bretonibus more*)." In Chapter IV. we read how King Tuduvallus was cured of an intolerable disease in the head and of blindness by the touch of the saint and the sign of the cross. The next chapter relates how a priest, falsely accused of unchastity, was triumphantly vindicated in church before a great gathering of clergy and people by an infant of one day old. The new-born babe, when adjured by the saint, stretched forth his hand, and pointing to his real father, exclaimed in a manly voice (*vox virilis*), "That is my father; your priest, O bishop, is innocent, and there is naught between him and me but participation in that human nature which is common to us both." I think there is something more portentous in the acquaintance of the infant with

[1] The passage occurs in the *Ecclesiastical History* (lib. iii. c. 4).

the metaphysics involved in the conception of our common human nature than in the "manly voice," which has suggested to the sceptical a suspicion of saintly ventriloquism. This is a story, we may observe in passing, which is told, with modifications, of various saints in different countries. A study of comparative Christian mythology shows us that it was a favourite. Chapter VI. is an amplification of the fact that Ninian laboured among the Southern Picts as missionary and bishop. In Chapter VII. we are told how leeks, which the gardener had just planted, were found full-grown and in seed when the saint required them for the refectory table. It is added, "the guests looked at one another"; and well they might. In Chapter VIII. it is related how the saint would protect his cattle by drawing a circle round them on the ground with his staff, how robbers dared to penetrate inside the enclosure thus formed, how one of them was gored to death by the saint's bull, and afterwards raised to life, admonished, and forgiven. Meanwhile, the other thieves do not seem to have been able to escape outside the magic circle. Chapter IX. tells a story that has obtained currency, I fancy, because of its picturesqueness, and what is supposed to be its "edifying" character; how the saint, saying his Psalter in the open air, was surrounded by an invisible canopy impenetrable by the rain which fell around, save once, apparently, when a wandering and idle thought for one moment crossed his mind, whereupon the shower wet both him and his book, and recalled him to his duty. But in Chapter X. we have, as our author says, "miracle added to miracle." A youth belonging to the saint's school, desiring to escape a punishment about to be inflicted on him, ran away, carrying off St. Ninian's staff. In his terror he incautiously put out to sea in a wicker-framed coracle, over which the hide had not been drawn. After a little the water came pouring in, and with pale countenance he beheld the waves ready to avenge the injury done to his master. When at length coming to himself, and believing that St. Ninian "was present in his staff," he besought him by his most holy merits that aid might come to him from God. He then stuck the staff into one of the holes, and this took place that posterity might understand what St. Ninian could do even on the sea. "On the touch of the staff the element trembled, and did not presume to enter further through the open holes." To be brief, the youth landed safely and planted the staff on the shore, where the dry wood took root and bore branches and leaves; and at the root of the tree a most limpid fountain springing up, sent forth a crystal stream delightful to the eye, sweet to the taste, etc. Chapter XI. consists in an eulogy on the saint, and relates his burial in a stone coffin near the altar; while Chapter XII. concludes the book with relation of certain miracles wrought by his relics.

After the perusal of this record of marvels, those who have acquired experience in such studies will, I believe, not hesitate to declare that these are for the most part not the mere outcome of the misunderstandings of a credulous age, but in great part, at all events, the deliberate concoctions of a dull romancer.

Of course we are well aware that even our most trusted sources of information on the history of the Church at certain periods contain narratives of supernatural occurrences that are scarcely likely to commend themselves as strictly representing actual facts, when weighed by the modern historian, who comes untrammelled to the investigation. But from among the general body of ecclesiastical documents of the middle ages, an acquired tact will enable us to make a distinction between miracles and miracles, and to discriminate, often with a high measure of probability, between, on the one hand, the narration of the careful writer who recorded what, on some fair show of evidence, he rightly or wrongly believed to be true, and, on the other, the wild romancing of a professional miracle-monger. In the former class we are very frequently rewarded by a sense of contact, at many points, with reality; in the latter, we find abounding the unmistakable flavour of the unscrupulous story-teller. We are in a different world when we pass from Bede's narratives of the supernatural to the succession of astounding prodigies related by Jocelyn of Furness.[1]

It would be wearisome were I to deal with the *Life of St. Kentigern* chapter by chapter. One's appetite for the marvellous is quickly satiated. And while an occasional prodigy may enliven a story, my experience is that reading a rapid succession of them is as dull

[1] Problems of a special kind are presented by Adamnan's *Life of St. Columba*, and they will be considered separately when the history of the Irish mission is dealt with.

work as the systematic perusal of a jest-book. Nevertheless, I would fain convey some taste of the flavour of Jocelyn's confections. Well, then, when Kentigern as a boy was under the instruction of St. Serf at Culross, some of his youthful school-fellows in their rough play pulled the head off a pet redbreast of the master, and then sought to lay the blame on Kentigern; but he placed the bird's head upon its body, and signed it with the sign of the cross, when away it flew. On another occasion, while still under the tuition of St. Serf, it was Kentigern's duty to light the lamps of the church, but no fire could be found. Whereupon Kentigern took a bough of a growing hazel-tree, and when he had signed it and blessed it in the name of the Trinity, fire fell from heaven and kindled the bough, which, like Moses' bush, burned but was not consumed. The bird and the tree that figure heraldically in the arms of the city of Glasgow were suggested by these legends; while the salmon with the ring in its mouth that is represented on the dexter side of the shield is supposed to be a memorial of a less edifying story of Jocelyn's, in which we are told how a certain queen, Languoreth by name, who had been an unfaithful wife, is able, through the miraculous aid afforded by the saint, to pose successfully before her husband as a slandered and innocent woman. But I do not know that any of the stories takes my fancy more than that of the saint's ram, which ran faster after its head was cut off than it did before it was slaughtered; while the head, turned into stone, remains at Glasgow " even unto this day," writes

Jocelyn, "as a proof of the miracle, and, though silent, declares the merit of St. Kentigern."[1] The titles of chapters were doubtless intended not only to summarize the contents, but also to whet the curiosity of the reader. Some of these are as follows: "How Saint Kentigern placed in the plough under one yoke a stag and a wolf, and how, sowing sand, he reaped wheat";[2] "Concerning a cook raised from the dead by the prayers of St. Kentigern"; "How a jester, despising the gifts of the king, demanded a dish of fresh mulberries after Christmas, and how, through St. Kentigern, he received them"; "Concerning two vessels full of milk sent by St. Kentigern to a certain craftsman, and how the milk was spilled into the river and became cheese"; "How the Lord protected the saint's garments from being wet by the smallest drop of rain, snow, or hail." All these, and many more, are entertaining stories, if one does not indulge in too many of them at a time; and, to do him justice, Jocelyn does his best to draw a moral from each.

From a biography such as Jocelyn's it is a task of the greatest difficulty, if indeed it be not an absolute impossibility, to extract historical material as to which we can feel complete confidence. We may be able to

---

[1] The story of the ring and the salmon may be briefly told. The king finds on the finger of one of his knights, who was asleep, a ring given by the king to his queen; he throws it into the Clyde, and then asks the queen to show him the ring; the queen, in her distress, asks the aid of the saint, at whose command a salmon is caught in the river, and the ring is found in the body of the fish and given to the queen.

[2] The same marvel is told of St. Ternan in the *Aberdeen Breviary*, pars hyem., fol. lv.

say of one incident perhaps, "This may well have been; it falls in with what we learn elsewhere"; or of another, "It possesses more of local colour than we can readily attribute to an inventor"; but beyond this we feel that our footsteps are on very uncertain ground.

Jocelyn tells us that Kentigern, "matured in merit," died at the age of 185. After what we have seen of the character of Jocelyn's romancing, is it really worth while to adduce in relation to this statement (as is done by the acute and learned Dr. A. P. Forbes, late Bishop of Brechin) examples of great longevity, such as that of the famous Countess of Desmond, "Old Parr," and some instances referred to by the physiologist Haller, all of which come to us on evidence that at least deserves consideration? It seems to me a remarkable example of how the judgment of an able, learned, and cultivated man may be warped by a "tendency," in this instance (as I take it), a misplaced reverence for what is certainly ancient and had a show of piety. "Temperance," writes Bishop Forbes, "sweet temper, and faith tend to length of days;" and, as Bishop Forbes is plainly not indisposed to believe many of the alleged miracles, he might well have added that in the moist climate of the west of Scotland, and before another Scotchman had invented the "mackintosh," it must have been of immense hygienic value never to have worn wet clothes. For here Jocelyn is very express: "All bear witness who knew the man, as well as those that conversed with him, that never in his life were his clothes wetted with the drops of pouring rain, snow, or hail, dropping upon the earth. For many a time placed in the open air while the inclemency of the weather increased, while the pouring rain flowed along like a sewer, and the spirit of the storm raged around him, he stood immovable, or went where he wished, and always continued untouched and uninjured by a drop of any kind."[1] In the region of ecclesiastical no less than of civil history, our first thoughts should ever be not of what is "edifying" or what is "pious," but of what is *true*. To the kind of criticism indicated above, there can be no question of the superiority of the critical spirit shown by the Bollandists, who in many instances apply what I shall venture to call the "canon of common-sense" as trenchantly as the most sceptical of modern inquirers. Again, in our own day, an Irish scholar of distinction,[2] who certainly cannot be justly accused of a tendency to unreasonable incredulity, does not scruple to test some of the legendary histories of Irish saints (though perhaps with some inconsistency of application) by ordinary common-sense considerations applicable to the events of every-day life. Thus the St. Ninian of Scotland

---

[1] Bishop Forbes, in the end of his discussion (*Historians of Scotland*, vol. vi., p. 369), asserts that "the difficulty in the case of St. Kentigern arises from chronological considerations," and cites an admirable passage from Mr. Skene, who shows that "if you deduct the 100 (*i. e.* from 185), you will bring out a chronology very consistent with other events." Exactly so; *if* you deduct 100, which would bring the age of St. Kentigern to the not very unusual 85 years.

[2] Dr. John Healy (Roman Catholic), Coadjutor Bishop of Clonfert.

appears in Ireland (with the common honorific prefix *mo*[1]) as St. Mo-nenn. In former times there was a disposition to identify St. Moinenn of Clonfert with St. Ninian or Mo-nenn of Candida Casa, but the critic to whom I refer declares such an identification to be "manifestly out of the question," as it would have made St. Ninian of Candida Casa "at least 200 years of age."[2] The disposition to dignify the Celtic saints with extraordinary longevity is common among the Irish hagiographers. Thus St. Ultan of Ardbraccan dies, according to the *Martyrology of Donegal*, at the age of 189. The authors of the lives of St. Ciaran, St. Declan, and St. Ailbe give to these saints lives extending from 200 to 300 and even 400 years; while, according to a writer who scorns round numbers and will be accurately precise, St. Ibar died at the age of 353.[3]

We have already hinted that for dealing with the legendary lives of the saints a valuable qualification would be extensive reading in hagiological literature generally. If the student confines himself to only one or two documents, he will, I think, spend more time and take more trouble in sifting some marvellous tale, and labouring to find what he might imagine to be the nucleus of truth contained in it, than he will feel himself justified in doing if he finds the same startling and effective story appearing again and again

---

[1] *Mo* = "my," a term of endearment.
[2] *Insula Sanctorum et Doctorum; or, Ireland's Ancient Schools and Scholars*, by the Most Reverend John Healy, D.D., etc., p. 223.
[3] See Bishop Healy's *Insula Sanctorum*, etc., pp. 136-7.

in various lives with or without modification. Indeed, quite independently of any search for biographical facts, the examination of such materials for a comparative Christian mythology as are supplied, for instance, in the long row of great folios that make the *Acta Sanctorum* of the Bollandists, would form a study entirely worthy of the scientific inquirer. The task would doubtless necessitate the expenditure of much time and trouble; and probably we shall have to wait till some patient German of large erudition and indomitable perseverance undertakes it. I may illustrate what I am thinking of by one or two examples. We have seen already how St. Kentigern, while still a youth, is greatly embarrassed for the want of fire, which had been extinguished throughout the monastery of St. Serf; he takes a branch of a green hazel-tree, breathes upon it, signs with the sign of the cross in the Name of the Trinity, and it immediately bursts into flame. Now this same Jocelyn, who so well hit off the prevailing taste, was requested by the Irish Archbishop of Armagh and the Bishop of Down to write a life of St. Patrick, and here we find St. Patrick, while still a child, miraculously making a good fire, not this time with green hazel branches, but with a lapful of icicles, which, similarly, he breathes upon and signs with the cross. Again, St. Mungo has the dead body of Fergus, "a man of God," placed in a wain drawn by "two untamed bulls," which move to the appointed burying-place. This miracle, we are told,[1] was repeated in the cases of

---

[1] *Historians of Scotland*, vol. v., Notes, p. 329.

several other saints, who are named as St. Fursey, St. Florentinus, St. Tressanus, St. Joava, St. Fachult, and St. Patrick. In the case of St. Gall, the story is varied; unbridled horses take the place of oxen or bulls.[1] We have noticed in the *Life of St. Ninian* how the saint cleared a priest of false accusation by the voice of a new-born child. St. Aldhelm, the Saxon scholar of the seventh century, in a similar manner, when at Rome, extracts a declaration from a child nine days old which cleared the credit of Pope Sergius I. St. Brigid of Kildare, by a like adjuration, proves the innocence of a bishop; and this story appears in one of the Lessons on the festival of that saint in the *Aberdeen Breviary*.[2] A similar story is told in the mediæval Lectionary of the Church of England of St. Britius, whose name still appears in the calendar of our Prayer-Book at November 13,[3] with the slight variation that the saint himself is the accused and the child is a month old. Nor does even this instance exhaust all the parallels.

One other illustration may be offered of this tendency to the recurrence of certain striking stories. There may be differences of opinion as to the date when St. Baldred flourished, but we need have no doubt that a hermit of that name took up his abode upon the Bass-rock, which forms so remarkable an object at

---

[1] I have not gone to the trouble of discovering who is meant by St. Joava, but I am sure the story is as true of him or her as it is of the others better known.

[2] Pars hyem., fol. xlvi.

[3] See *Sarum Breviary* (edit. Procter and Wordsworth), Fascic. iii., col. 1033.

the mouth of the estuary of the Forth, and that he laboured in good works among the people of the neighbouring parts of Lothian. He taught the faith, we are told, in three churches of that region—Aldhame, Tynynghame, and Preston. On the death of the saint there was an eager contention which of these churches should have the honour of possessing his body. Prayer was made that a sign from heaven might be given to settle the question in debate; and, lo, on the morrow, three bodies were found exactly alike, each laid out "with the same exequial pomp," and each congregation carried off one, which was ever after held in the greatest reverence.[1] Bishop Forbes has pointed out a parallel to the triplication of the saint's body in the case of the great Welsh saint, St. Teilo; while two bodies are produced in a legend of St. Patrick and in a legend of St. Monnena.[2]

Valueless, or worse than valueless, as these stories may appear to us, it is the part of the historian to remember that in former times such narratives entered largely into the religious beliefs and largely affected the religious sentiments of both clergy and people. None of them were too absurd to be read in the appointed Lessons of the Church,[3] and they possessed all the qualifications for impressing and holding the imagination of a credulous and ignorant people.

It is worthy of mention that as late as the sixteenth

---

[1] See Forbes' *Kalendars of Scottish Saints*, p. 274.
[2] Smith and Wace, *Dict. of Chr. Biog.*, s.v. Baldred.
[3] The story of the multiplication of St. Baldred's body will be found in the *Aberdeen Breviary*, pars hyem., fol. lxiii., *sq.*

century the story of the triplication of St. Baldred's body appears in one of the philosophic writings of an eminent Scottish theologian, John Major, or Mair, who, after studying at Cambridge, became famous at Paris as a lecturer on Theology at the Sorbonne.[1] In his commentary upon the Fourth Book of the *Sentences* of Peter Lombard, a recognized text-book of the theological schools, Major, when treating of the Holy Eucharist, argues from the story of the body of St. Baldred that it is possible with God "that the same body can be placed *circumscriptive* in different places at the same time."[2]

Once more; in examining the ancient documents which are concerned with the lives of the saints, the critic is bound to take into consideration *moral improbabilities*, and what I may call *miracles in the moral and spiritual world*, as well as miracles in the physical world. The cases where real discrimination and the exercise of sound judgment are needed (and such are very numerous) are, of course, very different from cases involving palpable absurdities like the following, which I adduce as affording illustrations,

---

[1] In 1518 Major was induced to leave Paris for Glasgow, where he was made Principal Regent of the College, and continued to reside for five years. John Knox, the leader of the Scottish Reformation, was matriculated at Glasgow while Major was in office; and Dr. Æneas J. G. Mackay—in his scholarly life of Major, prefixed to the translation of Major's *Historia Majoris Britanniæ*, printed by the Scottish History Society (1892)—conjectures that the fame of Major may have been the cause of Knox going to Glasgow rather than to St. Andrews.

[2] See *A History of Greater Britain* (1892), p. 87, note.

on a magnified scale, that will carry conviction even to the least suspicious of those addicted to hagiological literature. In a manuscript *Life of St. Serf*, preserved in Archbishop Marsh's library in Dublin, which has been printed in the Appendix to Dr. Skene's *Chronicles of the Picts and Scots* (pp. 412—423), we read how St. Serf was first Patriarch of Jerusalem for seven years, then Pope of Rome for seven years, and finally settled himself at the village of Culross on the northern shore of the Forth. Now, even if the records of the episcopal succession at Jerusalem and at Rome were more patent than they are of this startling allegation, it will be admitted that, to say the least, this is a highly improbable story. For myself, I could quite as easily credit that St. Serf, as we read in the same narrative, was miraculously born to his parents, Obeth, King of Canaan, and his wife Alpia, daughter of the King of Arabia, that on his way *from Canaan to Jerusalem* he crossed the Red Sea, like Moses, on dry ground, and that an angel cut for him a staff of the wood of the tree from which the Cross of Christ had been made. Again, when St. Serf, having surrendered the throne of St. Peter at Rome, despite the expostulations of the whole people, had advanced to the coast of France, he crossed the sea to England on dry ground, with 7,000,000 companions of his pilgrimage.[1] This large number of

---

[1] After reading this narrative, it will not surprise the reader to learn that St. Adrian, who is also of royal descent, should come from Hungary to labour among the Picts, accompanied by 6606 companions, who were all martyred by the Danes. (*Aberdeen Breviary*, pars hyem., fol. lxii.)

fellow-travellers is doubtless a little surprising; but we cannot assert that it involves a suspension of the physical laws of nature.[1] Is it, however, more probable than their mode of crossing the channel? We certainly cannot wonder that when St. Serf met St. Edheunanus at the island of Inchkeith, after they had spent a great part of the night in secret converse, he should put to his friend the awkward question, "How am I to dispose of my family and companions?" After these things the reader becomes impatient of the subsequent stories of his healing the blind, raising the dead, and other such commonplaces. A brief stimulant to our jaded sense of wonder is supplied by the narrative of how the saint cured a man afflicted with an insatiable appetite by thrusting his thumb into the patient's mouth, and so expelling a devil by whom he had been possessed; of how a pig which a poor man had killed for the saint's supper was found next morning safe and sound; and lastly, of how a sheep-stealer, who was declaring his innocence by oath on the saint's wonder-working staff, was painfully convicted by the animal bleating inside the culprit.[2]

[1] The text of the MS., as printed in the *Chronicles of the Picts and Scots*, reads *cum septem milibus milium*. Skene (*Celtic Scotland*, vol. ii., p. 256) seems to take *milium* as an error for *militum*, and to understand the word as meaning *monks*. But the story is too absurd to be improved by the conjectures of the textual critic. The word *miles*, it may be added, needs some such addition as *Dei* or *Christi* to signify a monk.

[2] Archbishop Usher was acquainted with this *Life of St. Servanus*, and describes it as "packed with the most stupid lies"— a verdict that will probably be assented to by all (*Brit. Eccl.*

The extravagances and absurdities of many of the lives of the saints of the ancient Scottish, Irish, and British Churches were distinctly recognized in the seventeenth century by one who may justly be reckoned as in the very first rank of authorities on hagiological literature, the learned Jesuit, John Bollandus (1596—1665), who initiated the vast design that has resulted in the long series of the *Acta Sanctorum*, volume after volume of which has been appearing, at varying intervals, from 1643 up to our own day. The attitude of the Church of which he was a member towards the miraculous scarcely permitted him that freedom of critical investigation which is open to others; and he himself was certainly by no means over-sceptical. But he was plainly somewhat staggered by the records of our national hagiology. He in a marked way particularizes in this connection the lives of the saints of Ireland, Scotland, and of the ancient British Church, rightly including among the latter the saints of Gallic Brittany. In other words, the narratives of Celtic origin, in his opinion, have a portentous wildness of statement which is characteristic. It is as much as could

---

Antiq., p. 353, edit. 1687). Yet these stories of the recreated pig and the bleating mutton formed part of the faith of the people of Scotland. They both are read in the Lessons for St. Serf's day in the *Aberdeen Breviary*. The Rev. T. Olden has been so good as to point out to me a similar story in Jocelyn's *Life of St. Patrick*. St. Patrick's he-goat, employed by the saint in carrying water, was stolen, killed, and eaten. The suspected thief declared his innocence on oath; but "a vile-sounding bleating" in the stomach of the culprit revealed the truth. (*Vita S. Pat.*, cap. xv.)

be expected of him when he declares them to be "almost incredible."[1] And I am afraid it is only too true that the Celtic saints occupy this position of unenviable pre-eminence; though I am bound to say the hermit saints of Egypt come in a good second.

Some may, I fear, think that I have been unsympathetic in my treatment of the lives of the saints of the Celtic period. But dealing, as I was, with the trustworthiness of the documents, I do not know that I could have adopted any other line. I am quite willing to admit that, in many cases, the writers themselves believed the marvels that they reported. Allowance must, in all cases, be made for temperaments characteristic of race. An excitable, sentimental, and highly-emotional people will be judged by a different standard from that applicable to those of a cold-blooded and phlegmatic disposition. Rude and uncultivated minds cannot be expected to possess the natural critical acumen which we find among peoples who have been subjected for generations to a strict mental discipline. Even at this day, how difficult it is for us to discover the real truth from the highly-coloured descriptions of contemporary events in Ireland.

Nor should we omit to notice, as contributing something to the influences affecting the work of the old Celtic writers, the wild and sometimes awe-inspiring aspects of Nature in the midst of which they dwelt. Life upon desolate moorlands, or amid

---

[1] General Preface to the *Acta Sanctorum*, Jan. Tom. i., p. 34.

mountains often shrouded in mysterious gloom, or by the wild shores of the Atlantic, may well have fostered a natural tendency to strange fancies and superstitious fears. Even now Ireland and the Scottish Highlands can breed portents and prodigies which cannot breathe the air of regions occupied by people of Saxon descent. Those who have read the recently-published *Journal of Sir Walter Scott* may remember how, in 1827, Sir Walter was informed by Clanronald of a carefully-organized attempt made, apparently shortly before, to catch a *water-cow*, which inhabited a small lake near the house of the chieftain. And the excellent editor of the *Journal*, Mr. David Douglas, adds the illustrative note that yet more recently the proprietor of Loch-na-Beiste, " moved by the entreaties of the people and *on the positive testimony of two elders of the Free Church* that the creature was hiding in his loch, attempted its destruction by pumping and running off the water; this plan having failed, owing to the smallness of the pumps (though it was persevered in for two years), he next tried poisoning the water by emptying into the loch a quantity of quicklime." But the water-cow does not seem to have suffered materially, as it was seen in the neighbourhood as late as 1884. "This transaction," adds Mr. Douglas, "formed an element in a case before the Crofters' Commission at Aultbea, in May 1888." · Surely, if we will not be very hard upon the grave and reverend " Free Church elders" towards the close of the nineteenth century, we must make allowance for the witness-bearing of the members of another Scottish Church a thousand years earlier.

It seems to me certain that "the law of demand and supply" prevails in regard to "miracles" as well as to other commodities. Where the ordinary interests of life are numerous and varied, there is little taste for the marvellous. Where, on the contrary, men's thoughts have small scope beyond the events of a somewhat monotonous existence, a ghost, a prodigy, or a miracle is eagerly accepted. It serves to stir the dull blood, and becomes a valued possession. Now, when men crave a stimulant of this kind, a supply is sure to be forthcoming among an imaginative people. The long evenings of winter spent by households gathered in the firelight supplied the fitting environment for the development of the myth. Exaggeration and embellishment were absolutely certain; and will any one, knowing what human nature is, doubt that there was a good deal of deliberate invention? But when a striking story that reflected honour on some local or national saint once got currency, it would have been felt by most as nothing short of irreverence or profanity to question its truth. And so, by and by, the silliest legends found their way, not only into the popular lives of the saints, but into the Service-books of the Church.

CHAPTER VI.

ST. COLUMBA.

IN treating of the career of the third great figure that is presented to us in the history of the evangelization of Scotland, we are fortunate in possessing records of a very different kind from those with which we had to deal in the cases of St. Ninian and St. Kentigern. One of the most precious relics in the early records of any people is the *Life of St. Columba,* by the Abbat Adamnan. No wide interval of time intervened in this case between the writer and the subject of the biography. In his early years, Adamnan must have had " frequent opportunities of conversing with those who had seen St. Columba." All materials, written or oral, which Iona could supply were at his disposal. He wrote his account in the island home of the saint, and "surrounded by objects, every one of which was fresh with the impress of some interesting association." Though Adamnan was the ninth abbat of the monastery of Iona, the succession of its chief officers had been rapid; and it was only one hundred years after the death of the saint that he drew up his inestimable memoir. He had before him at least two written documents dealing with his subject, and of these he makes use.[1] Whatever may be thought of his narratives of miraculous occurrences, there is no reason to suppose that he was not an honest relater of what he heard from others or found recorded in writing. And the innumerable notices of the ordinary incidents in the story of the founder of his house bear the unquestionable stamp of truthfulness. The whole work abounds in material by the help of which it is not difficult to reconstruct with much reasonable confidence the constitution of the brotherhood and to picture to ourselves the daily life of its members. The Scottish antiquary, Pinkerton, does not perhaps overrate the merits of Adamnan's work when he declares it to be "the most complete piece of such biography that Europe can boast of, not only at so early a period, but even through the whole Middle Ages."[2] And the latest and most learned editor of the work declares that "Adamnan's memoir is to be prized as an inestimable literary relic of the Irish Church: perhaps, with all its defects, the most valuable monument of that institution which has escaped the ravages of time."[3] And we must add that the inquirer into this period of Scottish ecclesiastical history is fortunate not only in the possession of this early memoir, but also fortunate to a very high degree in the consummate learning and judgment

---

[1] Dr. Reeves, *Historians of Scotland*, vol. vi., p. xx.
[2] *Enquiry*, etc., vol. i., p. xlviii.
[3] Reeves, *ut supra*, Preface, p. xxxi.

exercised in its illustration by the late Dr. William Reeves, afterwards Bishop of Down and Connor.

The consideration of the supposed miraculous occurrences recorded by Adamnan will be considered in a separate chapter. We shall here endeavour to sketch the life of Columba, as it may be gathered from this work and from other ancient records.

In our sketch of the planting of the Christian Church in Scotland there now comes to be related an event, seemingly insignificant, but in reality pregnant with profound consequences to the future of religion, not only in Scotland but in Britain generally, and, indeed, not without its considerable influence on the fortunes of the faith in various parts of the continent of Europe.

One day, in the year of our Lord 563, there landed upon a small island off the west coast of Scotland an Irish monk, Columba by name, with twelve companions, who had accompanied him from his native land.

It was not uncommon, in those days of violence, rapine, and frequent tribal quarrels, for men who had made choice of the life of monastic devotion to seek for the more complete retirement and greater security which were attainable by removing themselves out of the track of wars, with the danger of enforced military service, and away from the fear of the fierce marauding bands, from whose savagery few parts of the mainland were long exempt. Hence one of the characteristic features of Irish monasticism—its fondness for island homes. The islands off the west coasts of Ireland and Scotland abound to this day in ecclesiastical memories; and many shadowy traditions gather round the remains of broken cross, ruined cell, or roofless chapel, over which have swept the spray-laden Atlantic storms of a thousand years.

In the particular case before us, other motives may have been at work in determining the choice, in the first instance, of Iona as a place of settlement, or, at all events, the continued preference shown for it. The little island that Columba made his home and head-quarters for thirty-five years, while being indeed a place of secure retirement, when retirement was sought, proved also a serviceable basis of operation in active missionary enterprise. Along the deeply-indented coast-line of the west of Scotland a boat with oars and sails gave the missionary of the sixth century almost as many advantages as he would possess at the present day. He could not, indeed, as we can with the aid of steam, defy wind and tide; but, watching his opportunities, he could move about with ease, and choose his own places and his own time for landing and leaving.

In the monastic system of Ireland and Celtic Scotland, as elsewhere, the continuous round of Divine worship, the cultivation of the spirit of devotion, the study of Divine truth, the practice of self-discipline, were all duly cared for; but with these were conjoined on the part of the Celtic monks a missionary zeal so earnest and an ardour of diffusive Christian love so glowing, that the lives of their recluses and anchorites are seldom thought of, and our minds naturally dwell on the active and untiring missionary labours which have achieved such great things for the evangelization of our own land, and which subsequently extended their beneficent influence even to the remote regions of Germany and Switzerland and Italy.

But who was this Columba? His story has been often told, and can never gain a hearing without stirring men's hearts, for it is indeed the story of a noble life, a life of high aims and unceasing endeavour, a life full of loving sympathy with his fellow-men, and of loving devotion to his Lord. And if Columba was not without his failings and faults, they are faults and failings that beset men of naturally warm hearts, strong will, and eager temperament, and such as are often found associated with the characters of those who have made a deep impression upon their fellows, and have gained for themselves commanding stations in the history of the world, or of the Church.

Columba was born in Donegal in the year 521. He belonged to the clan of the O'Donnels, which has again and again figured largely in the subsequent history of Ireland. He was descended on both father and mother's side from the families of powerful provincial princes.

We have seen that tradition has represented the two other great figures that attract the eye when we view the early history of religion in Scotland, St. Ninian and St. Mungo, as also of royal blood. And this, taken together with what we now learn was told of St. Columba, may perhaps raise a suspicion in some minds that there is something of romancing in these old stories. But I do not think that further consideration will bear out the suspicion—I mean as regards this particular feature of the histories. It is true that there was a temptation to the ancient hagiologists to glorify their heroes by representing them as of exalted birth; but taking all the evidence into account, we may, I think, come to the conclusion that while in the case of Columba his royal descent and connection must be regarded as absolutely certain, in the other cases, more particularly that of St. Ninian, there is no sufficient reason to seriously question the statement. Again, we should remember that the bringing up of a child amid the traditions of a historic family, the inspiring effect of the stirring tales of forefathers and relations, and the comparative breadth of view that must have been found in the circle of a great chief, as contrasted with the mere personal cares and petty occupations of the common crowd, would all have helped to stimulate the imagination, and have made easier the influence of ideal motives in initiating great things. High courage and the spirit of adventure often comes amid such surroundings; and both were indeed needed by the early Christian pioneers in Britain. In the case of Columba, as we shall see, his royal connections helped probably to determine his choosing his settlement among the islands of the west of Scotland. Again, we shall not be wrong in believing that, among a people so keenly alive to the claims of hereditary rank as the Celtic populations of Scotland

and Ireland, the advantages possessed by Columba must have added vastly to his influence as preacher, missionary, and monastic ruler.

At his baptism the boy was given, as is supposed, the two names—Crimthann, a "wolf," and Colum, a "dove." The former name, which might have been very appropriate had the noble child devoted himself in after life, like so many of his ancestors and relations, to war and rapine, was dropped by the Christian priest and missionary; and Colm, or, in its Latin form, Columba, is the name under which he has become famous in Church history.[1]

Columba, it is said, was from early years devoted to attendance on the services of the Church. We do not find in his case, as in that of some others who in the days of their subsequent penitence did great things for Christ, that he was in early days led astray by the seductions of the world or of youthful pleasures. He is represented as from boyhood devoted to the practice of piety, and as an eager student. He first attended the monastic school of St. Finnian of Moville, at the head of Strangford Lough; and there he was ordained deacon. He next moved south into Leinster,

---

[1] In after time the word "kille" was sometimes added to the word "Colm"—either on account, as is said, of the great number of churches founded by him, or on account of his early devotion to attendance at church. The name Colum in different forms was a great favourite. The suffix *an* is a diminutive, and has given us the very common name of Colman=Columan. Dr. Gammack (in Smith and Wace's *Dictionary of Christian Biography*) supplies notices of 41 Colmans; and Archbishop Usher says that upwards of 230 of that name are to be found in records of Irish saints.

and placed himself under the instruction of a secular teacher—the "bard" Gemman. At a subsequent time we shall find him exerting himself successfully for the protection of the Irish bards (the professional poets and chroniclers of Ireland), at the great Council of Drumceatt. He was himself a skilful writer of verse, and we possess, not only some remarkable Latin hymns, but also some poems in his Irish vernacular, which have been, not without reason, attributed to his pen.[1] Thus we see he did not despise what was the chief form of secular culture known to his age and country.

We next find Columba attending the most famous school of ecclesiastical learning of that day in Ireland —the monastery of Clonard, situated on the upper waters of the Boyne, under another St. Finnian.[2] Clonard, in respect to the vast number of its monks and students, reminds one of a mediæval university. Usher seems to accept the statement that reckons its scholars as three thousand. And here Columba remained for several years.[3]

It is of much interest to note that Columba, in attending the schools of the two Finnians, became probably acquainted with the monastic systems of

---

[1] See Appendix I. for a translation of the poem *Altus Prosator* attributed to Columba.

[2] The name in the forms Finian, Finan, Fintan, Findan, etc., is very common. It is the diminutive of Finn = white, *i. e.* probably "the light-haired." Finnian of Moville is sometimes referred to under the name Find-bar = white head.

[3] The numbers at Clonard find a parallel in the case of the Irish Bangor.

both the north British school of Candida Casa (where Finnian of Moville had studied), and also of the south British, or Welsh, school of St. David (under whose instruction at Menevia, Finnian of Clonard had been a pupil). In Columba the influence of St. Ninian in Galloway came back to another part of Scotland by a strange route.

It is also interesting to know that both these St. Finnians are commemorated in Scottish mediæval calendars, and that Finnian of Moville, appearing under the form Vinnin or Wynnin, has, as has been thought, given his name to the town of Kilwinning in Ayrshire.

At Clonard Columba gained much skill in the art of the copyist, which, in other hands, was brought afterwards to such marvellous artistic perfection, as we find in the superb decorations of the *Book of Kells* and other Irish manuscripts. It was while a resident at Clonard that Columba was ordained Presbyter; and the story that refers to the incident is so curious and instructive, that it is worth being related. Its historic value, indeed, is of the slightest. Reeves declares it to be a fiction of a later age, but it illustrates very well some of the ecclesiastical usages of the time. St. Finnian, who was at the head of the great monastery, was not himself of higher rank than presbyter, but perhaps he desired to have Columba as a resident bishop, who would perform all the needed episcopal duties of the place. Accordingly, as the story runs, he sent Columba to Etchen, bishop at the monastery of Clonfad (in Westmeath), with a request for his consecration. On reaching Clonfad and inquiring for the bishop, Columba is informed that he is ploughing in a neighbouring field. On finding the bishop and disclosing his errand, he is received in a very kind manner, but through some error as to the wishes of St. Finnian, or some other unaccountable mistake, Columba is ordained only priest, and not bishop. Now let us observe what may be learned from this legend, supposing it to reflect the ecclesiastical notions current at a very early date in Ireland. We saw already that St. Mungo was consecrated bishop by only one Irish bishop, and the same practice—which, as I have said, has always been reckoned by the Church generally as *valid*, though *uncanonical* and *irregular*—seems to have continued, at least on occasions, till the twelfth century. Certainly Lanfranc, Archbishop of Canterbury (1070—1093), complained of the practice as existing in Ireland in his day; and the complaint was repeated by his successor, Anselm (1093—1114).[1]

This curious story not only points to the practice of consecration by a single bishop, but suggests the notion that what is known as consecration *per saltum* (that is, that consecration to the higher grade without formally passing through the lower) was then recognized. Very many hundred years afterwards, when James VI. desired to restore the episcopal succession to Scotland, this question of *per saltum* consecration was discussed, and the bishops of the Jacobean episcopate were consecrated (with the sanction of the

[1] Usher, *Vet. Epist. Hibern. Sylloge*, xxvii., xxxv., xxxvi.

most learned theologians of England) without being required to go through the inferior grades of deacon and presbyter. The conferring of the higher office was held to include the authority to exercise the functions of the two lower.[1]

Columba appears never afterwards to have sought the rank of bishop; and the sentiment that it was unbecoming that any of his successors should possess a higher dignity than their great patron became a well-defined practical rule of the Columban monasteries.

But we must hasten over the remainder of the story of Columba in Ireland. After spending some time at another monastery, that of Glasnevin (now a suburb of Dublin, where are situated beautiful Botanic Gardens and a great public cemetery), he devoted, according to Bishop Reeves, some fifteen years to planting churches and monasteries in various parts of Ireland; and in view of his subsequent settlement in Iona, it is not uninteresting to observe that some of his Irish monasteries were situated in islands off the coast, as, for example, Lambay, Rathlin, Tory, and Inishowen.[2]

---

[1] After the great rebellion, however, when in 1661 episcopacy was again restored to Scotland, two Scottish divines—Leighton and Sharp—consecrated bishops at Westminster, were required to submit to previous ordination as deacons and presbyters. The validity of the former consecrations to the episcopate (in 1610) was not indeed questioned, but it was probably thought wiser to anticipate and prevent the raising of doubts at a later time.

[2] St. Columba's labours in Ireland have gained for him the distinction of being reckoned in Ireland as one of "the Three Patrons" of the country—St. Patrick and St. Brigid being the other two.

We now come to the time when Columba entered upon his labours in Scotland. This was not till he had reached forty-two years of age, but the remaining thirty-four years of a very active life were spent almost wholly either in his home at Iona, or among the other islands, or on the mainland of Scotland, engaged chiefly in the work of converting the heathen Picts of the north, and in teaching and building up the scattered and enfeebled Christian communities of men of his own race already existing in the western highlands.

Why did Columba leave Ireland? Different reasons have been assigned. Some contend that the love of God and of his brethren was to him a sufficient motive, and that his immediate objects were the instruction of the Christian Irish of the principality in Argyll, and the conversion of their neighbours, the Northern Picts.[1] It is necessary to be acquainted with the fact that for some considerable time before Columba's day, Scots from the north coast of Antrim, and belonging to the district called Dalriada, had been emigrating to the west of what is now Scotland, passing over the narrow channel that separated them from the Scottish mainland. They probably might easily land in Cantire, and spread up along the western coast of Argyll; and so they founded another principality of Dalriada, and laid the foundations of that other Scotia or Scotland,

---

[1] See Dr. George Grub, *Eccl. Hist. of Scot.*, vol. i., p. 49, and Dr. Skene, *Celtic Scotland*, vol., ii. p. 79; and this view seems to be accepted as the more probable by Prof. Stokes, *Ireland and the Celtic Church*, p. 112 *sq.*

which eventually took sole possession of the name. The great body of these Dalriads was Christianized before their emigration to Britain. Conal, the reigning prince of the British Dalriads at the time of Columba's first visiting that region, was a kinsman of the saint. Those who care to trace the genealogy and family history of Columba can do so with the help of Bishop Reeves; but it must suffice here to say that Columba's royal descent and connections served him in good stead in his work among the Scots in the region of Argyll and the more southern islands.

Professor Stokes, who here substantially follows Skene,[1] suggests (and I think he has here rightly gauged the high spirit and chivalrous temper of the man) that the imminent danger to which the new colony was exposed of extinction at the hands of the pagan Picts, stirred the heart of Columba to go to the effective assistance of his brethren, by bringing to their aid, "not the might of temporal warfare, but of those spiritual weapons which alone can curb and restrain unregenerate nature." Certainly it was only two or three years before the arrival of Columba among the British Scots that they had received a terrible defeat from the Northern Picts, under their warlike and, as Bede calls him, "most powerful king," Brude, whom we shall presently meet again in the history of Columba. What would have deterred timid natures may well

---

[1] Skene says plainly, "This great reverse (*i. e.* the defeat of the British Scots by Brude) called forth the mission of Columba, commonly called Columcille, and led to the foundation of the monastic Church in Scotland." *Celtic Scotland*, vol. ii., p. 79.

have acted as a powerful attraction to the generous, ardent, and right-royal soul of Columba.

Such seems a probable account of the reasons that actuated Columba in seeking this new field of labour, as they commend themselves to some among our ablest recent historians.

Bishop Reeves, however, is evidently not disposed to regard as altogether valueless the account which, from a very early date, had currency and acceptance in Ireland, and which represents the settlement of Columba at Iona as an involuntary exile, due to ecclesiastical censures passed upon him for the part taken by him in originating and urging on a war in which much Christian blood was shed on both sides.[1] At any rate, there might be just cause of complaint against me if I were to omit a story which, even if without historical foundation, is often referred to, and which should therefore, if for no better reason, be known to those who claim to possess acquaintance with the life of the saint.

Briefly told, the story runs as follows. His old teacher, St. Finnian of Moville gave on one occasion permission to Columba to examine, for the purpose of study, a manuscript of the Book of Psalms, or, as some say, a manuscript of the Gospels, which was Finnian's property. But Columba was not content

---

[1] The Rev. H. J. Lawlor has observed very justly that the two accounts are not inconsistent. "St. Columba (1) determined to engage in missionary work: this may have been in consequence of the judgment of Molaise; (2) he chose a *particular* sphere of work: to this he may have been guided by the considerations referred to by Skene and Stokes."

with only reading the book; he forthwith proceeded to make a transcript of it. When the account of this infringement of copyright reached the ears of St. Finnian, it roused him to warm indignation. He demanded that the copy should be handed over to him, together with the original. This demand Columba stoutly refused; and eventually it was resolved that the question in dispute should be referred to the decision of the King of Meath. The king in full court decided against Columba. The principle on which the decision was based was one laid down in the Brehon law; and the judgment was delivered, " To every cow her calf belongs, and so to every book its child-book." Columba's proud temper would not brook this adverse ruling, and he resolved to resort to arms with the aid of his clansmen, the Northern Hy-Neill. No doubt he would represent it to himself as a struggle, not on account of a paltry book, but for the sake of a principle of justice and right. We know how easy it is for good men when angry to find that they are not contending for self but for principle. A battle was fought at Cooldrevny (somewhere between the town of Sligo and the neighbouring Drumcliffe). Victory went with the Ulster allies of Columba, and 3000 men of Meath were reckoned among the slain.

I offer no opinion on the probability of this story; I would only say that in estimating the evidence we should not fail to take into account the fierce spirit of the age. Again, we must not omit to remember the very slight occasions that have at almost all times been found sufficient in Ireland to stir up clan-feuds; nor, finally, the historical fact that at that time, and long after, it was not considered derogatory to the members of the monasteries to bear arms and take an active part in bloody wars.

The story in one of its forms then goes on to say that Columba, after the slaughter at Cooldrevny, consulted his "soul-friend," *i. e.* his confessor and spiritual adviser, Molaise, who then lived on the wild island of Inismurray, six miles off the Sligo coast.[1] Perhaps Columba was already suffering the excommunication by an ecclesiastical synod of which we hear in another account. Indeed, we have the authority of Adamnan for saying that he was for a time excommunicated; Adamnan says for trivial faults, and, as it afterwards appeared, unjustly. At any rate, Molaise is said to have enjoined upon Columba as a penance to leave his dear Ireland, and to devote himself to missionary labours among the heathen Picts until he had converted to Christ as many souls as his recent conduct had brought down to death upon the battle-field.

In accord with the story I have now related, is the further feature of the legend (which is certainly not without a tender and poetic beauty of its own), that Columba, attended by twelve companions, having sailed from Ireland in compliance with the penance enjoined upon him, first landed at the island of Oronsay; but finding that from the highest point of the

---

[1] See an extremely interesting account of this island and its ecclesiastical remains, quoted by Stokes, *Ireland and the Celtic Church,* vol. i., p. 184 *sq.* I have visited Inismurray, and can testify to the profoundly interesting character of the place.

land he could still see the distant coast-line of his beloved Ireland, he again embarked, and finally settled at Iona, after having satisfied himself that no longer was Ireland visible.[1]

From the documents sifted and examined in the historic spirit, it would appear that a grant of the island of Iona was made to Columba by his kinsman Conal, the reigning prince of the colony of Dalriads in Scotland; and it seems not improbable that before the landing of Columba on Iona, the island already contained a Christian community. But, however this may have been, henceforth Iona was to be for ever associated pre-eminently with the name of Columba.

The eventful landing of Columba in Iona is to be placed, as has been said, in the year of our Lord 563.

Columba, having built a church and monastic cells of a rude kind, and generally organized his little community in the island, soon turned his attention to labour among his Irish brethren in British Dalriada, and more especially to the grand design of Christianizing the enemies at once of his countrymen and of the faith—the northern pagan Picts.

At this time the kingdom of the Pictish king, Brude, the son of Mailcon, was powerful and widely extended. The principal residence of the king was situated not far from Inverness.[2] Columba was at-

---

[1] It has been conjectured by some that Columba's leaving Ireland was a self-inflicted penance.

[2] Reeves places the royal residence at the vitrified fort of Craigphadrick, the remains of which are still to be seen; but Skene, as I think, with more reason, is disposed in favour of Torvean, or else the eminence known as the Crown. *Celtic Scotland*, vol. ii., p. 106.

tended on his journey to the fortress of Brude by some of his trusty companions. Two of them, both famous in Church history, were Picts by race, though of the Irish branch; and it looks like what might be called an "undesigned coincidence" to find them associated in the narrative with the mission to the Picts of the north. One was Comgall, abbot of the famous monastery of Bangor in the county of Down. The other was Cainnech or Canice, who has given his name to the ancient city and cathedral of Kilkenny. He was known in Scotland as Kenneth, and, judging from the number of churches dedicated under his name, he was second only to St. Columba and St. Bride (*i. e.* Brigid) in popularity.[1]

The Christian monks, when they arrived at the palace of King Brude, were met by closed and fastened doors; but before the sign of the cross, as the story is told, the locks flew back, the gates opened, and Columba and his companions entered.

The *Life of St. Columba,* by Adamnan (of which we shall have to speak more fully later on), abounds from beginning to end with stories of the miraculous, and, as we shall hereafter have occasion to observe, many of them are intractable by any fair process, and must either be accepted as they stand, or else be set down as pure inventions, or at all events inventions with only the smallest grain of truth for a basis. In this particular instance, however, it is easy to see how some metaphorical expression as to the wonderful removal

---

[1] See, for a list of dedications, Forbes' *Kalendars of Scottish Saints,* p. 297.

of formidable obstructions to the preaching of the faith, and "the opening of a door" (in Pauline phraseology) for the servants of the Cross might have originated the story.[1] King Brude is represented as awe-struck by what had happened; he receives the missionaries with reverence, and in due time renounces heathenism, and is baptized into the faith of Christ. With the conversion of the king came rapidly the conversion of the people, after the manner not uncommon among the Celts, with whom the honour due to the chief is often regarded as demanding that his people shall follow his wishes in respect to creed and religion as in other things.[2]

Here it is natural to ask the question: What was the character of the paganism of the Picts? Skene has investigated the subject with his customary thoroughness, and has come to the conclusion that it did not differ substantially from the paganism of the Scots of Ireland. Accordingly, the documents relating incidentally to the early religions of both countries may be considered together. Unfortunately the notices of Irish and Scottish heathenism are not very numerous, and nowhere do we get a detailed description of it. But the result of inquiry leads one to believe that there was certainly no largely developed or elaborate mythology. The late learned Dr. James Henthorn Todd goes indeed so far as to say that "there is no evidence of their having had any personal gods."[3] The

---

[1] See 1 Cor. xv. 9; 2 Cor. ii. 12; Col. iv. 3.
[2] Illustrations of this statement may be found in the Scottish Highlands within modern times. [3] *Life of St. Patrick*, p. 414.

sun, the moon, and the stars, the sea, the rivers and wells, the clouds and the mountains, were certainly objects of religious veneration, but whether only as the habitations of the earth-gods (whom the Christian missionaries regarded as demons) or not, it is difficult to say.

In the early lives of the Celtic missionary saints their most vigorous opponents are certain persons called *Druids* (*Druadh*) or, in the Latin records, *magi*. But these Druids do not recall to us the sacerdotal figures that are pictured under that name in Cæsar's familiar account of the religion of the Gauls; they are presented rather as sorcerers, magicians, and, if we may borrow the name from South African paganism, "medicine-men." It is now generally acknowledged that the stone circles and cromlechs that are to be found in various parts of the country do not exhibit to us the remains of heathen temples and altars, but are, in truth, sepulchral monuments. The magi of the Columban records are not apparently priests, but wizards, who have gained control over the powers, personal or impersonal, that underlie the forces of nature. There was much, in this Druidism, of the religion of fear. Magical rites, spells, and incantations, designed to ward off the ill-will of the dread mysterious powers, or to stimulate and direct their energies against enemies, are a common feature in the narratives.

It is of deep interest to observe how these pretensions of the magi, or Druids, were met by the Christian missionaries. In general, it would seem that the missionaries themselves accepted the supernatural character of the power possessed by the Druids, but regarded it as obtained, through God's permission, from evil spirits. Hence there is no attempt made by the missionaries to disprove the Druids' miraculous performances, no attempt to expose them, as would probably be the mode of procedure with our modern missionaries in similar circumstances. Columba and the other ancient saints are not represented as explaining away the marvels of their opponents, but as out-rivalling them. And the contests that are pictured to us at once recall to mind the trials of strength between Moses, the servant of the Lord, and the magicians of Egypt, in the Old Testament story. To take an example from the history of St. Columba. On the saint letting it be known on what day he was about to leave the Court of King Brude, the powerful Druid, Broichan, told him that on that day he could not depart, for that he (Broichan) would raise a contrary wind, and bring down the darkness of mist from the mountains. Columba replied that all our actions are in the hands of God, who would do as seemed to Him fit. On the day fixed, as the Druid had foretold, a contrary wind arose and increased to a tempest, while great darkness came down upon the lake (Loch Ness). But Columba, despite the murmurs of the sailors, embarks, orders the canvas to be spread in the teeth of the gale, and sails his boat triumphantly *against the wind*, to the amazement of the assembled crowd. Adamnan, commenting on this, observes that it is not to be wondered at that God should at times permit the demons to exercise their power upon the winds and waves. There is no attempt at explaining the storm on that day by suggesting that it was a coincidence, any more than there is an attempt to rationalize the wonder of Columba's navigation, as some might do, by supposing him to be sailing " very close to the wind."[1]

Now, if we succeed in reconstructing in imagination the then existing conditions of social life, I think we shall be satisfied that it must have been far easier to effect the conversion of the people on the principles accepted by Columba and his followers than it would have been had the missionaries attempted to show that the much-honoured magi were mere impostors, and the prevailing faith in the supernatural utterly baseless. As it was, the missionaries admitted the reality of the heathen miracles, but declared that He whom they served could do yet greater things, and manifest His superior power. There is no escaping the conclusion that the Celtic missionaries and the Fathers of the Celtic Church were themselves unhesitating believers in what would in our time be regarded as puerile superstitions. But we may well believe that in the providence of God such a nearness of intellectual level between teacher and taught materially assisted their evangelistic labours. And we are instructed in the lesson, which we shall again and again have to bear in mind, that a great body of baseless superstitions may be held compatibly with large measures of Divine truth, with the most sincere piety, and with high intellectual ability and acumen.

[1] *Vita S. Columbæ*, lib. ii., c. 35.

On the part of most modern writers dealing with the lives of the great pioneers of the Faith in Britain, there seems to be a shrinking from telling those portions of their histories that indicate the wide difference in the intellectual standpoints of those times and of these. The feeling is prompted, I dare say, by the sentiment of reverence for those great servants of God. Yet I am sure that if we only attain to a true understanding of the situation, neither respect nor reverence will be wanting, even when we are at first tempted to smile at the grotesque forms in which the beliefs of those distant days very frequently took their shape.

The conversion of the Northern Picts was the great triumph of Columba's missionary efforts. The labours involved in this undertaking are unfortunately scarcely touched by his biographers; but we can gather that his whole life was one full of activity, and occupied by many interests. Beside his toils among the heathen, there were many toils among his Christian brethren of the mainland and of the neighbouring islands. His own community on Iona held a place of first importance in his heart. But the care and oversight of very many daughter monasteries and churches in the islands and in Ireland could not be escaped; and we find him not confining himself to his island home, but from time to time, as the occasion required, visiting the Western Isles, the mainland of Scotland, and even Ireland. Affairs of general interest, at times affairs of political interest, would lay hold on him. Thus he takes the important step of "ordaining" Aidan to be King of

Dalriada, although the right of succession and his private preference indicated another for that dignity. Again, in the year 575, he attends a great gathering of chieftains and ecclesiastics held at Drumceatt (situated not far from Newtown-Limavady, in the county Londonderry). He accompanied the King of British Dalriada, and was himself attended (if we may trust the saint's poetical panegyrist, Dallan Forgaill) by twenty bishops, forty priests, fifty deacons, and twenty students. At this "Synod" of Drumceatt—a very important assembly, which is said to have lasted for fourteen months—Columba helped to effect the exemption of the settlers in Albanian Dalriada from the payment of tribute to the chief King of Ireland. Another result of the intervention of Columba on this occasion is said to have been the mitigation of the harsh measures which it was designed to apply to the Irish "bards"—a class hitherto formally recognized, and possessing important privileges. The "bards" were at this time extremely numerous, and vexatiously exacting in their demand for maintenance for themselves and their retinue[1] as they travelled through the country. Any reluctance to yield to their requests was met by a threat that satirical verses could be readily produced, and might prove disagreeable. In fact, the "bards" had, by their large numbers and by their excessive greed and annoyance, become a nuisance, and the Irish Congress, or "Synod," was about to abate the nuisance by abolishing the order of the bards alto-

[1] *Coinmed* (= refection) was the name euphemistically given to this claim of the bards.

gether.¹ Columba successfully pleaded for them, and laid down limitations as to the number of followers to be allowed to each bard, with a view to lessening the grievance not unnaturally complained of.² On this occasion also, Columba exerted himself to obtain the release from captivity of Scannlan Mor, a prince of Ossory. In the attempt he was perhaps unsuccessful, but we see from the proceedings at Drumceatt, what is elsewhere confirmed, that Columba possessed a force and vigour of character that was capable of displaying itself in social, public, and state affairs, not less than in the more obscure field of missionary effort and of ecclesiastical economics and government. Had Columba lived in later days and amid different surroundings, he might perhaps have presented to us, in one aspect of his character, the figure, as we may imagine, of a great cardinal or other powerful prelate, adroit in state-craft, and zealous in advancing the claims of the party which he had espoused. Nor do I think there is anything improbable in the supposition that Columba was concerned, after the founding of the settlement in Iona, in the battle of Coleraine, fought on account of a dispute, probably about ecclesiastical jurisdiction, between him and St. Comgall, of Bangor.³ The name of Columba is also connected, though in a less definite way, with a third battle, fought only ten

---

[1] Ædh, the Irish king, had already issued against them a decree of banishment.

[2] It was in gratitude for Columba's exertions on behalf of the bards that their head, Dallan Forgaill, composed his *Amhra Choluimchille*, or *Praises of Columkille*, see p. 111.

[3] In County Down, on Belfast Lough.

years before his death, between the northern and southern branches of the Hy Neill. At this distance of time, and with little or no information as to the circumstances, we are quite incapable of forming a judgment on the rightness or wrongness of Columba's supposed participation in these quarrels and the consequent bloodshed. We know that in days of savagery or semi-barbarism it is not uncommon to find that physical force is the only remedy that can be employed against the violence of injustice. And we have to remember, as already observed, that the sentiment of the time was in no degree outraged or wounded by members of the monastic brotherhoods bearing arms and engaging in the bloody wars of tribal factions.[1]

The quick, high-spirited, and passionate natural temperament of this great man must not be dropped out of sight if we are to do him justice. But it is to other aspects of his character that we more readily turn. His spirit of self-denial, his devotion to the cause of Christ, his considerateness for others, his

---

[1] "It was not until 804 that the monastic communities of Ireland were formally exempted from military service. . . . That even among themselves the members of powerful communities were not insensible to the spirit of faction appears from numerous entries in the ancient annals. Of these, two—of which one relates to a Columban house—may here be adduced as examples: A.D. 673, 'A battle was fought between the fraternities of Clonmacnois and Durrow, where Dermod Duff was killed . . . with 200 men of the fraternity of Durrow . . .' A.D. 816, 'A battle was fought by Cathal, son of Dunlang, and the fraternity of Tigh-Munna, against the fraternity of Ferns, in which 400 were slain.'" Reeves' *Introduction to Adamnan's Life of St. Columba*, xlviii. (*Historians of Scotland*, vol. vi.). Other illustrations may be found in Prof. Stokes' *Ireland and the Celtic Church*, Lectures V. and X.

affection and tenderness for the brethren, his kindness even to dumb animals, and similar traits, make us able to understand how it was that he secured the enthusiastic love of the members of the fraternity at Iona, and indeed of all his monasteries.

"What did St. Columba look like?" some one may ask. "What do we know of his personal appearance?" Questions of this kind are the first I myself wish to have answered when I come to study any man's biography. "What like was he?" was the question which the great historical painter—if I may not call him the great historian—Thomas Carlyle, was wont, *more Scoticano*, to ask about each character of the past that caught his fancy. In a letter of Carlyle's which, though little known as being buried ten fathom deep in the *Proceedings* of one of our learned societies, is full of interest, we read: " I have to tell you, as a fact of personal experience, that in all my poor historical investigations it has been, and always is, one of the most primary wants to procure a bodily likeness of the personage inquired after; a good *Portrait*, if such exists; failing that, even an indifferent if sincere one. In short, *any* representation, made by a faithful human creature of that face and figure which *he* saw with his eyes, and which I can never see with mine, is now valuable to me, and much better than none at all . . . Often I have found a Portrait superior in real instruction to half-a-dozen written 'Biographies,' as biographies are written; or rather, let me say, I have found that the Portrait was as a small lighted *candle* by which the Biographies could for the first time be *read*, and some human interpretation be made of them; the *Biographical* Personage no longer an impossible Phantasm or distracting Aggregate of inconsistent rumours." [1]

Now, a contemporary portrait of Columba, in the sense here intended by Carlyle, we do not possess; nor, if we did possess one, would it be of much value, for however admirably skilled the Irish decorative artists were in other directions, they seem to have been ostentatiously, even grotesquely, indifferent to any exactness of realism in the attempted portraiture of the human face and figure. All we can do then is to look for some vivid description of the personal appearance of this great missionary and saint, and failing that, to piece together as best we may the incidental notices that help to show us in any degree what manner of man he was. Even in this respect, unfortunately, the material is scanty, and lacking in the definiteness and precision that our age so eagerly demands. We may perhaps believe that Columba was tall and dignified in bearing, and that he had brilliant eyes, as later authorities aver. Adamnan tells he was "like an angel in appearance," and was "endeared to all, for a holy joy always beamed from his countenance, manifesting the inner gladness with which the Holy Spirit filled his heart." [2]

A powerful voice of great sweetness is referred to

---

[1] Letter to David Laing on the subject of Scottish Historical Portraits, *Proceedings of the Society of Antiquaries of Scotland*, vol. i., part iii.
[2] *Vita, secunda Prefatio.*

more than once, and the distance at which the words, and even syllables, were distinctly heard when he sang the Psalms seemed to his biographers to point to the miraculous—more especially, as to those who stood in the church with him his voice did not seem louder than the voices of others.[1] The advantages of such a sonorous and yet musical voice to a preacher, many of whose sermons must have been delivered in the open air, was doubtless very great. There are other suggestions in Adamnan's *Life of Columba* of a physical vigour and energy, which independently we might be led to suspect from the laborious character of the career of the saint.

The outlines of his mental, moral, and spiritual portrait may be more clearly gathered. When the head of a large and widespread community commands, as Columba did, the respect and admiration as well as the affection of its members, we cannot doubt his possession of many intellectual endowments. His biographer represented the general sentiment when he declared that Columba's intellectual abilities were of

---

[1] "The voice of the venerable man, when singing in the church with the brethren, raised in a marvellous manner, was heard sometimes at a distance of four stadia, that is 500 paces, sometimes at a distance of eight stadia, that is 1000 paces." The poet Dallan Forgaill may be excused for the poetic licence of augmentation when he sang—

> "The sound of his voice, Columcille's,
> Great its sweetness above all clerics;
> To the end of fifteen-hundred paces,
> Vast spaces, it was clear."

Adamnan is careful to note that this peculiarity was only rarely observed.

the highest order and his practical wisdom great.[1] His tenderness and readiness to sympathize with the sorrows and joys of others, united with a certain reserve and dignity that are not commonly found in combination with effusive sympathies, made a marked feature in his character. His indignation at injustice and cruelty, his affection for the brethren, his more than perfunctory hospitality to strangers, are constantly showing themselves in the incidents of his life as recorded by his successor. Like a true Celt, as he was, he gave ready expression to his emotions. We read of his smiles and his tears—sometimes of tears in copious abundance. Columba has been accused even by admirers[2] of a vindictive temper; and the evident satisfaction with which his biographer multiplies instances where men of violence, murderers, and oppressors of the innocent were overtaken by death or misfortune, as foretold by the saint, seem at first to the hasty reader to lend colour to the charge. But the exact line where righteous indignation ends and the sin of vindictiveness begins it is not easy for the moralist to define. The wild life of that period of miserable disorder was not such as to promote the growth of the gentler virtues among any who were brought into contact with it. It was certainly not personal slights or indignities, as such, but wrong and injustice to others that ordinarily roused the anger of Columba.[3]

---

[1] "Ingenio optimus, consilio magnus," *Secunda Præf.*
[2] For example, by Montalembert.
[3] Again, his biographer represents the saint rather as predicting than as invoking a just retribution upon wrong-doers.

The laborious and untiring industry of Columba is testified to by Adamnan. Not an hour of the day passed without its occupations in prayer, or reading, or writing, or some other task. His fastings and his vigils were carried to an extent that seemed to surpass the powers of man's endurance, and yet he maintained the sweetness and the brightness of disposition that do not always accompany vigorous self-discipline.[1] He had all the tender and passionate affection of the Celt for the land of his birth. Again, his widely diffused benevolence did not check the ardour of devoted personal friendships.

Nor can we pass over, as contributing to the fullness of the portrait, glimpses that show us a real sympathy with the brute creation. For example, Columba on one occasion gives directions to one of the brethren to feed and tend a poor crane, which, completely exhausted by its long flight from Ireland, fell upon the western shore of the island of Iona;[2] while the story has been often told how, on the evening before the death of the saint, the pack-horse that used to carry the milk-vessels to the monastery, thrusting his nose into the bosom of the aged man as, in his weariness, he rested himself by the road-side, received from his grateful heart a farewell benediction.[3]

Any one who reads Adamnan's *Life of St. Columba* will not regard the praises Dallan Forgaill bestowed upon his memory as a mere professional *éloge*. The

---

[1] *Secunda Præfat.*
[2] *Adamnan*, lib. i., c. 35.
[3] *Id.*, lib. i., c. 24.

words of the bard are felt in the main to express just the impression which the study of the biography has left behind, and they are comparatively free from the mere generalities of epitaph laudation. Mr. Skene thus cites the words of the poet, who describes the people as mourning over him who was "their souls' light, their learned one, their chief from right,—who was God's messenger, who dispelled fears from them, who used to explain the truth of words,—a harp without a base cord, a perfect sage who believed in Christ; he was learned, he was chaste, he was charitable; he was an abounding benefit of guests, he was eager, he was noble, he was gentle, he was the physician of the heart of every sage; he was to persons inscrutable; he was a shelter to the naked, he was a consolation to the poor; there went not from the world one who was more continual for a remembrance of the cross."[1]

It has been claimed for one of the greatest men of letters in modern Europe[2] that his heart, which few knew, was as great as his intellect, which all knew. I shall not venture to say whether in that particular case facts justify the claim. But it is certain that great and widespread *personal* influence has been oftenest found where the warmth of the affections and the richness and sensibility of the emotional side of nature bulk large in combination with intellectual capacity and force of purpose. It is then that those with whom a great man comes in contact become not only his

[1] *Amhra Choluimchille*, as cited by Skene, *Celtic Scotland*, vol. ii., p. 145.
[2] Goethe.

admiring disciples, but his ardent and enthusiastic followers. The affection, the loyal personal devotion which he inspires, far outweighs in practical value the ill-effects that are produced by the occasional errors of a hasty judgment, and of an impulsive and eager temperament. Columba's influence was due, we can scarcely doubt, in large measure to his combining in his own person the various and rarely united sources of power to which I refer.

Columba's labours included several voyages to Ireland, and journeys among the Irish monasteries. He also at times penetrates into the country of his converts, the Picts, beyond "the dorsal ridge of Britain." From time to time, probably for the sake of retirement and opportunities for more undistracted devotion, he visits and sojourns for a while in the little island of Hinba, which Reeves and Skene would identify with Eilean-na-Naoimh, a little further to the south of Iona, north-west of Scarba, and where the ruined remains of a little church and of two bee-hive cells are still to be seen.[1]

His was a busy life of unceasing labour. After thirty years in Iona had been completed, he seems to have felt his infirmities crowding upon him. He told his disciples that for many days he had been praying for his release that he might go to his "heavenly fatherland." But, as he added, "the prayers of many churches" had gone up to God that he might stay longer with them, and four years were to be added to his life. At the completion of the four years his end

[1] See p. 294.

was approaching. Following the account of Adamnan, and for the most part merely translating his words, we learn the affecting story of the saint's last days. It seems to me to possess a singular air of truthfulness; and I give it in all its quaint simplicity. One day in the month of May, the old man, now worn-out with age, was drawn in a cart to visit the brethren at work in the western plain of the island, about a mile from the monastery, and calling them to him he began to say, "During the Paschal solemnities in April with desire I desired to depart to the Lord Christ, as He

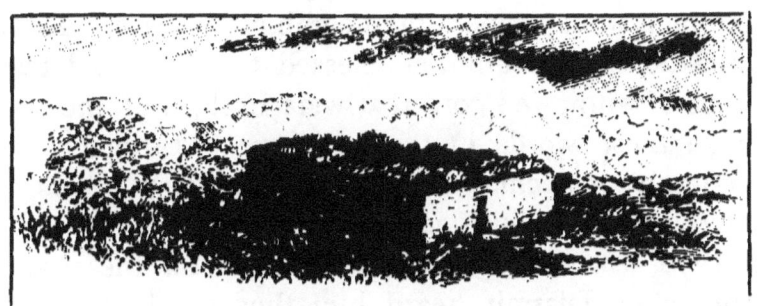

had granted that I should if I preferred it. But lest for you the festival of joy should be turned into mourning, I chose to put off a little longer the day of my departure from the world." At this saying the monks were deeply grieved, and he sought as well as he could to cheer them with words of consolation. And then, still seated in the cart, he turned his face to the east, and blessed both the island and them that dwelt therein. When he had finished the words of blessing he was carried back to the monastery. A few days afterwards, when he was celebrating mass as usual upon the Lord's Day, the face of the venerable man, as his eyes were raised to heaven, seemed brightened with a ruddy glow. Afterwards, in answer to the inquiries of the brethren, he told them how he had seen the angel of the Lord, who had come "to seek for a certain *deposit* dear to God." At a later time they came to understand that he spoke of his own soul.

The following Saturday (*dies Sabbati*) was the last day of his life. On that day, accompanied by his faithful and attached attendant, Diarmit, the venerable man went to bless the neighbouring barn. And, when he had entered, he blessed the barn and two heaps of winnowed corn that were in it; and then he spoke these words in thanksgiving: "I rejoice exceedingly, my children of the monastery (*monachi familiares*), that this year also, if I must depart from you, ye will have a supply sufficient for the year." And when Diarmit heard him thus speak, he said, "O Father, thou grievest us by so often making mention of thy departure." The saint made answer, "I have a secret to tell thee in few words, and if thou wilt faithfully promise to disclose it to no one before my decease, I shall be able to speak more plainly about my departure." When Diarmit had promised on bended knees, as the saint desired, the venerable man spoke and said, "This day is called in the sacred books the *Sabbath*, which, being interpreted, is *Rest;* and to me in very truth this day is the Sabbath, for it is for me the last day of this life of toil, the day upon which, after the anxieties and troubles of my labours, I go to rest (*sabbatizo*). In the middle of this approaching night of the sacred Lord's Day I shall, in the language of the Scriptures, go the way of our fathers; for now my Lord Jesus Christ vouchsafes to call me, and to Him, I say, who calls me, in the middle of this night shall I depart. For so it has been revealed to me by the Lord Himself." When his attendant heard these sad words he began to weep, while the saint tried to comfort him as well as he could.

After this the saint comes forth from the barn; and as he returned towards the monastery and had gone half-way, he sits down at the place where afterwards the cross was erected, fixed in a mill-stone, where it may be seen at this day, says Adamnan, by the side of the road. And while the saint, wearied with age, was sitting there, and resting a little while, the white horse,[1] that obedient servant that had been accustomed to carry the milk-vessels backwards and forwards between the cow-shed and the monastery, approached, and coming close to the saint—strange to say—laid his head in the saint's bosom and began to whine, and, like a human being, to shed tears in abundance upon the breast of the saint, and with water dropping from his mouth began to make his

---

[1] A recent writer relating this incident calls the animal an "old" horse. But a horse may be "white" without being old. The same writer, a few lines later, exercising the same spirit of reading into the narrative his own fancies, tells us that "at midnight he (Columba) *crept* into the chapel." Now that is what might be well supposed of a sick old man; but the original

moan. Diarmit wanted to drive off the sorrowing creature, but the saint forbade him, saying, "Suffer him, suffer him, since he loves me, to pour out his grief into my bosom. Thou, though thou art a man with a rational soul, could in no way have known of my departure if I had not told thee; but to this brute and unreasoning animal the Creator in His own way has revealed that his master is about to leave him." And then he blessed the sorrowing horse as he turned away from him.

After this the saint arose, and ascending the little hill above the monastery, he stood for a little on its top, and standing there, he lifted up both his hands and blessed the monastic buildings, saying, "This place, though it be mean to look at and narrow in its bounds, shall be honoured with great and distinguished honour, not only by the kings and people of the Scots, but by the rulers of barbarous and foreign nations with their subject peoples. And even the saints of other churches shall hold it in great reverence."

After these words he descended the little hill, and returning to the monastery, he sat writing the Psalter in his hut; and when he came to that versicle of the thirty-third Psalm [1] where it is written, "They that seek the Lord shall want no manner of thing that is good," he said, "Here at the end of the page I must stop; and what follows let Baithene write." At this point Adamnan interposes his comment, that as the last

---

tells us that he *ran* in before the rest, and if one were disposed to rationalize, we may suppose that a coroner's jury would have attributed the saint's death to a failure of the action of the heart.

[1] In our English versions, Psalm xxxiv. 9.

verse written by St. Columba was very appropriate to one about to enter on the good things of the eternal kingdom, so the next was equally appropriate to the new abbat, father and teacher of his spiritual children —" Come, ye children, and hearken unto me : I will teach you the fear of the Lord."

When the saint had completed writing the verse, he entered the church for the vesper office preceding the Lord's Day, and when it was finished he returned again to his little chamber, and rested for the night on his bed, where he had, instead of straw, a bare flag with a stone for a pillow, which at this day, adds Adamnan, stands like a kind of monument beside his grave.[1] While he was resting thus upon his bed he gave his last commands to the brethren; but Diarmit, his attendant, was the only one who heard him speaking. "O my children," said he, "receive ye these last words of mine. Have peace and unfeigned charity among yourselves; and if ye thus follow the examples of the holy fathers, God, the Comforter of the good, will be your helper. And I, dwelling with Him, will intercede for you. And He will not only supply you with a sufficiency of the things needed for this life present, but will also bestow on you the eternal rewards prepared for them that keep His commandments." After these words, as Adamnan goes on to relate, the holy man kept silence. And at

---

[1] The visitor to Iona may see deposited in the east end of the cathedral a rounded stone, which it has been found necessary to protect from relic-loving tourists by an iron cage. This is shown as, and may be in fact, " St. Columba's pillow."

midnight, when the bell sounded, he rose in haste and passed to the church, and running more quickly than the others, he entered alone, and on bended knees he knelt beside the altar in prayer. His attendant, Diarmit, with some others, as they were coming up a little after, saw the whole building filled with a heavenly light, but when they came to the door the light faded suddenly. Then Diarmit, entering, called repeatedly in a voice broken with sorrow, " Where art thou, father?" And before the brethren had brought the lights, feeling his way in the darkness, he found the abbot lying in front of the altar. He lifted him up a little, and sitting beside him, propped his holy head upon his bosom. In the meantime the body of the monks ran in with the lights; and when they saw their father dying they burst into lamentations. Then Diarmit raised the holy right hand of the saint that he might bless the assembled monks. And the venerable father himself at the same time moved his hand as well as he could, so that, though he could not speak, he might by the motion of his hand be seen to bless the brethren.[1] After which he immediately expired. Then the whole church resounded with loud lamentations of grief. When the matin hymns were finished, the body was carried by the monks, chanting Psalms as they went, from the church to the little hut; and after three days of solemn obsequies, it was laid to rest in the burial-ground of

[1] We have instances, in the *Life*, of Columba making the sign of the cross in blessing (lib. ii. 15, 28, 30), and this last action of his was in all probability an attempt to make the accustomed movement of the hand.

the monastery. Such is the account given us by Adamnan of the closing hours of a holy and noble life. Dr. Reeves, after a careful chronological investigation, decides that the death of the saint took place "just after midnight between Saturday the eighth and Sunday the ninth of June in the year 597." [1]

The greater monasteries of the Columban monks were, with the exception of Iona, all situated in Ireland; but some smaller foundations were to be found scattered in the western and northern islands of Scotland and in Pictland. We know that in the life-time of St. Columba, Tiree had its houses; there was a house for a few of the brethren at Eilean-na-Naoimh, and a monastery at Oronsay may perhaps be attributed to the same date. Our records are so scanty that we can say little for certain as to the spread of the Columban houses in Scotland. Abernethy and Dunkeld may have been early Columban foundations; but the numerous dedications of churches in the mainland and the northern islands afford but hazardous grounds for any sure conclusion.[2] The church of Lismore, in the long and narrow island of that name, which lies in the mouth of Loch Linnhe, and is now daily skirted by steamers from Oban going

[1] In the *Booke of Common Prayer for the Use of the Church of Scotland*, 1637, Columba is commemorated in the Kalendar at June 9, following the example of the mediæval Church.

[2] Dr. Reeves gives a list of thirty-two "Columbian foundations" in Scotland, and considers that the list "admits of considerable enlargement," but very many of those recorded are no more than churches dedicated under the name of the saint, and may date from a period long subsequent to St. Columba.

north, is supposed to have been founded in the lifetime of Columba by a bishop, Moluag by name.[1] It was in after times the seat of the bishopric of Argyll. Another contemporary foundation was Kingarth in the south of the island of Bute; here, too, the founder was a bishop. Another missionary contemporary of Columba was St. Donnan, who settled in the island of Eigg. There are several Kildonans among the Scottish churches; and doubtless this is largely due to his having, according to the common account, obtained the glory of martyrdom. It is strange with what little opposition Christianity won its way in Scotland; but in this case Donnan and fifty-two of his monks fell victims to the fury of the "queen" of the island; though it should be stated that, according to another account, they suffered death at the hands of pirates. An Irish legend, which recurs in part in the *Breviary of Aberdeen*, assigns the origin of the Church in Aberdeen to a disciple of St. Columba, Machar by name. He was a bishop, and set out with twelve companions to preach the gospel. He was ordered to travel till he came to a river which exhibited a curve like a bishop's crosier. This sign he found near the mouth of the river Don at Aberdeen, where the cathedral was afterwards dedicated under his name. Another missionary, named Maelrubha, a monk of St. Comgall's monastery at Bangor, settled (673) at Apurcrossan (Applecross, in Ross-shire), where he presided for forty-nine years. The Irish accounts represent him as dying a natural death; but it is pro-

---

[1] See pp. 307, 312.

bably due to the Scottish story of his martyrdom by Norwegians that dedications to him are numerous in Scotland. It is interesting to note that, however great the fame of Columba justly is, other independent missionaries of monastic foundations distinct from his had their share in the work of evangelizing Scotland. Those who desire further information and further conjectures will consult the pages of Reeves and of Skene.[1]

[1] As to Maelrubha, see more particularly Dr. Reeves' paper in the *Proceedings of the Society of Antiquaries, Scotland*, vol. iii., p. 258. This saint is said to have founded a church on one of the islands in the beautiful lake in Ross-shire, Lochmaree, which takes its name from him.

CHAPTER VII.

IONA: ITS PHYSICAL FEATURES—THE CONSTITUTION OF THE COLUMBAN "FAMILY"—LIFE IN THE BROTHERHOOD AT IONA.

IONA is a small island about three and a half miles long (in length lying north-east and south-west), and in its widest part about a mile and a half in breadth. It is separated from the great island of Mull[1] by a deep and narrow channel, or "sound," about a mile broad, through which the tides run with much force. It presents to the Atlantic a bold front, with outposts of isolated crag, or rocky islets, on the north-western, south-western, and southern side. From the south the heights slope down by a heather-covered surface of great irregularity to the middle of the island, where a comparatively flat plain (the corn-fields of the monastery) runs from the western to the eastern shore. Then the level again rises.

On the eastern side, close to the shore, and a little north of the central plain, stood the monastery of St. Columba. To the north-west of the monastery is the

[1] This island is twenty-four miles long and thirty miles broad, and as seen from Iona is indistinguishable from the mainland.

highest point—a rocky hill rising to over 300 feet,[1] known as Dunii.[2] From this height on a clear day (which, in the moist climate that prevails, the visitor will find of less frequent occurrence than could be wished), a magnificent prospect is obtained. To the west is the wide sweep of the Atlantic; on the east are the red-granite cliffs of the Ross of Mull, the trap terraces of Bourg, and, further inland, the mountain of Benmore, rising to a height of over 3000 feet. When the air is very clear the jagged faint blue outline of the Coollin Hills of Skye may be distinguished in the far north; while the Paps of Jura may be seen in the south rising over the near Ross of Mull. The distance between these two extreme points north and south is ninety-six miles. Many other islands are visible in the distance, while the islet of Staffa is so close at hand that the characteristic columnar formation of its basalt rocks is readily distinguishable through the glass.[3]

In the choice of their settlements the Irish monks seem to have looked for islands not very remote from the mainland. Avoiding the greater islands, of which they could not hope to secure exclusive possession, and which would not supply the security and the isolation which they sought, they made their selection from among those that, without being very large, were yet sufficiently extensive to supply wholly, or in the

---

[1] The Ordnance Survey gives the height as 327 feet.
[2] Pronounced Doon-ee, with the accent on the last syllable.
[3] For further details, see the minute and accurate description given by Skene (*Celtic Scotland*, vol. ii., p. 89 *sq.*). See also the charming and most vivid account of the island and its surroundings in the Duke of Argyll's *Iona*.

main, the tillage-ground and pasture required for the maintenance of the community.[1]

Columba landed in a little bay or creek[2] in the south of the island, but his monastery was constructed about two miles farther north, and if not situated exactly in the places occupied by the mediæval buildings and enclosures that now remain, was certainly only a little removed from them.[3]

The original monastery would seem to have been of wood, or of wattles and clay. If bee-hive cells of stone then or afterwards occupied the ground, their material would probably have been used in the construction of the mediæval buildings. No vestige of the original structure can now be distinguished.

If we would picture to ourselves what the monastery at Iona looked like in the days of Columba, we must fancy, at a distance of some two or three hundred yards from the shore, a large enclosure, surrounded by a high rampart or embankment (*vallum*) constructed of earth or perhaps of a mixture of earth and stone.[4] Within this rampart was a space round

---

[1] It would appear that as the community at Iona grew in numbers, it was necessary to supplement home supplies. Even in Columba's time, Tiree (the *Ethica Insula* of Adamnan) had become, according to Reeves, "the farm-land of the mother island." *Historians of Scotland*, vol. vi., p. 309.

[2] Known now as *Port-na-churraich* (or port of the coracle), marked by a brilliantly-coloured beach of "green serpentine, green quartz, and the reddest felspar" (Duke of Argyll's *Iona*, p. 80). It has been lately asserted that jade has been found there.

[3] About a quarter of a mile to the north of the present remains, as Skene contends, see *Celtic Scotland*, vol. ii., p. 100.

[4] The rampart or cashell (a corruption of the Latin *castellum*) in some Irish monasteries was as much as fifteen feet high and nine or ten feet broad.

which the lodgings of the monks were situated, and somewhat apart from the rest, on a little rising knoll, was the hut (*turguriolum*) of the abbat. The church, close by, with a little room abutting on it, and, as it would seem, having a door on the outside, and also one opening into the church, like many of our modern vestries, was probably the largest building on the island. There were also a refectory, and one or more guest-chambers, and without the enclosure, a mill, a kiln, a cow-shed, a stable for one or more horses, and a barn.

A large community on a small island, however sparing in their diet, must have had some difficulty in finding an adequate supply of provisions. The land on the western part of the centre of the island was in tillage. In the harvest-time we read of the labouring monks reaping and bringing back loads of corn on their backs. There were sheep on the island. The cows may have been numerous, and their milk was largely used.[1] "Fish were abundant, and could be obtained at all seasons. The large flounders of the Sound of Iona are still an important item in the diet of the people. The rocks and islets all around swarmed with seals, and their flesh seems to have been a favourite article of food."[2] One of the alleged instances of Columba's prophetical powers relate to his foretelling the depredations made by a robber in a

---

[1] In our own day the island, we know, could maintain more than 200 cows and 140 calves, about 600 sheep and 25 horses, beside some pigs. Duke of Argyll's *Iona*, p. 92, edit. 1889.

[2] Duke of Argyll, *ut supra*. The statement that seal's flesh was "a *favourite* article of food" seems unsupported.

breeding-ground of seals, which belonged to the monastery.[1] The food resources of the island were supplemented by the corn-land of the neighbouring island of Tiree.

As might be expected, boats, large and small, of pine and oak, or of wicker covered with skin (*curachs*), propelled by oars, or with sails, figure largely in the history. Indeed, again and again the narrative of Adamnan, even in its unconscious romancing, has caught and reflected with singular truth the varying tints, the light and shadows, the life and movement, the grace and mystery of the shifting currents of the ocean among the western islands. Whiffs of the sea breezes reach us with their briny odour. The authentic note of a dweller among the impressive surroundings of his island home may be caught in almost every page.[2]

It is worth observing that the familiar name by which St. Columba's island is now commonly known seems to have arisen through an error of transcription on the part of copyists. The name habitually given to the place by Adamnan is the "Iovan island" (*Ioua insula*). So it appears in the earliest extant manuscript of the *Life*, that of Reichenau, assigned to the beginning of the eighth century, that is, close to the date of the death of the author (703). In this form the word appears also in the two next oldest manuscripts of the *Life*—one of the ninth, and the other of the tenth century. Any

---

[1] *Vita*, lib. i., c. 33.
[2] In the summer of 1889 I spent two delightful days upon the island, in company with the Bishop of Argyll. We each had a copy of Reeves' *Adamnan*, and felt that it could be but half appreciated when read elsewhere.

one familiar with the difficulty of distinguishing *n* from *u*, as written in mediæval texts, will see at once how the error may have crept in. But it was fostered by some confusion, such as we find in our Scottish historian, John Fordun, arising probably from the stress laid by Adamnan, in the beginning of his work, on the fact that *Iona* (Jonah of the Old Testament) and *Columba* mean the same thing—the one being the Hebrew, and the other the Latin, for a "dove."

In the early Irish records the name of the island appears as Ia, Hya, or Hy. And this last form (pronounced *ee*) is still used in reference to the island by the Gaels of the Western Highlands.

Adamnan's *Life of St. Columba*, naturally enough, as written not for the information of later ages, but primarily for the use of his contemporary brethren of the monastery, enters into no detailed account of the constitution of the establishment, or of the every-day life of the community. But much may be gathered by the careful student from incidental allusions scattered in abundance through the work. Dr. Reeves has, in a masterly way, grouped together such occasional references, and illustrated them from the stores of his copious erudition. In what follows I have seldom done much more than extract the more important features of his exhaustive discussion.

(1) It is very doubtful whether Columba composed any systematic Rule like that of his great contemporary, the founder of the Benedictines. But there is every reason to believe that the brethren were bound by the rules of Obedience, Chastity, and Poverty. The

authority of the abbat extended to all the members of the community, whether living in Hy—the *insula primaria*—or in the daughter and affiliated houses, the heads of which all received their charge from him. The whole community was known in Irish as the *Muintir Choluimchille*, or Family of Columkille.

(2) The founder named his own successor, his cousin Baithene; and it was not till after the year 716 that a free election of the head appears to have been allowed. Of the first eleven abbats in succession to Columba, nine were certainly of the same family as Columba, and only one was certainly not of "founder's kin." The founder's successor was styled the *Comarb*, or *Heir*, of Columkille. The word *comarb*, which is pronounced almost as if written *co-arb*, is explained by Dr. J. H. Todd (*St. Patrick*, p. 155) as follows:—The word "properly signifies co-heir or inheritor; co-heir or inheritor of the same lands or territory, which belonged to the original founder of a church or monastery; co-heir also of his ecclesiastical or spiritual dignity. In the absence of territorial designations, this term was employed in the Irish Church to designate bishops or abbats who were the successors or inheritors of the temporal and spiritual privileges of some eminent Saint or founder. Thus the co-arb of St. Patrick was the bishop or abbat of Armagh; the co-arb of Columkille was the abbat of Hy; the co-arb of Barré was the bishop or abbat of Cork . . . The Bishop of Rome himself is frequently called co-arb of Peter, and sometimes also abbat of Rome, showing how completely the abbatial and co-arban

authority, implying, as it did in Ireland, the rank of a feudal lord of the soil and chieftain over the inhabitants of the soil, swallowed up, as it were, and obscured the accident of a co-existing episcopal or sacerdotal character in the co-arb or spiritual chieftain." Sometimes the term *Ard-comarb*, or *chief co-arb*, is met with. Thus, while there were co-arbs of Columba at the Columban monasteries of Derry, Durrow, and Swords, the ard-co-arb of Columba was the Abbat of Hy.

(3) Perhaps it was, as suggested by the name *Abbat* (or *Father*) applied to the head, that the body of the monks (and sometimes even those who lived as serfs or clansmen on the territory of the abbat) were styled the *family* (*muintir, familia*). And certainly as regards Columba himself and his followers, the relations, as disclosed in the *Life*, were those of constant, affectionate, and watchful care on the one part, and of filial reverence on the other. It would be difficult to find anywhere a more beautiful picture of loving solicitude and loving and reverential obedience than is revealed by innumerable unconscious touches in the work of the saint's biographer. Some of the monks are spoken of as "seniors," but I cannot satisfy myself whether they formed a distinct class, or were so termed only on account of their age or standing in the monastery.

(4) The monastic life in our records is frequently spoken of as a "warfare" (*militia*), and the term "soldier of Christ" (*miles Christi*) is a term very commonly used when it is meant to designate a monk, for which it is indeed employed as a simple equivalent. It was a name that would doubtless have special significance

and special attractions in that warlike age. The monastery, with its surrounding *cashell* or rampart, was, indeed, in more senses than one, a fortress.

(5) The life of the monk was primarily and essentially a devotion to the warfare of Christ in the world, but the weapons of that warfare were not carnal. Prayer, praise, and the hearing of God's Word formed a large part of the daily duties of the community. I do not know that we need doubt that the services of the "canonical hours" were duly held, with perhaps the exception of "compline." Vespers, a night service, and matins are very clearly referred to. The references to the lesser "day hours" are less distinct.

The Holy Eucharist was celebrated, it would seem, only on Sundays and festivals, and on special occasions at the order of the abbat.

(6) Even if the spiritual advantages of physical labour had not been fully appreciated, yet much manual work was absolutely necessary for the maintenance of the community. And so we have abundant references that show us that much time was expended in the island upon agriculture and the tending of cattle. The monks are shown ploughing, sowing, reaping, storing the corn, and grinding it into flour. A mill and a kiln are mentioned. A Saxon monk in Columba's time officiated as baker. Both cows and sheep appear on the island, and milk seems to have formed an important part of the diet of the establishment. Fish, too, are caught; and the care and management of boats of all sizes must have occupied the time of many of the brotherhood.

We possess, too, a very clear and interesting reference to the skill shown by the monks of the island in working in metals (lib. ii., c. 30).

(7) Wednesdays and Fridays were ordinarily observed as fasts, but this rule did not extend to the weeks between Easter and Pentecost. The forty days of Lent were kept. It is an interesting feature to observe that a relaxation of a fast was permitted to the community in welcoming a stranger to the island.

(8) The monks slept on beds covered apparently with straw; but the great founder, even to the day of his death, slept on the bare rock with a stone for his pillow. Dr. George Petrie (*Round Towers*, p. 426) mentions that in the upper apartment of the building known as St. Columba's house at Kells, a flat stone is shown, six feet long, which is called "St. Columba's penitential bed."

In Adamnan's *Life* there is no detailed description of the dress of the monks, but they seem to have worn an inner garment called the *tunic;* and Columba's cowl (*cuculla*) is expressly mentioned, but in such a connection that it seems to me to suggest that either the ordinary monks did not at that time wear the cowl, or that Columba wore one of a distinctive shape or colour.[1] The monks appear to have worn sandals.

---

[1] "One of the wicked associates (of the sons Conall) was instigated by the devil to rush on the saint with a spear on purpose to kill him. To prevent this, one of the brethren, named Findlugan, put on the saint's cowl and interposed, being ready to die for the holy man." *Vita*, lib. ii., c. 25.

(9) It is not unlikely that, as in so many monasteries, there may have been at Iona, in Columba's day, a school for the instruction of youths; but the solitary mention of one Berchan, "a pupil (*alumnus*) learning wisdom" (lib. iii., c. 22), would seem to be too slight a foundation upon which to build a confident conclusion.

(10) The references to the copying of books are numerous. The saint himself is frequently described as thus occupied. And even in the feebleness of his old age, on the evening preceding his death, on returning to his hut after what is described as a fatiguing visit for the aged man to the barn, he sat down to his task of transcribing the Psalter, and continued till he reached the foot of the page. In an earlier part of the history we find Baithene, who was afterwards his successor, seeking for one of the brethren who would collate and correct a copy he had made of the Psalter. When the collation had been made, it was found that the copy was perfect but for a single omission of the letter *i* (lib. i., c. 17). Beside Psalters, we have it recorded (lib. ii., c. 8) that Columba wrote with his own hand a "Book of Hymns for the week" (*hymnorum liber septimaniorum*). And other transcriptions are elsewhere mentioned (lib. ii., c. 45). There is no hint, so far as I have observed, of the transcriptions being adorned with artistic decoration; and though I am conscious of the danger of an argument from silence, yet I can hardly doubt that anything like the elaborate ornament we are familiar with in some

Irish manuscripts would certainly have been noted by the biographer.

(11) The chief subject of study was the Holy Scriptures, as well with the abbat as with other members of the community; and there is an interesting story of how, on one occasion, some of the difficulties of the Word of God upon which he had meditated were supernaturally made clear to the saint.

(12) The abbat maintained such a measure of reserve as became his dignity. He not only slept, but studied and wrote, in his little hut somewhat apart from the main body of the buildings. There he was attended by his faithful servant and companion, Diarmit. And sometimes we find two of the brethren standing in attendance at the door of the hut. Strangers arriving at the island had formally to request an interview (lib. i., c. 2).

(13) Strangers visiting the island were numerous, and were received with hearty hospitality. Water was provided for the washing of their feet, and the guest-chamber was made ready for them. Of Baithene, the saint's successor, we are told expressly not only that he was "holy and wise, and experienced both in teaching and writing," but that he was *affabilis et peregrinis appetibilis.*

(14) Voyages of the monks to the neighbouring islands, to the mainland, and to Ireland, are of frequent occurrence. Timber had to be fetched from a considerable distance. Messages from the abbat had to be conveyed, and often excursions

were made across the great mountain ridge that forms the Scottish water-shed into the remoter regions of the Picts.

These notices, drawn almost exclusively from Adamnan's *Life of Columba,* may suffice to give some distinct conception of the constitution of the monastery and of the life of the brotherhood of Hy. The consideration of the position of bishops in the ancient Scotic Church will be dealt with, and some account of certain peculiarities of ritual observance will be given, in separate chapters.

CHAPTER VIII.

THE HISTORICAL CHARACTER OF ADAMNAN'S 'LIFE OF ST. COLUMBA': THE MIRACULOUS ELEMENT.

THE work of Adamnan, to which the Christian Church is so deeply indebted for the story of the life of St. Columba, invaluable as it is for the unquestionably truthful glimpses of the ecclesiastical and social life of a remote and obscure period of Church history, is written in a manner that is very unsatisfactory and often vexatious to the student who would follow in consecutive order the narrative of the saint's career. The *Life* is divided into three books, arranged on a somewhat artificial system. The first is devoted to recounting instances of Columba's powers of prophecy, the second to his miracles, and the third to supernatural appearances connected with the saint, such as visions of angels seen by him, or the visits of angels to him as seen by others, or the appearance of heavenly glory around his head or on his face, etc. And as regards time and place, the various occurrences here detailed are hopelessly jumbled together.

The value of Adamnan's work really consists not in what he was most desirous to tell, but in what he incidentally lets slip or alludes to in passing. For myself, I do not care much to investigate whether it is really true that the saint prophesied that somebody would knock down his ink-horn and spill his ink. I am much more interested in the fact that he possessed an ink-horn (lib. i., c. 19). It may have an interest for some that the saint blessed a knife in such a way that it would never wound either man or beast, but it is to me more interesting to know that the monks were so skilled in the working of metals that, in complete faith in the miraculous property of the knife, they melted it down and were able to apply a thin coating of the metal to all the iron tools used in the monastery (lib. ii., c. 30). Knowing how differently different men are affected by the same evidence, I shall not scoff at any one who believes that a formidable wild boar in a wood in the island of Skye fell down dead at the prayer of the saint; but I am myself more interested in learning that the wild boar was hunted in Skye in the sixth century (lib. ii., c. 27). I do not care to discuss whether it is really true that on the occasion of St. Columba's visit to the monastery of Terryglas in Tipperary, the locked doors of the church flew open at the word of the saint; but it does seem worth noting that in those early days the doors of the monastic churches had their fastening of lock and key (lib. ii., c. 37). Adamnan records how Columba supernaturally detected the rank of a disguised pilgrim to Iona. Whether it was by natural or supernatural agency the saint discovered the truth, it is to all students of ecclesiastical history of real consequence to know the fact that Columba recognized his guest as possessing, on account of his rank as a bishop, special privileges and honours in the ritual of the Church not allowed to presbyters (lib. i., c. 35).

I will return presently to the miraculous features of the story, and will state frankly what I have come, after some consideration, to think about them. But I must here repeat that the *Life* of Adamnan gives us but little help in a chronological arrangement of the incidents related. We can gather, however, from the narrative enough to picture to ourselves the chief features of the saint's daily round of duty. How he was commonly attended in his little hut, built a little apart from the other buildings, by the faithful Diarmit; how he occupied much of his time in writing, part at least of which was the work of transcribing portions of the Holy Scriptures; how with the monks he attended the services of vespers and matins in the church; and how to the church the saint repaired when he felt moved to make special supplications for the preservation or relief of friends in danger or distress; how he took an interest in the farm-work of the monastery, and from time to time inspected it himself; how, in his later years, as his strength failed, he was drawn about in a little cart; how the welfare of the various daughter-houses was dear to his heart; and how very frequent were communications between Iona and its dependencies. These and scores of other precious pieces of information we gather from the *Life*.

There can be no question that even in his lifetime Columba was almost universally looked on with profound respect and veneration. On his proposing, for example, to visit St. Ciaran's monastery of Clonmacnois, the whole body of the monks of that establishment, both those engaged in the fields and those occupied in duties within their walls, assembled in the enclosure and went out, headed by the abbat, to meet the saint, " as if he had been the angel of the Lord." When Columba came within sight they bowed themselves with their faces to the ground, and when they met him they saluted him with kisses of reverential affection. Hymns and praises were then sung as they walked in procession towards the church. And to prevent the saint being inconvenienced by the pressure of the crowd, he was protected by being placed under a kind of wooden canopy borne by four men walking beside him (lib. i., c. 3).

Nor can there be a doubt that even in his lifetime Columba was very generally regarded as possessing the power to work miracles, or by his prayers to obtain the supernatural aid of Heaven. I am also satisfied —and this is a most important fact, if it be established —that Columba was himself convinced that he was granted, at least in some measure, the powers that were attributed to him. And further, I am satisfied that his biographer Adamnan, who wrote the *Life*, perhaps within a hundred years of the death of his hero, was not himself a deliberate inventor of fictions. And yet, after having read all that is alleged about the antecedent probability of miracles being vouchsafed in circumstances like those of St. Columba, I have to confess that I am not satisfied that we have evidence before us as to the miracles of a kind that ought to carry our judgment to a verdict of "proven."

Now, though I acquit Adamnan himself of inventing miracles, I am unable to acquit of blame "some person or persons unknown," who, either by gross exaggeration of facts in some instances, or in others by deliberately concocting what passed for facts, have largely contributed to the material of this biography. I am afraid I must say that this remark applies to the great majority of the prodigies with which the book abounds. A few can be accounted for by a mere unconscious spirit of imaginative amplification exerted to do honour to a holy man. Stories went from mouth to mouth, and grew as they travelled. When listeners are found eager to believe, story-tellers will not be over-scrupulous. And to have been sceptical would in those days have been regarded as irreverence. Think, again, how a child with open eyes of wonder, and with no intention to deceive, gives an account absurdly inaccurate of something strange or unusual that has happened. His own fancies and fears become part of the history; and, without moral blame, the facts assume the shape and colour of the marvellous.

A few of the alleged miracles of St. Columba—though I have to admit they are very few—may be accounted for on natural principles, or as being mere coincidences. The most obstinate unbeliever need feel no interest in denying that Columba's mother had a dream before the child was born about an old man who brought her a beautiful cloak, which was afterwards carried away by the wind, and who comforted her by telling her that her son would be counted as one of God's prophets, and would bring innumerable souls to the heavenly country.[1] And it may very well have actually happened that King Oswald dreamed that Columba came to him and promised him victory the day before the defeat of his enemy. Nor am I disposed to deny that some "wicked and blood-stained men," who sang in Irish the songs in Columba's praise, had a marvellous escape from flame and sword, while on the same occasion a few who had regarded these songs of little value perished.[2] But by far the larger number of the "miracles" are, in my opinion, to be regarded as valueless, with no residuum, or only the smallest residuum, of fact as a basis. Adamnan, when he began his *Life*, was naturally on the look-out for miracles, and they came in in abundance. They reach us generally third or fourth hand; and certainly, honest as he was, Adamnan clearly shows that he had no disposition to sift them thoroughly. It is very interesting to note that the one marvel which he himself vouches for (the occurrence, some fourteen years before the time of his writing, of copious rain after a long and unusual drought, which he attributes to their shaking three times in the air a tunic that had been worn by the saint, and the reading aloud of some of the books written by the saint's hand) need not neces-

[1] lib. iii., c. 2.
[2] It is plain from the conclusion of the story that these *carmina* were used as *charms* in cases of danger.

sarily be accounted for by a suspension of the ordinary laws of nature (lib. ii., c. 45). It is also of much interest to observe that Adamnan makes boast that the stories which popular fame had made current could not stand comparison with the wonders which he had to relate. It is to no purpose that he tells us that in some cases he followed previous writers. These may have been more credulous than himself, nay, they may have been dishonest, as he certainly was not. And we know nothing of the capacity or intellectual qualifications of the old men who retailed to him many of his stories (*Præfationes*).

I have already spoken of how important it is to the investigator to be familiar with a wide range of hagiological literature. Legendary types have a singular tendency to recur. And with regard to the lives of Scotic saints, when reading the bardic stories we find ourselves in an atmosphere quite akin. It was universally felt that there was little worth relating which was not a marvel.

As illustrating the popular beliefs of his time, the stories related by Adamnan, however incredible, are full of interest; and much more is to be learned from them than many modern writers, in their contemptuous impatience, have been ready to acknowledge. The stories reflect the religious notions current in the writer's day, and so supply us with a most precious source of information as to a period of the history of religious thought in this country otherwise singularly obscure. Some illustrations of this truth will be offered in another chapter. It is not, I think, less interesting to know what men believed and what they thought, than what kind of dress they wore, what kind of houses they lived in, what weapons they carried, and what food they ate.

Again, that in many instances unfavourable winds shifted round to a favourable point after the prayer of the saint, will, in our own day, be differently regarded by pious men—that is, either as coincidences or as answers to prayer in a region of physical phenomena where such answers are still vouchsafed. Of a similar kind is the account of the fall of rain after the unusual drought. This last is, I think, a well-authenticated story. The events happened only fourteen years before Adamnan wrote, and he himself seems to have been present on the occasion. The months of March and April had been without rain, and the monks feared greatly for their crops. After consultation they resolved to go out among the cornfields and wave three times in the air the white tunic of the saint, and to read aloud some books which the saint had written with his own hand. This was done, when suddenly the sky became overcast, and presently the rain fell in copious abundance. One may accept the truth of the narrative, and yet, I hope, may not be suspected of irreverence or culpable scepticism in remarking that *post hoc* is sometimes confounded with *propter hoc*.

Cases of recovery from sickness upon the prayer of the saint are not matters that require special comment. But I have to confess, with respect to many of the alleged miracles, I should like to cross-examine the witnesses before accepting the testimony that has reached us second or third hand.

There is a story of Samuel Taylor Coleridge, which relates that on some occasion when he was asked, did he believe in ghosts, he replied, "I have seen too many of them to believe in them." And, similarly, how much one must discount from the stories of the Celtic population of Ireland and the Western Highlands of Scotland can only be learned by living for some considerable time among these people. For myself, I have lived too long among ghosts, banshees, clurichauns, merrows, and fairies, the interest being occasionally diversified by miraculous cures at holy wells, or miraculous appearances, like that of "our Lady of Knock," to estimate testimonies to supernatural occurrences with the seriousness and deliberate consideration with which those unfamiliar with such experiences may be disposed to regard them. The disposition to bring things to the test, to be thorough, to get at the bottom of a wonderful story, was certainly not more developed in the sixth century than it is in the nineteenth. The testimonies to the supernatural powers associated with witchcraft in the sixteenth and seventeenth centuries are immeasurably weightier than those for any miracle in the entire hagiology of Scotland or Ireland.

CHAPTER IX.

ST. ADAMNAN : IONA IN THE EIGHTH AND NINTH CENTURIES.

IT would not serve the purpose I have in view to trouble my readers with a list of the succession of the abbats of Iona. The only name of outstanding eminence is that of the ninth in order from Columba, his biographer, Adamnan, who filled the office of abbat from 679 till his death in 704, when he had reached seventy-seven years of age. On his father's side Adamnan was of the family of Columba, like whom, he appears to have been a native of Donegal. He attained a high repute for piety and for learning; and his extant writings show that the repute was not ill-founded.

The Northumbrian prince, Aldfrid, who had been in exile, probably in Iona, was among his friends, and on at least two occasions he visited him at his court at Bamborough. On the first occasion his visit was prompted by the desire to obtain the liberation of some Irish captives; and he appeared before Aldfrid as the commissioned ambassador of the Irish people. He was successful in his mission, and returned to

Ireland with sixty of his fellow-countrymen. On the occasion of his second visit to Aldfrid, he presented to the king, as it would seem, a copy of his book, *Concerning the Holy Places*, of which we shall presently speak. On this occasion, too, he visited, among other churches, that of Jarrow, where the abbat Ceolfrid discussed with him the vexed questions of the Tonsure and Easter, and by his arguments and winning persuasiveness converted him to the Roman view. On his return to Iona, Adamnan sought to win over the brotherhood to his new way of thinking, but in vain. In Ireland he was, by arguments urged with gentle moderation, more successful, though there too the houses of the Columban foundation resisted his efforts. In 697 he attended a synod, or rather mixed council of princes and ecclesiastics, held at Birr, in Ireland; and at his instance a law, afterwards known as the "Law of Adamnan," was enacted, which for the first time exempted the women of Ireland from the obligation of bearing arms and going to battle. He also took part in another Irish synod at Tara, which was attended by forty-seven chiefs and thirty-nine ecclesiastics; and in Ireland he spent his last Easter, keeping it according to the Roman computation. He returned to Iona, and again sought to persuade the monks to adopt his views on the controverted points; but he was not destined in his lifetime to see the fruit of his labours in this respect. It was not till twelve years after his death that Iona adopted the Roman ways.

K

In 710, as we learn from Bede, Naiton (or Nectan), king of the Picts, conformed to the Roman Easter. Ceolfrid, already mentioned as having effected the change in Adamnan's opinions, had sent to Naiton, in response to inquiries, a wisely-written exposition of the question, and to him may be attributed the adoption of the Roman Easter by the Pictish nation. But the Columban monasteries in Pictland still adhered to their old ways, even after the Mother House of Iona had abandoned them; and, in 717, Naiton took on him to exhibit the fervency of his orthodoxy by driving west across the mountains of Drumalban the recalcitrant Columban monks. The battle was, however, now practically won; and before many years the Easter of the old Irish cycle, which had been abandoned long before (634) in the south of Ireland, was heard of no more. There can be no doubt that the high reputation of Adamnan for learning contributed largely to bring about this result. When one so wise and so good had changed his belief and practices, men felt there must be something in the contention of their opponents. Yet the final surrender of the monks of Iona must be attributed to the wise instructions of an aged Northumbrian priest named Egbert, who had for many years lived as a monk in Ireland, and had obtained there a singular repute for piety and ascetic severity. He was, in his old age, very desirous to make a pilgrimage to Rome, but was warned by the dream of a brother-monk that his duty was to visit the brethren at Iona "because their ploughs did not go straight." In 716 he removed to Iona, where he was held in great veneration. He spent the last thirteen years of his life there, and died, after celebrating mass, on Easter-day in the year 729. And after that date, at all events, if not a few years earlier, the old Celtic computation of Easter was abandoned for ever.[1]

Celtic names often underwent strange transformations; but few of them exhibit more numerous variations of shape than that of Adamnan. The word (which in signification is a diminutive of Adam, and sometimes appears as Adaman) passed, through the form Ownan, into Eunan, the name under which the cathedral church of the Irish diocese of Raphoe was dedicated. While in Scotland the saint's name can be traced, according to Dr. Reeves, under such disguises as Ainan, Arnty, Eonan, Eunan, Teunan, Thewnan, Skeulan, and, most odd of all, Arnold.[2] In the Scottish dedications of churches and the names of wells, etc., we have indications that he was venerated not only in Cantire and the island of Sanda (Inchawyn) off its coast, but in Aberdeenshire at Aboyn, and Furvie (which is specially connected with his name in the *Aberdeen Breviary*); in Banff at Forglen; in Perthshire at Campsie; in Forfarshire at Tannadice; in West Lothian at Dalmeny; and in the island of Inchkeith in the Forth, which we are now familiar with for

---

[1] See Bede, *Eccles. Hist.*, lib. v., c. 21.
[2] Reeves, article "Adamnan" in Smith and Wace's *Dict. of Christ. Biog.*, and *Historians of Scotland*, vol. vi., p. clxviii; Forbes, *Kalendars of Scottish Saints*, p. 266.

its lighthouse and its fortifications, lately armed with heavy guns for the protection of Edinburgh. You will observe that the large majority of these dedications were in the dominion of the Picts, and I cannot help offering the conjecture that the concurrence of Adamnan's changed views with those adopted by the zealous Pictish monarch may have stimulated the special veneration felt for him in that kingdom.

The most important of the writings of Adamnan is undoubtedly the *Life of St. Columba*, which has been discussed; but something should be said here of his other principal work, entitled *Concerning the Holy Places*.[1] We learn from Bede (lib. v., c. 15) that Arculf, a bishop, and a Gaul by nationality, was wrecked on the coast of Britain on his return voyage from a pilgrimage to Palestine and the East. It is not difficult to understand how, if he were sailing to some port on the western or northern coast of France, he might by tempests have been blown far north, and on landing have come within reach of the fame of Adamnan. After many unrecorded adventures he reached Iona, and from his lips Adamnan took down on waxen tablets Arculf's account of the most interesting places visited by him, including, besides Jerusalem, Alexandria and Constantinople. He had also seen something of Crete and of Sicily on his return journey. His narrative, as we see from the work itself, was drawn from him in large measure by the intelligent questions of his host. It was afterwards

---

[1] This work is printed in the *Acta Ord. Benedict.* sec. iii., pars ii.

transferred by Adamnan, in an abbreviated form, from the tablets to parchment. It forms, in truth, a really valuable account of the places in the Holy Land visited by the pilgrims of that day, and contains several ground-plans (sketched by Arculf) of the churches built upon the sacred sites. It was made the foundation of Bede's work on the same subject. We may note in passing that in the Galilean part of his tour Arculf placed himself under the guidance of a hermit, Peter by name, a Burgundian by birth, who hurried him from place to place with a speed which he little relished. The incident has a life-like air of truthfulness.

Unfortunately, the work contains, in its pertinent narration, scarcely any information that would throw even a side-light upon the usages of the Scottish Church. One point, however, I have noted with much interest. Adamnan observes that the initial letter of Tabor (the mountain) is the Greek Theta [θ], indicating that it should be pronounced "with an aspiration," and that the final o is long, being Omega [ω]. Now, through the chink of this fact of the interest of Adamnan in such a little question, we may get a passing glimpse of the considerable measure of culture which existed in the Scottish monasteries. When men are interested in questions of philology and pronunciation, it indicates that they have progressed a considerable way in intellectual pursuits.

The conclusion of the work contains a story reported by Arculf of a warrior in the East, who, going out to the wars, "commended himself and his horse" to the care of St. George, and was kept in safety in many fierce battles. It was not unnatural for Arculf to take a special interest in St. George, as that hero had been long venerated in France. But we may conjecture that Adamnan's book may have helped largely to spread his fame among the warlike people of Britain.

Among other subjects of inquiry, Adamnan desired to know whether, in the desert of St. John Baptist, Arculf had seen any locusts or wild honey. Small locusts, the traveller replied, he had seen; but he gives it as his opinion that the "wood-honey" (*mel silvestre*) was the sweet leaves of certain trees which he had tasted.

Adamnan also seems taken with the view of Arculf, that our Lord in the phrase, "Ye are the salt *of the earth*," meant to refer to salt dug out of the earth as distinguished from *sea-salt*. The traveller had seen and tasted some rock-salt in Sicily, and declared it to be the saltest of salts (*sal salsissimum*). Now, foreign as both these interpretations are to those familiar only with our English Bibles, and baseless as the latter seems to be, the view that the honey, which formed part of the food of the Baptist, was some sweet exudation on the leaves of trees, has been maintained by very many scholars of modern times.[1] My object, however, in noticing these things is to show that they give us a glimpse of the real interest taken by Adamnan in getting at what he

---

[1] Meyer (on Matt. iii. 4) cites Suidas, Salmasius, Reland, Michaelis, Kuinoel, Fritzche, Bleek, and Volkmar.

thought the true sense of the Scripture narrative. It is easy to picture the eagerness with which, in the remote little island in the western sea, he questioned the traveller from the distant regions of the East.

Again, before transcribing his guest's narrative, he made himself acquainted, he tells us, with other accounts of the Holy Land, which fact gives us another glimpse of the learning of Iona.

The treatise, *Concerning the Holy Places*, is written in a more careful and studied style than the *Life of St. Columba*, and is seldom disfigured by barbarisms and obscurities such as are not infrequent in the latter work. The book concludes with the request, so common in these old writings, that the reader would pray for Arculf, who supplied the facts, and for the "wretched sinner" who wrote them down.

Everything we know of Adamnan makes us disposed to willingly accept the judgment of Bede, that he was "a good and wise man, and pre-eminently learned in the Holy Scriptures." We have only to add that the error which made Adamnan, under the name Eunan, *bishop* of Raphoe, recurs in the Kalendar of the Scottish Prayer-Book of 1637, where, at September 25th, we find "Adaman B."

After the death of Adamnan, the learned Skene (*Celtic Scotland*, vol. ii., p. 289) infers, from a comparison of lists of abbats of Iona, that each of the two rival parties—the Celtic and the Roman—elected their own abbat, and that this schism was continued for many years. The different lists are certainly perplexing, but in default of more light, I cannot but think the inference is weightier than the evidence will bear. It seems to me quite inconceivable that so grave a state of things as the existence of a prolonged schism would not have been expressly referred to.

The later annals of Iona during the period with which we are concerned are for the most part only brief jottings; but we may notice a few events of importance and interest. Their island home, exposed to the wild sweep of the Atlantic, must have subjected the brotherhood of Iona to frequent perils of the deep. The monastery of Apurcrossan (now Applecross, in Ross-shire) had, in 737, lost its abbat, with twenty-two others, out at sea, and twelve years after (749) the monastic family of Iona met a similar disaster. The language of the Irish annalist, Tighernac, would suggest that it was attended with even greater loss. Under the year 749 he notes, "A great storm. The family of Iona drowned."[1]

In 778, Niall Frassach, who had been king of all Ireland for seven years, and had retired to the monastery of Iona, died there apparently after eight years' residence among the brethren. Four years afterwards, another Irish monarch, Artgaile, king of Connaught, went on his pilgrimage to Iona, and died there after eight years' residence.

---

[1] Skene's *Chronicles of the Picts and Scots*, p. 76. Perhaps *demersi* may mean "buried" in the ruins of their destroyed houses.

During the course of the eighth century the remains of St. Columba were disinterred, enshrined, and removed to Ireland, where they were deposited in the church of Saul Patrick, in the county of Down. The cause of this translation of the relics is generally, and probably rightly, attributed to the terror which the Danish piratical fleets were spreading everywhere along the coasts. We know from the *Saxon Chronicle*, that, in 793, the sacred island of Lindisfarne was ravaged by the heathen Danes; and it may well have been that the dread of a similar calamity prompted the removal, to a place of greater safety, of the most precious treasure of Iona, the body of the holy founder. However this may be, in 802 the blow fell, and the monastery of Iona was pillaged and burned. Four years later a second attack was made upon the island, and sixty-eight of the brethren fell by the sword. The intense love of the brotherhood for their home is affectingly manifested by their persistent efforts to re-establish their position the moment the immediate danger was removed. In 818, the abbat Diarmait returned to the island with the shrine of Columba. And at this time, as Skene (*Celtic Scotland*, vol. ii., p. 298) gives good reason for believing, the monastic buildings were constructed of stone, in a situation better suited for defence. But once more a terrible and murderous onslaught on the brotherhood was made by the Danish hordes in 825, in the account of which the monk Blaithmac, the son of an Irish prince, appears prominently, as having been slaughtered before the altar where he was celebrating mass. The desire to secure the precious metals that formed the shrine of Columba, which they believed was hidden in the island, was on this occasion, as we are expressly told, one of the objects of the Danish attack. Some of the monks saved themselves by flight. After having seen the companions who remained with him put to death before his eyes, Blaithmac was asked to reveal the place where the holy relics were deposited in concealment. He replied that he did not know, and that if he knew he would not tell, whereupon he was instantly hewn in pieces. "It was fitting that Iona, the sacred nursery of so many doctors and confessors, should also have its martyrs in the saints of God."[1] Some of the particulars just related are derived from a Latin *Life of Blaithmac*, written in one hundred and seventy-two hexameter verses by his contemporary, the erudite Walafrid Strabo, who, as a monk of St. Gall, and afterwards abbat of Reichenau, lived in a region where contact with visitors from Irish monasteries was frequent.

We now approach an event of singular importance in the secular as well as the religious history of the country—the union of the Scottish and Pictish kingdoms under the rule of one monarch, Kenneth MacAlpin, who transferred the primacy from Iona to Dunkeld. Whether Iona had preserved its privileges in the kingdom of the Picts after the expulsion of the Columban monks is doubtful. "Among the

[1] Bishop Healy's *Insula Sanctorum et Doctorum*, p. 347.

Picts," says Dr. Grub (*Eccl. Hist. of Scotland*, vol. i., p. 142), "the Church appears to have been reduced to vassalage by the temporal power. During the contests of the two nations, the difficulty must have been experienced, which is always felt when an inhabitant of one state exercises ecclesiastical jurisdiction over the inhabitants of another." But now this difficulty ceased, and Kenneth, having built a new church at Dunkeld, removed to it some of the relics of St. Columba (850); and henceforth the primatial authority was claimed for Dunkeld, though the claim may not have been readily or at once acknowledged by all the Columban monks in the west of Scotland. Tuathal, the abbat of Dunkeld, is also styled "first bishop" (*primus episcopus*) of Fortrenn—the name given to the kingdom of the Southern Picts.[1] As abbat of Dunkeld, a church dedicated to St. Columba, and possessing some of his relics, he would claim obedience from the Columban monasteries of Scotland, and as bishop of Fortrenn, he was head of the Pictish Church.[2] I have learned, after a long acquaintance with his admirable work, to have a profound respect for the judgment of Dr. Grub, who weighs his evidence with all the impartiality of a trained lawyer on the judicial bench; but on the question of the sense of the phrase, "primus Episcopus Fortren," in the *Annals of Ulster* at 865, I am inclined to believe Skene is right in saying that it "means first in

---

[1] *Annals of Ulster*, A.D. 865.
[2] Skene, *Celtic Scotland*, vol. ii., p. 308.

time and not in dignity" (*Celtic Scotland*, vol. ii., p. 308). By this we should understand that he was the first bishop having episcopal *jurisdiction*. Bishops, as we shall see (chap. xiv.), were numerous, but hitherto they had, by an unusual arrangement, been subject, as members of the monastic communities, to the authority of the abbats.

CHAPTER X.

INFLUENCE OF IONA IN THE SOUTH: ST. CUTHBERT IN LOTHIAN.

It is not my intention to narrate at any length the wonderful story of the Irish mission in England. It has been often told; and close as its connection is with the monastic foundation of Columba at Iona, it would open a field too wide for brief treatment, and, in part, too remote from the religious history of Scotland. Some notice, however, must be taken of the events connected with the memorable time when the streams of Celtic and Latin Christianity first met in the north.

It must be learned elsewhere how the half-Christianized tribes of Angles in the north-east of England and the adjoining south-east of Scotland had been overwhelmed by the power of the pagan Penda, and how the arms of Oswald had restored (634) the kingdom to the hands of a Christian. Oswald, on the death of his father, Ethelfrid (616), had fled with his brother and sought refuge either in Ireland or, as seems for many reasons very much more probable, among the Irish Christians of British Dalriada. During his exile he had been baptized (Adamnan, *Vita S. Columbæ*, lib. i., c. 1). And, if we may rationalize, it was the memory of the wonders he had heard about their saintly patron from the Columban monks in Iona which suggested to him on his return to England the dream which he dreamed the day before his successful engagement with the forces of Cadwalla. Columba seemed to approach, bright with angelic glory and of a stature so great that he seemed to touch the clouds. Then the saint in the dream uttered the words, "Be strong and of a good courage; behold, I will be with thee;" and added the command that he should not delay to attack the enemy, for victory would be his. After his triumph and settlement in his kingdom of Bernicia, Oswald sent a message to Iona, beseeching the brethren to send him a bishop as a missionary to help in bringing back his people to the Christian faith. His petition was answered. A bishop (to whom the late writer, Hector Boece, gives the name Corman) was sent from Iona. But this man, who is described by Bede (*Eccles. Hist.*, lib. iii., c. 5) as of too austere a temperament, met with no success, and soon returned back to Iona.

With the aid of Bede (*Eccles. Hist.*, lib. iii., c. 5) we can picture to ourselves the scene on the return to Iona of the unsuccessful missionary. The "seniors" of the island monastery are summoned together; and Corman declared to them that no progress could be made among men so intractable, so stubborn and barbarous as the Angles. Then there was much discussion among the assembled brethren as to what was to be done, for they were desirous to grant the blessing which had been sought for the people who still sat in darkness. Then a monk named Aidan, who was present in the council, addressing the returned missionary, who must have been giving some details of his mode of working, said, "It seems to me, brother, that you were more harsh with your unlearned hearers than was reasonable, and did not first, as the Apostle has taught us, offer them the milk of less solid doctrine, until, gradually nourished with the Word of God, they would have been able to accept a more advanced teaching and stricter rule of life."

When they heard these words, the eyes of all who sat in the council were turned upon Aidan, and after a careful and full discussion of what had been said, they resolved to send Aidan himself to supply the place of Corman. And so, when they had ordained him bishop, they despatched him (635) to Northumbria. His wisdom and loving moderation fully justified their choice. Under Aidan Christianity made rapid progress in the dominions of Oswald, which extended northward as far as the Forth.

The episcopal see of Aidan was fixed by the king in the island of Lindisfarne, off the coast of Northumberland. Though unlike Iona in being accessible from the shore at low water, it resembles the Scottish "Holy Island"[1] in extent, being about two miles and three-quarters in length, and in breadth about a mile and a half. Like Iona, too, it

[1] See *Lindisfarne or Holy Island*, by the Rev. W. W. F. Keeling.

contains no vestige of the original Celtic church and monastery; and, like Iona, the ecclesiastical ruins now to be seen on the island are of the mediæval period. This sacred spot was the seat of sixteen bishops in succession, and a centre of missionary labour scarcely, if at all, inferior to the mother house itself. That it was within easy reach of the fortress of Bamborough, a principal residence of the king, must have been serviceable in maintaining and increasing the influence of its spiritual chiefs.

It was under the rule of Aidan that the most famous monastery in the south of Scotland, Melrose, had its origin at a spot some two miles lower down the Tweed than the site of the ruins of the noble Cistercian abbey which now attract the attention of the visitor. The place occupied by the original monastery is still known as Old Melrose, and is situated on the right bank, where the river's course makes a horse-shoe curve nearly surrounding the enclosure of the monastery.[1] Of this monastery the first abbat was Eata. He had been one of twelve native Northumbrian boys whom St. Aidan had taken "to be instructed in Christ."[2] He afterwards appeared as the first bishop of Hexham, and the fifth of Lindisfarne. It was during Eata's rule as abbat of Melrose —the "Mailros" of Bede—that, in 651, the young shepherd Cuthbert, who tended his flocks upon the

---

[1] Bede (*Eccles Hist.*, lib. v., c. 12) says the monastery was almost surrounded by the winding of the river Tweed.

[2] Another of these twelve boys was the famous St. Chad (Ceadda), bishop of Lichfield.

banks of the Leader Water (a tributary of the Tweed, which flows from the southern slope of the Lammermuir Hills and enters the larger river near Melrose), presented himself for admission at the monastery. And it was from Melrose, after a few years, that he accompanied his abbat to found the monastery at Ripon. Differences with their princely patron at Ripon on the subject of the Easter computation drove back (661) these followers of the Celtic practice to Melrose. In 664 Eata removed Cuthbert to Lindisfarne, where he was appointed prior or provost.[1] Here his connection with Scotland ceases; and it is not my province to relate the story of his great work and wonderful life in England. It is of interest, however, to gather together all that we can learn of him during his stay in the country that forms our present Scotland.

Our great authority is Bede, who deals with the life of Cuthbert, not only in his best-known work, the *Ecclesiastical History*, but also in a separate biography of the saint written in lucid and beautiful prose, as well as in a metrical biography of less value, though not without its merits. Bede had, however, made use of, and, in part, incorporated in his own work, an earlier and much shorter *Life* by an unnamed monk of Lindisfarne, which should certainly be studied together with Bede's work, as occasionally we find in it some graphic touch or some little piece

---

[1] The word "præpositus" is the word habitually used in the documents of Celtic monasticism for the officer who, under the abbat, administered the affairs of each religious house.

of information which Bede expunged or glossed, to our loss.[1]

Not a word is said by Bede or the anonymous author about the birth or parentage of Cuthbert. Perhaps the reason is that nothing was known about it; and I can only express my wonder that Skene is to be found (*Celtic Scotland*, vol. ii., p. 205) in any measure coquetting with the Irish story which makes him born, out of wedlock, of a mother who was an Irish king's daughter. The whole narrative, crammed full of absurdities, has for its source a fourteenth-century manuscript now preserved in the Diocesan Library at York.[2]

I do not know that we can even claim, with any confidence, the great saint as a native of North Britain, though it appears that his early years were passed at no very great distance from Melrose; as we are told by Bede, in recounting a miracle where the saint saved a house from fire by his prayers, that he frequently visited (apparently from Melrose) a good woman who brought him up as a child, and whom he therefore used to style "mother."

The first thing we learn about Cuthbert is that

---

[1] This *Life*, "by a contemporary monk of Lindisfarne," is printed by the Bollandists (*Acta Sanctorum*, Martii tom. iii., p. 117), and by Stevenson, *Bedæ Opp. Minora*, p. 259.

[2] Skene suspects that this early part of Bede's narrative, dealing with the parentage of the saint, was "expunged at the instance of the critics to whom he had submitted his manuscript." This part of the story of the Irish manuscript has, it seems to me, a strong resemblance to the legend about the birth of St. Kentigern, and may have been suggested by it to the Irish hagiologist.

he was fond of, and foremost in, all manner of noisy boyish games, and delighted in the companionship of his fellows. He was active and quick-witted; and in leaping, running, and wrestling was proud to be able to beat, not only all boys of his age, but even some of his seniors.

The anonymous author, with a greater frankness of detail than Bede, describes how one day, when Cuthbert was eight years of age, the boys indulged themselves (some of them stark naked) in the sport of standing on their heads with their legs wide apart in the air. This a child of three years old, who was possessed of the gift of prophecy, considered an unbecoming attitude for a future bishop, and rebuked the saint accordingly, who did not take well the comments of his three-year-old mentor. It is amusing to find Bede refining on this story in his prose life, while in his verses, as was natural, the humorous or unbecoming element is entirely suppressed. Still further, in the First Lesson for St. Cuthbert's Day in the *Aberdeen Breviary*, we read the very tame account—" Cuthbert was a youth of good disposition, and one day, when he was playing with boys, a certain boy of about three years old came to him and said, with tears, "O most holy Bishop Cuthbert, it does not become thee, whom the Lord has destined to be the ruler of those older than yourself, to play among boys." This is a specimen of the process of rehandling, as to which the student must be always on the alert. To most of us, I suppose, the child's prophecy is of much less interest than the picture presented of the merry, light-hearted, vigorous, and athletic boy, in whom the prophecy was fulfilled. He who afterwards underwent so many hardships and toils had then his early physical training.

The next incident in the anonymous *Life* is how a swelling in Cuthbert's knee (which might very easily occur in the life of this frolicsome boy) was cured by an application of a mixture of flour and milk, cooked together and *put on hot*, a recipe recommended to him as he lay in the sun outside the house by a man in white robes who came riding by on a splendidly-caparisoned horse. "After a few days," says the biographer, "he was perfectly cured," and Cuthbert perceived that his adviser on horseback was an angel.[1] This story is reproduced faithfully enough by Bede in his more elegant style, except that he adds the very important statement that Cuthbert tells his angelic visitor that "the skill of none of the doctors" had been able to do him good. Perhaps the doctors had never tried a poultice of hot milk and flour.[2]

Perhaps it was in his early youth that Cuthbert

---

[1] Canon Browne (*Venerable Bede* in the *Fathers for English Readers*) observes: "Curiously enough, Bede's only doubt in the matter is whether all readers will believe that an angel rode on horseback. To satisfy the scruples of such, he refers them to the passage in the Maccabees, where angels came on horseback to the aid of Judas Maccabeus."

[2] Should any one care for the recipe in Latin hexameters, here it is—

Sic fatus, "Similae nitidam cum lacte farinam
Olla coquat pariter ferventis in igne culinae,
Hacque istum calida sanandus inunge tumorem."

served as a soldier—a fact testified to by the anonymous biographer, but, strangely enough, not recorded by Bede. The notice is very brief; the admiration of the anonymous monk is roused by the statement that Cuthbert, living in camp, with the enemy in front, and subsisting on scanty rations, still throve and flourished, like Daniel and the Three Holy Children on their poor fare. The place which this story occupies in the secular life of Cuthbert, and, indeed, its very terms, preclude the notion that the anonymous biographer understood the story in any other than a literal sense.[1]

From the time when his knee was cured, we are told the youth devoted himself much to prayer, seeking more particularly for angelic aid. His prayers were on one occasion effectively made on behalf of some ships in danger at the mouth of the river Tine (*Tinus*). Now, what river was this? Was it the great river Tyne that divides Northumberland from Durham, or the little river of the same name in East Lothian that enters the sea a few miles north of the town of Dunbar? It seems to me that there is little or no evidence to determine which is meant. The Bollandists give judgment in favour of the Scottish stream; and Scotchmen will probably prefer to regard it as a Scottish miracle. But it is certain, if we credit the anonymous *Life*, that Cuthbert, during his secular life, had made journeys south of Durham.

There is a more general agreement that the river Leader (*Leder*) of the anonymous *Life*, by which he

[1] See Stevenson's *Opp. Hist. Min. Ven. Bedæ*, p. 124.

was tending the herds of some richer man, when he saw by night the vision of St. Aidan's soul being carried to heaven " in a ball of fire " by the angels, is the stream already referred to as a tributary of the Tweed.[1] It was this wonderful sight which, according to Bede, determined Cuthbert to abandon the secular life, and devote himself to the monastery.

We are told that Cuthbert was specially drawn to choose Melrose for his place of profession by the high repute of the provost of the house, Boisil by name, " a monk and priest of exalted virtues." This, I think, tends to confirm the belief that the place of his labour as a herd was not very remote from Melrose. Cuthbert rode to the monastery spear in hand,[2] as was not unnatural for a traveller in those wild times. Boisil, who was standing outside the door of the monastery as he approached, received him kindly ; and Eata, the abbat, who had been absent, arriving after a few days, on the provost's recommendation admitted Cuthbert to the " family," or brotherhood of monks.

Cuthbert threw himself eagerly into the duties of the monastic life at Melrose. " In reading and praying, working and watching," he seemed to surpass his fellows. It is especially noted of him that he strictly abstained from every intoxicating drink, but was not at this time rigid in the matter of food, "lest he might

---

[1] Lauderdale takes its name from this river.
[2] Indeed, the protection of the herds from plunder was probably one of his chief duties, as he watched by night. The stout young soldier would have been well suited for it.

be less fitted for work." His strength and vigour of body, fit for any kind of labour, is expressly mentioned.

After some years, Cuthbert was taken with him by his abbat to found the monastery at Ripon, and there he was elected by the "family" to be "provost of the guest-chamber," which was esteemed an honourable office and one requiring much discretion.

There is a story told of St. Cuthbert while at Ripon, which, though concerned with his life on the other side of the border, is worth relating, not for the miraculous element, but because it illustrates the duties of the post which he occupied at that place, and which was one of importance in the monasteries of Celtic foundation. I choose the earlier anonymous *Life*, rather than Bede's, as my chief source of information. Very early one morning in winter a traveller presented himself at the guest-house. He was kindly received by Cuthbert, as was his manner. Water was supplied for washing the hands and feet of the stranger, and Cuthbert, having dried his feet with towels, rubbed and warmed them, for they were cold, with his own hands. The stranger was anxious to resume his journey at once, but was prevailed upon by Cuthbert's entreaties to wait till nine o'clock (the third hour), when food would be served. When the bell for the third hour had sounded, and the prayers of Terce were finished, Cuthbert made ready the table, and placed on it some food which he had by him. By some chance there happened to be no bread in the guest-house, but only a few crumbs which he gathered together and put on the table "for blessed bread."[1] Cuthbert then left the guest-house, and proceeded to the monastery to get some more bread, but none was yet to be had, for the loaves were not yet taken out of the oven. When he returned to the guest-house the traveller was gone, and not a trace of him could be found, though Cuthbert at once looked for his footprints in the fresh snow with which the ground was covered. His senses, however, as he entered the guest-chamber were greeted with the smell of bread of the sweetest kind, which he soon perceived came from three hot loaves. But how did they come there? It was plain that his guest was an angel.

As already mentioned, Eata and Cuthbert, with the other brethren, had soon to leave Ripon. They were given their choice to adopt the Roman Easter or to depart. They chose to return to Melrose.

After his return, the pestilence, which was then widespread through Britain, attacked the monastery. Among the sufferers were the prior, Boisil, and Cuthbert. The former died, having been attended sedulously by Cuthbert, who read aloud to him, at his request, during the week before his death, the Gospel according to St. John. The village of St. Boswells, a

---

[1] There is a passage in Adamnan (*Vita S. Col.*, lib. ii., c. 12) which illustrates this. I take it that the practice of the Columban monks was to break their fast, whether at the third, or, on fast-days, at the ninth hour, by first partaking of some "blessed bread." In Adamnan it is called *eulogia*. Whether this bread was part of the bread offered at the altar, but unconsecrated, or had received some other kind of special benediction, is not certain.

few miles from Melrose, now best known for its great sheep-fair, the largest in the south of Scotland, still perpetuates the name of the good provost.

Cuthbert during his own illness was told how the brethren had been praying all night for him. At once he exclaimed, "Why do I lie here? We cannot think that God will despise the prayers of so many good men. Give me my staff and my sandals." And he thereupon rose, and attempted to walk with the help of his staff. He gradually recovered his strength and health, though almost throughout his whole life he felt in some degree the injurious effects of that formidable illness.

On the death of Boisil, Cuthbert was made provost of the monastery of Melrose, and he followed the good example of his predecessor, not only in the performance of the duties within the monastic house, but also in his labours for the welfare of the country folk all around, whom Bede speaks of as Angles by race. For many of them had led bad lives, or were given over to gross superstitions, and some, even in the time of the pestilence, neglected "the sacrament of their faith," and resorted for protection to spells and incantations and other idolatrous remedies. Cuthbert went frequently among them through the surrounding villages, sometimes on horseback, but oftener on foot. And he took more particular care to preach in the hamlets among the wild hills, where other teachers were little inclined to go. Sometimes he would spend a week in this work, or even two or three weeks; sometimes it was a whole month before he would return home. The results that followed were very marked. Cuthbert was a skilful instructor, and possessed a winning and persuasive manner, and " the light of his angelic countenance " was such that none that were present dared to hide from him the secrets of their hearts, but openly confessed their deeds, because they believed that it was impossible to hide them from him. Nor did they fail, as Bede assures us, to follow his directions for their amendment.

Such is the account that has come down to us of the labours of St. Cuthbert at Melrose.

We find that on one occasion Cuthbert, accompanied by two of the brethren, paid a visit to the country of the Niduarian Picts—that is, the Picts of Galloway. But this was not for missionary purposes, but on some business connected with the monastery, the nature of which is not told us. They travelled partly by sea, taking boat, we may suppose, at some place well up in the Solway.[1]

On another occasion he went from Melrose to the monastery at Coldingham (on the sea cliffs of Berwickshire), on the invitation of the royal abbess, St. Aebba. This Aebba was a daughter of Ethelfrid, king of Northumbria, and sister of St. Oswald. Coldingham (*Coludi Urbs* of Bede), as founded by Aebba, was a double monastery—that is, of both monks

---

[1] I have placed in the text the commonly accepted view of the words "to the land of the Picts, who are called Niduari" (Bede's *Vita S. Cuthb.*, c. iv.) ; but it is by no means certain that these were not Picts north of the Forth.

and nuns, who, though residing apart, were subject to one head. The great house of St. Brigid at Kildare had long before set an example of such twin communities. Similar was the House of St. Hilda at Whitby; and other examples of this practice are shown us by history at Repton, Barking, and Wimborne; and in France at Brie, Autun, and Fontrevault.

The monastery of St. Aebba was placed on the wild headland not far from the site of the lighthouse that now marks the promontory of St. Abb's Head, which takes its name from her.[1]

Connected with Cuthbert's visit to Coldingham is a story that shows us the saint practising a form of ascetic discipline that was a favourite in the monastic life of the time, and for that reason it is worth recording. St. Aebba had asked St. Cuthbert to come and preach to the inmates of her House. He felt that he could not refuse, and so he went, and for some days he remained there preaching the way of righteousness. And according to his manner, says Bede, at night, when the rest were sleeping, he went forth alone to pray, and so continued during the long watches of the night till the hour of service in the church called him back. One night a prying brother of the monastery privately followed him. The saint was seen descending the cliffs to the sea-shore, and then entering the water till the swell of the waves reached his shoulders

---

[1] As in so many instances, the mediæval Benedictine Priory of Coldingham (founded in 1098 by King Edgar) is situated at a considerable distance, inland, from the site of the earlier foundation. The ruins of the Priory Church still give some notion of its former dignity.

and neck. And there he stood during the dark hours of the night mingling his praises with the noise of the sea (*undisonis in laudibus*). When dawn approached he came to land and began to pray afresh, as he knelt on the shore.

This is a very interesting picture, yet it is likely that it might never have been preserved for us, but for the marvel that followed. While he was praying, two small creatures coming from the sea—Bede says they were "otters"—approached him, and sought to dry him with their furry coats, and to warm his feet with their breath. This service done, they received his blessing and glided back into their native waves.[1] Cuthbert then returned to the monastery and joined with the brethren in singing the morning psalms.

If Stevenson (*Bedæ Opp. Hist. Min.*, p. 268) is correct in his conjecture that the name of the river "Tesgeta" is an error of the scribe of the anonymous *Life*, and should be read "Tevyota"—the Teviot—we have another incident of Cuthbert's life that is to be placed on the north of our modern border.[2] He

---

[1] Bede's expansion and adornment of the story in the anonymous *Life* is worth a study. The anonymous *Life* describes the two creatures as *pusilla animalia maritima:* in Bede they are *quadrupedia quæ vulgo Lutræ vocantur.* If there is any foundation at all for this part of the story, could the creatures have been young seals, seen dimly from a distance and in the gloom—the imagination of the prying brother contributing something?

[2] Indeed, we need not assume any transcriptional error so far as the letter "g" is concerned, as many instances may be found of the change of *g* into *y*. Thus "Mayo," see p. 179, is in *Bede* "Mageo." "Ely" was "Elge." Our affirmative "yea" appears in *Bede* as "gæ." See Mayor and Lumby's *Bede*, p. 308.

had gone one day towards the south, teaching and baptizing among the country people, and was accompanied in his journey by a boy as his attendant. They had brought no provisions with them, and as the day went on Cuthbert asked his companion, "Are you thinking who has prepared your dinner for you to-day?" The boy confessed that he had not much hope of dinner that day. The saint replied, "Be assured, my son, that the Lord will provide food for those who trust in Him, for He has said, 'Seek ye first the kingdom of God and His righteousness, and all these things shall be added unto you'; and again in the Prophet, 'I have been young and now am old, yet saw I never the righteous forsaken nor his seed begging their bread.' 'For the workman is worthy of his hire.'" Presently an eagle comes in view on the bank of the river with a large fish which it had caught. The boy ran forward, and brought the fish to the saint, who at once rebuked him with the words, "Why did you not give part to our hungry fisherman?"[1] Then the boy took part of the fish back to the eagle, and the remaining part they carried with them, and when they got into inhabited places they cooked it, and ate, and gave to others, and being satisfied they gave glory to God, and went on their way. Kindness towards birds and beasts—nay, more than kindness, a real sympathy with them—is constantly exemplified in the lives of the ancient saints of Britain and Ireland. A truly beneficent influence such stories must have tended to

[1] Bede spoils this in the telling.

exert in those rude times when there was so little in the lives of the generality of men to foster the kindlier and more humane feelings towards the dumb creatures of God.

After some (Bede says "many") years at Melrose, the abbat Eata transferred Cuthbert to Lindisfarne, where he was appointed provost, and the story of Cuthbert in Scotland closes.

The true appreciation of the character of St. Cuthbert must, of course, be based on the review of his whole life, which has not been here attempted. I shall best consult the interests of the reader by merely citing the estimate of that character by one who had made himself intimately acquainted with the time and with the man.[1] "What was it," asks Bishop Lightfoot, "that won for Cuthbert the ascendancy and fame which no Churchman north of the Humber has surpassed, or even rivalled? He was not a great writer like Bede. He was not a first preacher like Aidan. He founded no famous institution; he erected no magnificent building. He was not martyred for his faith or for his Church. His episcopate was exceptionally short [two years], and undistinguished by any event of signal importance. Whence, then, this transcendent position which he long occupied, and still to a certain measure maintains? He owed something, doubtless, to what men call accident. He was on the winning side in the controversy between the Roman and English obser-

---

[1] Dr. Bright's admirable sketch (*Chapters of Early English Church History*) is too long for quotation.

vances of Easter.[1] Moreover, the strange vicissitudes which attended his dead body served to emphasize the man in a remarkable way. But these are only the buttresses of a great reputation. The foundation of the reverence entertained for Cuthbert must be sought elsewhere. Shall we not say that the secret of his influence was this? The 'I' and 'not I' of St. Paul's great antithesis were strongly marked in him. There was an earnest, deeply sympathetic nature in the man himself, and this strong personality was purified, was heightened, was sanctified by the communion with, the indwelling of, Christ. His deeply sympathetic spirit breathes through all the notices of him. It was this which attracted men to him; it was this which unlocked men's hearts to him. We are told that he had a wonderful power of adapting his instructions to the special needs of the persons addressed. 'He always knew what to say, to whom, when, and how to say it.' This faculty of reading men's hearts sympathy alone can give. And Cuthbert's overflowed, even to dumb animals. The sea-fowl, which bear his name [the eider-duck, called 'St. Cuthbert's duck,' which breed on the Farne Islands],[2] were his special favourites. .... Other tales, too, are told—perhaps not altogether legendary—which testify to his sympathy with and power over the lower creation. We are reminded

---

[1] Cuthbert had been content to accept the Roman observance, though at first he had followed the Celtic.

[2] When the saint's tomb was opened in 1827, figures of these birds were found worked in cloth of gold on the episcopal vestments which wrapped his body. Raine's *St. Cuthbert* (1828).

by these traits of other saintly persons of deeply sympathetic nature—of Hugh of Lincoln, followed by his tame swan, of Anselm protecting the leveret, of Francis of Assisi conversing familiarly with the fowls of the air and the beasts of the field as with brothers and sisters. But if the 'I' was thus strong and deep, the 'not I' was not less marked. 'Not I, but Christ liveth in me.' His fervour at the celebration of the Holy Sacrament manifested itself even to tears. 'He imitated,' says Bede, 'the Lord's Passion which he commemorated by offering himself a sacrifice to God in contrition of heart.' He died with Christ that he might live with Christ.'' (*Leaders in the Northern Church*, p. 81.)

CHAPTER XI.

THE END OF THE COLUMBAN EPISCOPATE IN NORTHUMBRIA—THE DIOCESE OF LINDISFARNE NORTH OF THE TWEED—MELROSE—COLDINGHAM—ABERCORN—THE SEE OF CANDIDA CASA AS AN ENGLISH FOUNDATION.

THE Scottish episcopate in Bernicia lasted not more than thirty years. Aidan, marked above most men by the "sweet reasonableness" of the Gospel, by unselfishness, humility, and simplicity of life, came from Iona in 635, and laboured unceasingly till 651. The work done by him was indeed wonderful. It is of him Bishop Lightfoot declared, "Not Augustine, but Aidan, is the true apostle of England." His staff of clergy was largely recruited from the Scottish monks, and from these he appointed the masters of the monastic schools which he established for the education of the children of the Angles. His successor, Finan (652—661), was also a monk from Iona. He was resolute and even "fierce" in his maintenance of the traditions of his forefathers. When Ronan, a fellow-countryman, who had travelled in Italy and Gaul and had come back with altered views, contended with him on behalf of the Easter computation which prevailed upon the Continent, he treated him with indignant protests. Like his two predecessors, the third bishop, Colman (661), was a Scot, and, like them, unyielding in his adherence to the Scottish usages. It was in the third year of his episcopate that the assembly was held at Whitby, which practically decided the question, and established the supremacy of the Roman rule in Northumbria. Bede's interesting narrative of that eventful meeting has been often related.[1] Though Wilfrid's overbearing zeal, and more particularly his insolence towards the memory of St. Columba, are painful to observe, yet he had, on the whole, the best of the argument. But, however the arguments on each side may have been regarded by the listeners, the *practical* question was settled by King Oswy, when he declared in language, in which the humorous plainly blended with the serious, "You both acknowledge that it was not to Columba but to Peter that the Lord said, 'To thee will I give the keys of the kingdom of heaven'; and I tell you that he is a doorkeeper whom I am unwilling to gainsay; but, as far as I know and have the power, I desire to be obedient to his injunctions, lest haply, when I come to the gates of the kingdom of heaven, there may be no one to unlock, if he is unfriendly who is shown to hold the keys."

And so Colman departed from Lindisfarne, accom-

[1] And nowhere better than in Bright's *Chapters of Early English History*, chap. vi.

panied by the whole of his Scottish brethren and about thirty attached monks of Anglic nationality. Some of the bones of the founder, Aidan, were reverently taken with them, and they travelled the sad journey of defeated men to Iona. It may well be that the House at Iona was unable to permanently maintain so large an addition to the community as was thus suddenly thrust upon it. At any rate, Colman before long removed his monks to Ireland, and settled them in Innisboffin (the " island of the white heifer "), situated two or three miles off the nearest point of the coast of Mayo, and wholly exposed to the wild sweep of the Atlantic. After a time, according to Bede, dissensions arose between the Irish and English monks, the latter complaining that the Irish used to shirk the harvest work by leaving the island in autumn and going about among friends, and that then on their return, when winter set in, they sought to lay claim to a share in the fruit of the others' labours. Colman solved the difficulty by buying a small piece of land from a chief on the mainland, and building there a monastery for his Englishmen.[1] He himself remained at Innisboffin till his death, which event has been placed by the Irish chronicler, Tighernach of Clonmacnois, in the year

[1] The English monastery of Mayo, known as "Mayo of the Saxons," increased in size and importance, and afterwards became the seat of a bishopric. St. Gerald, an Englishman, is said to have been the first bishop. Innisboffin derives its name, according to the general belief, from a white " water-cow " that lived in a lake on the island, and indeed still lives there, if one may accept the word of the islanders. Compare the story told at p. 78. See Bishop Healy's *Insula Sanctorum*, etc., p. 531. In acreage Innisboffin is a very little larger than Iona.

676. Thus closed in Northumbria the mission of the Scottish Church in its independence of Rome.

Men from the Scotic Church, whether from Ireland direct or through its houses in North Britain, continued from time to time to do good work for England, but after the departure of Colman it was only as adopted children of the Roman mission. Yet the inestimable services of the original Scotic mission can never be forgotten. The mission begun with Aidan did its work "with a rare simplicity of purpose. It brought religion straight home to men's hearts by sheer power of love and self-sacrifice; it held up before them, in the unconscious goodness and nobleness of its representatives, the moral evidence of Christianity. It made them feel what it was to be taught and cared for in the life spiritual by pastors who before all things were the disciples and ministers of Christ." [1]

One other glimpse we get of Melrose from the pages of Bede, and we eagerly take advantage of it, as after leaving Bede we shall be compelled to content ourselves with a few meagre notices of the chroniclers. We shall then pass from the clear light of his invaluable records, and shall have no choice but to grope about in gloom with only a few definite landmarks to guide us.

Provision was sometimes made in the monasteries of Celtic foundation for monks who, for a longer or shorter period, desired such seclusion for the purposes of devotion and the practice of increased austerities,

---

[1] Bright, *Chapters*, etc., p. 204.

as could not be had by those living in community. The seeking of a "desert" (as such places of retirement were called) is a common feature in the lives of Irish saints. In Iona, a place at some little distance from the monastic buildings was called the "desert." A story, related by Bede (*Eccles. Hist.*, lib. v., c. 12), shows us that at the monastery of Melrose a similar practice existed. A good man named Dryhthelm, who belonged to a district that has been commonly (though not satisfactorily) identified with Cunningham in Ayrshire, fell ill, and after some days died in the beginning of the night. Early next morning he came to life again, and sat up, to the dismay of the mourners, who, with the exception of his loving wife, all fled precipitately. After dividing his property into three parts—one of which was given to his wife, one to his children, and one to the poor—he repaired to the monastery at Melrose, where he continued till he died a second time, an event which the *Saxon Chronicle* places at the year 693. Bede relates at great length what Dryhthelm declared he saw in his disembodied state. The teaching of his experiences differs in nothing essential from the fully-developed Romish doctrine of purgatory, and it is expressly insisted on that many are relieved before the day of judgment "by the prayers, alms, and fasting of the living, but more especially by masses."[1] What

---

[1] The visions of the Irish monk Fursey (Bede, *Eccles. Hist.*, lib. iii., c. 19) of an earlier date bear the same complexion, but are not nearly so definite in their teaching. I suspect Bede, who had always an eye to pressing a point of dogma, was anxious to advance a view which was as yet less distinctly pronounced in the Irish Church.

he saw and heard in the world of spirits, Dryhthelm related to Aldfrid, king of Northumbria, among others, and it was at the king's request he was admitted into Melrose. In after times, when the king happened to be in those parts, he very often visited Melrose to hear the holy man.

A place of greater seclusion was granted to Dryhthelm in the monastery, where he practised special austerities, in daily fastings, and in a form of self-inflicted penance that one finds often recurring in the records of that period—the standing in cold water while prayers or the Psalter were recited. Dryhthelm would go up to the middle, and sometimes up to the neck, in the Tweed, and stand there as long as he could endure it. In winter he broke the ice for this purpose. And when those who witnessed him standing in the river with pieces of ice floating about would say, "It is wonderful, Brother Dryhthelm, that you are able to endure such extreme cold;" he would simply answer, for he was a man of simple wit, "I have seen greater cold." And when they said, "It is wonderful that you can endure such hardship;" he would reply, "I have seen greater hardship." And these things he said, doubtless remembering the hail and snow that formed part of the purgatorial torments he had witnessed, a cold so cutting that the wretched sufferers would leap back into the flames. On leaving the river, it was his practice not to put off his wet or frozen garments till they had dried upon his body.

Ethelwold, who afterwards became bishop of Lindisfarne, was abbat of Melrose at the time of Dryhthelm's admission. He had formerly been a minister of St. Cuthbert; that is, as I take it, he occupied the honourable position of personal companion and attendant of St. Cuthbert, an office probably similar to that which we may remember was in the life of St. Columba filled for him by the faithful Diarmit. And in honour of St. Cuthbert he had himself designed a beautiful cross of polished stone, which formed one of the treasures of Lindisfarne, and which accompanied the other sacred relics in their many wanderings. To his artistic taste also is due the splendidly ornamented and jewelled cover [1] of the "Lindisfarne Gospels," or "Book of Durham," which manuscript (now preserved in the British Museum) for the beauty of its decorative ornaments stands only second to the "Book of Kells," the chief glory of the manuscript collection in the Library of Trinity College, Dublin. The manual work of the scribe of the Lindisfarne Gospels, Eadfrid (Ethelwold's predecessor in the bishopric), is truly exquisite, but every minutest feature of the ornament is characteristically Scotic, and was the unquestionable outcome of the artistic tradition of the Scotic foundation. No relic of such artistic work has come down to us from the ancient monastery of Melrose; but we need not hesitate to believe that there, as in the mother house of Lindisfarne, at least under such a lover of art as Ethelwold, the illuminative work of the scriptorium would not have been neglected.

It may, with much reason, be questioned whether

[1] See pp. 317—320.

exact boundaries of the diocese of Lindisfarne north of the Tweed were ever clearly defined. A more correct way of putting the inquiry seems to me, In what parts of the country north of Tweed was the authority of the bishop of Lindisfarne acknowledged? In default of earlier sources of information, we have to resort to Simeon of Durham, a twelfth-century writer; but I see no reason to suppose that he, making use of sources of information not now available, has not indicated the actual facts with substantial accuracy. Generally, then, we may put it that from the east coast to where the river Leader flows into the Tweed a little below Melrose, was under the jurisdiction of the bishop of Lindisfarne. Then came lands, and even wide districts attached in some way to monastic houses, which acknowledged his rule, as Melrose and its lands to the west of the Leader, and the wide stretch of country from the northern slopes of the Lammermuir Hills, to the mouth of the Esk (at the town we now call Musselburgh), bounded on the north by the Firth of Forth, which district Simeon speaks of as pertaining to St. Baldred's monastery of Tyninghame, near Dunbar. Roughly, then, our modern counties of Berwickshire and Haddingtonshire formed the Scottish portion of the diocese of Lindisfarne; while outside these bounds the authority of the bishop was acknowledged further west at Edinburgh, and at the religious house of Abercorn higher up the Forth, and at the two Jeddarts by the Teviot in the south.

Visitors to the site of the old monastic house on

the lofty sea-beaten cliffs at Coldingham should recall that at that spot the Princess Etheldreda, whose memory was afterwards so closely associated with Ely, spent the first year of her conventual life (671). She had been twice married—married at least in name, for she had made a firm resolution of perpetual virginity; and the unhappiness caused by such a union with her second husband, Egfrid, king of Northumbria, soon brought about a divorce.[1] Aebba, abbess of Coldingham, was King Egfrid's aunt, and it was under her Etheldreda placed herself when she took the veil, which she received at Coldingham at the hand of the famous Wilfrid. Thomas, the monk of Ely, in the reign of Henry II., who has written at length about her life, alleges that the king, her husband, made an attempt in person to carry her off from Coldingham, and that she, accompanied by two sisters of the convent, had to leave the buildings and seek safety in the neighbourhood for a time. Perhaps it was due to this danger that she removed from the kingdom of Egfrid, to her old house in the south. At any rate, she herself was soon after made an abbess "in the country called Ely."

As not unconnected with our northern Church, we may notice that Etheldreda is said to have made with her own hands, as a gift for St. Cuthbert, a magnificent stole and maniple, adorned with gold and precious stones. In after years the abbess used to reproach

---

[1] Wilfrid's conduct in this affair contrasts most unfavourably with Columba's action in bringing a wife to a sense of her duty to her husband, as recorded by Adamnan (lib. ii., c. 42).

herself for having worn splendid and costly necklaces in her youth, and regarded a tumour in the neck from which she suffered as a sign that God by this chastisement absolved her from the guilt of that youthful vanity. May we venture on the conjecture that her discarded jewels went to the adornment of St. Cuthbert's stole and maniple?

It was only six or seven years after the departure of the royal Etheldreda (indeed, according to the *Saxon Chronicle*, in the very year of her death, 679), that a terrible calamity fell upon the monastery at Coldingham, which was burned to the ground. Bede tells us that the fire originated through carelessness, but goes on to show that what happened was really a Divine judgment on the self-indulgent lives of the inmates. There were always special dangers attaching to the system of double monasteries, but it does not seem as if, in this instance, the laxity of discipline was directly attributable to the appropinquity of the two houses. One of the monks of Coldingham, a man of the Scotic race, and bearing, like the biographer of Columba, the name of Adamnan, was wont to practise unusual austerities, being greatly given to vigils and prayers, and taking food only twice in the week, on the Lord's Day and on Thursday. One day he and a brother monk had occasion to travel to some distance from Coldingham, and as they returned and came within sight of the lofty buildings of the convent (*aedificia sublimiter erecta*), Adamnan burst into tears, and, on being questioned by his companion, he declared that a devouring fire was about to consume all those fair buildings. This saying being reported to Aebba, the mother of the community, she sent for Adamnan, and inquired of him how he came to speak as he had done. Then he told how, while watching one night and singing the Psalms, an unknown person had suddenly appeared and revealed to him that all except himself, both men and women, indulged themselves habitually in slothful sleep, or, if they were awake, were only awake "unto sin." "I have looked," said the mysterious visitor, "into every one's chamber and bed." The rooms built for prayer and study had become—so he declared— places of feasting, drinking, gossip and story-telling (*fabulationes*), and other seductions. The nuns, he went on to complain, with lives dedicated to God's service, spent their leisure time in weaving for themselves raiment of delicate texture, in which they would adorn themselves like brides, or even thus seek to attract the favour of strangers (*externorum virorum*). Adamnan comforted the abbess by telling her that the evil would not happen in her days; and a return to a stricter discipline was shortly afterwards effected. But after Aebba's death, as Bede relates, the inmates of the monastery went back to their evil ways, and the last state was worse than the first; and then came the destruction of the house by fire.[1]

In estimating the historical value of the narrative here

[1] "Fire from heaven," says the *Saxon Chronicle*, at A.D. 679. The date commonly assigned for St. Aebba's death—683—does not square with the story related by Bede. The burning of the monastery must have been later. See Bright, *Chapters*, etc., p. 300.

given, we must remember that the reproaches heaped upon the sisters and brethren of the Coldingham convent came from the mouth of a rigid ascetic, whose rule of food only twice a week might very easily beget a spirit of criticism that was unjust to others; and that he had nothing worse to tell makes one believe that after all the laxity of the monastic discipline may have been much exaggerated. A really valuable piece of information is that which shows us the nuns occupied in fine work at the loom. And if it be true that men not belonging to the institution were liable to be affected by the charms of the sisters in fine raiment, it shows us that the cloister was not as strict as it came afterwards to be in most religious houses.

There is yet one other incident of this period connected with Coldingham that deserves notice. Egfrid, after his separation from Etheldreda, had married again. And Ermenburga, his second wife, shared with her husband in a strong dislike to the assumptions of Wilfrid. It is outside our scope to tell his story, but it is well known with what contempt his "bull," procured at Rome, was rejected by the king and his witan. Wilfrid was imprisoned, and the reliquary, which he used to wear round his neck, appropriated by Ermenburga. This precious talisman hung in her bedroom, or in her carriage when she travelled. On the occasion of a stately progress through his dominions, the king and queen arrived at the monastery of St. Aebba at Coldingham. There the queen took ill with some kind of convulsions, and was at the point of death.[1] Their hostess, St. Aebba, believed the illness was a judgment on the king and queen for their treatment of Wilfrid. She declared that if Wilfrid were released and his case of relics restored to him, the queen would recover. And as she counselled it was done, and the queen was restored to health as the holy abbess had foretold. It adds to the interest of this incident on Scottish soil if we realize that at this very time Wilfrid was only some fifteen miles distant a close prisoner of the king, in chains at Dunbar.

We have already spoken of Abercorn (a few miles higher up the Forth than what is now South Queensferry) as a monastic foundation under the jurisdiction of the bishops of Lindisfarne. In 681, a bishop, named Trumwin, was consecrated by Archbishop Theodore for the extreme northern part of Egfrid's dominions. His residence was to be at Abercorn, and his labours were to be extended to the region of the Picts, over which Egfrid claimed the sovereignty—a sovereignty which was, however, rather nominal than real. But Trumwin's northern episcopate was of short duration. In 685 Egfrid with an army advanced to devastate the country of the Picts north of the Forth, and being cleverly lured among the hills by the enemy, who had made a show of flight, he was slain, and his troops routed with great slaughter at Dunnichen in Forfarshire.[2] Trumwin's position

---

[1] The violent partisan Eddi, in his *Life of St. Wilfrid*, speaks of this illness as a demoniacal possession.

[2] Skene (*Celtic Scotland*, vol. i., p. 266) connects a large number of stone coffins found in the neighbourhood with the slaughter of this battle.

became untenable at Abercorn, and he withdrew with his monks, who were distributed in different monasteries. He himself retired to Whitby, where he remained the comfort and support of Elfleda, the late king's sister, who had succeeded St. Hilda as abbess of the double foundation.

Egfrid's body, according to Simeon of Durham (*Hist. Dun. Eccles.*, lib. i., c. 9), was buried at Iona. He was an able king, and a most generous benefactor of the Northumbrian Church.[1]

It is worthy of notice that Bede does not tell us where King Egfrid's body was interred. He, with his strong convictions, would not have cared to think that the royal friend of St. Cuthbert, and the founder of bishoprics, was given his last resting-place among men who shaved their heads like Simon Magus, and kept Easter the wrong way. We cannot doubt that the interment in Iona was intended by the victors as an honourable distinction for the body of the vanquished king. It may have been requested by the abbat of Iona, at the instance of Aldfrid, the king's brother and successor, who either was then, or certainly had been shortly before, a guest of the monastery. It was a long journey across difficult country from the spot where he fell to the remote island in the west. Aldfrid, who succeeded to the throne, is described by Bede as a man "most learned in the Scriptures." He

---

[1] The sympathizers with Wilfrid could not readily forgive him, and in Eadmer's *Life of St. Wilfrid* (chap. xliii.), we are told that that saint, when celebrating mass in Sussex, saw two demons carrying off the soul of Egfrid from the fatal battle-field to the torments of hell.

had gone for the sake of study to Iona.[1] And it was there in all probability that he made that acquaintance with Adamnan which paved the way to the successful mission of the latter to the king's court with a view to urge the release of his captive fellow-countrymen, whom Egfrid had carried off from Ireland in his raid upon that country the year before his fatal expedition against the Picts.[2] The king's known love of learning doubtless prompted the gift, which Adamnan afterwards made to him, of a copy of the work, *Concerning the Holy Places*, already noticed.[3]

It belongs to the department of civil history to tell how the power of the Northumbrian kings became extended to the south-west of Scotland. But the revival of the bishopric of Candida Casa under English bishops has here to be recorded. The fifth and last book of Bede's *Ecclesiastical History* brings the story down to the year 732. And there (lib. v., c. 23), speaking of the four bishoprics which then existed in the Northumbrian kingdom—viz., York, Lindisfarne, Hexham, and Candida Casa—he tells us that the last-named had "lately" become an episcopal see on account of the increased number of the faithful in that part, and he mentions as its first bishop Pechthelm, who had been a deacon or monk of Aldhelm, bishop of Sherborne. Hence it has been commonly stated that the see was revived under the English about 730. We have no evidence as to whether the old British

---

[1] See anonymous *Life of St. Cuthbert*, § 28 ; and Bede's *Life of St. Cuthbert*, lib. i., c. 24.
[2] See p. 189.   [3] See pp. 148—151.

succession, originating in St. Ninian, had been maintained up to this time; nor, indeed, is it certain, though it is probable, that the monastery, once so famous as a school of learning, continued to exist. Its ancient repute for learning, and for sanctity, as containing the relics of St. Ninian, would have sufficed to determine the choice of Whithorn for the bishop's see. The Anglic succession of bishops of Candida Casa was continued in the persons of four other bishops for some seventy years, after which the frequent and destructive raids of the Picts and Scots made the position untenable for the English.[1]

[1] The authorities for these statements, and for the names of the successive bishops, will be found in Bishop Forbes' *Lives of St. Ninian and St. Kentigern* (*Historians of Scotland*, vol. v., p. xliv), and reference may be made to William of Malmesbury (*Gest. Pontific. Angl.*, lib. iii., c. 118), cited by Skene (*Celtic Scotland*, vol. ii., p. 225). Little beyond what has been stated above is known of the Church in Scotland and the neighbouring districts during this period. Skene, with reason, connects the numerous dedications to St. Cuthbert and St. Oswald in the south-west of Scotland with this period. See also Grub (*Eccles. Hist. of Scotland*, vol. i., pp. 121-4).

CHAPTER XII.

THE CHURCH IN SCOTLAND IN THE NINTH, TENTH, AND ELEVENTH CENTURIES—THE CULDEES.

FROM the writings of Adamnan and Bede, the student can gather materials for life-like and truthful pictures of the condition of the monastic Church in Scotland. The Church in the western islands and highlands is clearly figured for us by the former, the Church in Lothian by the latter. But when we pass from the bright light of their vivid presentations of men and things, we at once enter upon a lengthened period of gloom and obscurity, through which we grope our way with difficulty, and from which the most thorough inquirers emerge with but little knowledge. A few names of bishops or monks, a few dates, of which some are questionable, a few events associated with a monastery here and a church there, all recorded with the brevity of the baldest chronicler, supply us with almost the whole of our authentic information for some three hundred years and more. The legendary tales which we find in after times connected with the names of certain Celtic saints who make their shadowy appearance during this extended period, rarely reward an investigator with even the smallest residuum of ascertained fact. Adamnan died in 704, Bede in 735. It was probably in 1068 that the Saxon princess, Margaret, entered Scotland. With that event the history of the mediæval Church in Scotland makes a definite departure. But the interval between the death of Bede and the latter of these dates lies as a long stretch of time, of which the authentic notices concerning ecclesiastical affairs could be given in a few pages. Mr. Hill Burton is justified in calling this "the dark period" of Scottish history.[1] If the Church in Scotland during this period of its history was not absolutely barren of literature, no remains of any of its writers have come down to us. But we must make the best of what we have; and we thankfully recognize the value of the brief references to Scotland that are to be found in the Irish annalists. These, with a very few notices from other quarters and later sources, are all the materials at our disposal.

The general character of the information thus supplied may be better exhibited by a few examples than by any description. Thus, we read—

"727. The relics of Adamnan removed to Ireland, and the law renewed." *Tighernach, of Clonmacnoise, who died* 1088.

"The law" referred to was probably the *Cain Adhamnain*, called also the *Lex Innocentium*, or *Law of the Harmless*, which, as we have seen (p. 145), was

[1] *History of Scotland,* vol. i., p. 389.

enacted under the influence of Adamnan for exempting women from military service. The evil here condemned is to be found among the Picts of Galloway as late as the twelfth century.[1]

"737. Death of Ronain, abbat of Cindgaradh" [*i. e.* Kingarth in Bute].

"Failbe, son of Guairi, heir [*i. e.* co-arb] of Maelrubha, in Applecross, drowned at sea with twenty-two of his sailors."—*Tighernach.*

"766. Suibne, abbat of Ia [*i. e.* Hy or Iona], comes to Ireland."—*Annals of Ulster.*

"790. Artgal, son of Cathail, King of Connaught, died at Hy."—*Ib.*

"794. Ravaging of all the islands of Britain by the heathen."—*Ib.*

"800. The placing of the relics of Ronain, son of Berich, in a shrine of gold and silver."—*Ib.*

"802. Hy, of Columkille, burned by the heathen."—*Ib.*

"806. The community (*familia*) of Hy, sixty-eight in number, slain by the heathen."—*Ib.*

"807. Construction of the new city [*i. e.* monastery] of Columkille in Kells."—*Ib.*

"818. Diarmaid, abbat of Ia, went to Alban with the shrine of Columkille."—*Chronicle of the Scots.*

"825. Martyrdom of Blathmac by the pagans in Hy of Columkille."—*Annals of Ulster.*

"831. Diarmaid goes to Erin with the Mionna [*i. e.* as is supposed, the relics other than the body] of Columkille."—*Ib.*

"850. In the seventh year of his [Kenneth's] reign he carries relics of St. Columba to the church which he had constructed" [at Dunkeld].—*Chronicle of the Picts.*

"865. Tuathal, son of Artguso, first bishop of Fortren [*i. e.* the kingdom of the Picts] and abbat of Dunkeld, died."—*Annals of Ulster.*

"878. The shrine of Columkille and all his reliquaries

---

[1] See Robertson's *Statuta Ecclesiæ Scoticanæ,* vol. i., p. 15.

were taken [*i. e.* from Iona] to Erin to escape the foreigners."—*Ib.*

"908. In his sixth year [*i. e.* about 908] the king, Constantine, and the bishop, Cellach, solemnly vowed at the Hill of Faith [*collis credulitatis*] to preserve the laws and discipline of the faith, and the rights of churches and of the Gospels, equally with the Scots."—*Chronicle of the Picts.*[1]

"935. Angus, son of Muirchertach, a learned man, anchorite, and abbat-elect of Iona, died."—*Annals of the Four Masters.*

About 977. Kenneth "gave the great city [*i. e.* monastery] of Brechin to the Lord."—*Chronicle of the Picts.*

"986. The island of Columkille plundered by the Danes on the eve of the Nativity, and the abbat and fifteen clerics slain."—*Annals of Ulster.*

"Maelruannaidh Ua Maeldoraigh, lord of Cinel Conall, went over the sea [*i. e.* to Iona] on his pilgrimage."—*Annals of the Four Masters.*

"1027. Dunkeld, in Alban, entirely burnt."—*Annals of Ulster.*

"1055. Maelduin, son of Gillandris, bishop of Alban and ordainer of the clergy to the Gael (?), slept in Christ."—*Tighernach.*[2]

These entries, of very varying degrees of importance, are exhibited here, as they appear in the chroniclers, as specimens of the evidence which we possess for our Scottish Church history during more than three hundred years. Upon these much labour and ingenious comment has been bestowed by our historians. Such notices generally possess the advantage, denied by Adamnan and scantily supplied by Bede, of giving

---

[1] A little hill near Scone was the scene of this event.
[2] Reeves (*Historians of Scotland,* vol. vi., p. 340) renders the phrase *gloria cleri* Gaedhil.

us helps to a definite chronology. But the notices, even of events that keenly stir our interest, are of the meagrest and baldest kind. What little can be extracted from such material will be found, with conjectures and illustrations of varying values, in the pages of Pinkerton and Skene.

The repeated ravages of the Danes was one of the main causes for the decline of the influence of Iona. The head of the Columban houses was transferred from Iona to Kells (in County Meath), where a stone monastery was built (807—814). A sense of insecurity and overshadowing fear must have exercised in more or less degree a paralyzing effect upon the brotherhood. It is true the house at Iona was rebuilt, and now of stone. The shrine of Columba was brought back (818); but after seven years another onslaught of the northern pirates resulted in the martyrdom of Blaithmac (825). The centre of civil power was now established on the eastern side of the country; and the chief ecclesiastical authority, during the period with which we are dealing, became transferred—first to Dunkeld (850), then, perhaps, to Abernethy, and, beyond doubt, finally to St. Andrews.

It is probably to the second half of the ninth century should be assigned an attack of the Danes, which, according to the legend of "St. Adrian and his companions," resulted in the slaughter of a religious community that had settled in the Isle of May, which lies[1] at the widest part of the opening of the estuary

[1] The island is about a mile in length and three-quarters of a mile in breadth. It is about six miles from the coast of Fife.

of the Forth. The legend abounds in grotesquely absurd improbabilites (see p. 74). St. Adrian, who was of royal blood and born in Hungary, visits Scotland with 6606 companions. Mr. Skene expends here, as in some other similar cases, much misplaced ingenuity in attempting to show that Adrian was one of the Irish missionaries. There is, in truth, not a particle of what can be reasonably called evidence in support of his contention; and the whole story might be dismissed, like so many similar tales from the legends of the mediæval breviaries, as historically valueless, were it not that the local tradition certainly connected the later foundation in the Isle of May with a martyrdom of Christians in that place, and there are historical reasons for thinking that such an attack of the Danes, in the reign of Constantine (863—875), the son of Kenneth MacAlpin, was in no way improbable. David I., who was so eminently distinguished for the establishing of religious houses, was wont to choose for his foundations places already possessing some sacred associations, and it was perhaps on this account that he made the grant of the Isle of May to the monks of the Benedictine Abbey of Reading, in Berkshire, which had shortly before been founded by his brother-in-law, Henry I. of England. If in David's time the tradition already existed that Adrian was a native of Hungary and of royal race, there would be a further reason why the son of a princess, who was herself a native of Hungary (see p. 277), should honour the Hungarian martyr on the spot assigned as the place of his death.

The legend recounts the names of several of his companions; but it may suffice to mention the Hungarian Monanus, who, it is said, preached the gospel at Inverry, on the coast of Fife, and whose name survives in the parish and church of St. Monans between Ely and Pittenweem.[1] The cultus of both St. Adrian and St. Monan was well marked in mediæval times. Childless wives were frequent in their devotions at the Isle of May, and many miracles (including the extrusion of a barbed arrow from the body of King David II.) were attributed to the intercessions of St. Monan. But here we are concerned only with the possible truth of the martyrdom by the Danes; and we can go so far as to say that a martyrdom of religious in the Isle of May is by no means improbable at the date assigned.

The notices of the Church in the south of Scotland are even scantier than those relating to the parts of the country under Irish influence, and within the ken of the Irish chroniclers. An outstanding event was the burning of Melrose, about the middle of the ninth century, by Kenneth MacAlpin, monarch of the now united kingdoms of the Scots and Picts, in one of his numerous raids into the territory of the Angles.

A few years later (870) the other great monastery of the south, Coldingham, is said to have been burned by the Danes. A second Aebba appears as abbess; and the story runs that she and the sisters of the convent on the approach of the enemy disfigured themselves

---

[1] The church of St. Monans is picturesquely situated on a rock by the sea.

frightfully by cutting away their noses and lips as a protection against the licentious violence of the Danes. The abbess and nuns perished in the burning house.

The revival of the bishopric of Candida Casa under the Angles has been already noticed (p. 191).

Some brief account may here be given of the fortunes of religion in the northern islands. There is no doubt that the Gospel was preached among the Picts of the islands by missionaries of the Columban brotherhood. But in the northern islands the heathen Scandinavians (generally spoken of as Danes by our historians), who had at first only paid temporary visits for the purposes of plunder, came eventually to make settlements and to take possession. They extended their power even to parts of the mainland, and Caithness and Sutherland formed part of the earldom of Orkney under the suzerainty of the King of Norway. The efforts of the Columban Church to preserve Christianity and extend it among the heathen conquerors were inadequate for the accomplishment of the task. But when Christianity obtained possession of Scandinavia, at the end of the tenth and beginning of the eleventh century, it was impossible but that the conversion of the colonies and outposts would follow. Orkney, Shetland, and the Faroe Islands were compelled by the fierce and enthusiastic neophyte, King Olave Tryggvesen, to accept the Christian faith at the point of the sword, and it was the choice between baptism and death that gave us the first Christian Earl of Orkney. Even the king's more famous namesake, known as St. Olave, who succeeded to the throne in 1015, pressed the claims of the new religion by the terrors of confiscation, mutilation, and death.

This is not an unsuitable place to say something of the ecclesiastics commonly known as "Culdees," to whom an entirely fictitious importance has been given through the misunderstandings of later historians, and the unintelligent partisanship of religious controversialists.

The notices of the Culdees in Scottish records are few; but the investigation of the evidence, illustrated by the notices of ecclesiastics bearing a similar name in Ireland, leaves in the first place no doubt that they were bodies of clerics quite distinct from the Columban monks. In Scotland they were to be found almost exclusively in regions where the Columban influence was weakest. They were attached in several cases to important churches, and were responsible for and engaged in the conduct of the round of Divine service. It must be remembered that the great body of the Columban monks were laymen, and were necessarily much occupied with tillage, the care of flocks and herds, and the varied labour connected with the maintenance of the community.

The Keledei (for such is the Scottish form of the word), it would seem, were not large communities. They were enabled by gifts and the possession of endowments to devote themselves exclusively to private or public devotions. Writers of such eminence as Reeves (whose monograph, *On the Culdees of the*

British Isles, Dublin, 1864, is the classical authority on the subject) and Skene (*Celtic Scotland*, vol. ii.) point to resemblances between the Culdees and the "canons regular," first established by Chrodegang, archbishop of Metz (740—764). But the differences are as striking as the resemblances; for while Chrodegang's canons lived in one house and slept in one dormitory, unless especially exempted, the Culdees are, at least in some places, represented as living, what was styled in the ecclesiastical language of the day, an "eremitical life." That is, as is shown by the evidence, they lived in separate houses or cells within the same enclosure.

In the Chartulary of St. Andrews there is entered a record of an early grant made to the Culdees of Lochleven. It is, I think, the very earliest notice of these persons to be found in Scottish history. There we are told that Brude, son of Dergard, king of the Picts (whose death is placed in the year 706), "gives the isle of Lochleven to God Almighty, St. Serf, and the Keledei hermits dwelling there, who are serving, or shall hereafter serve, God in that island." The other places in Scotland which we find connected with Keledei are St. Andrews, Dunkeld, Dunblane, Brechin, Rosmarky, Dornoch, Lismore (all of them afterwards episcopal sees), and Abernethy, Monymusk, Muthill, Monifieth, and, at a late period (1164), Iona, where the Keledei are mentioned as distinct from the general body of the religious. The existence of corporations of endowed clergy at the seven places first named may perhaps have been one of the reasons why these places were eventually selected for the seats of bishoprics. The provision, when not irregularly alienated, was found to be already made, in whole or in part, for the maintenance of the round of services in the cathedral churches of those sees.

In the disorganization which affected the whole Church in the ninth, tenth, and eleventh centuries, the seizure and appropriation of Church property by laymen was only too common, and its tenure may have been facilitated by some nominal assumption by them of the titles belonging to the heads and other officers of the religious corporations. Discipline was grievously relaxed, and there may have been some foundation in fact for the statement made in the sixteenth century by Alexander Mylne (*Vitæ Episcoporum Dunkeldensum*, p. 4), so far as it asserts that the Keledei of St. Andrews at one time had wives. Similar irregularities (some of them indeed of a highly immoral kind) were to be found among the canon clerics, to whose organization the corporations of Culdees were most nearly akin in England and the Continent. The canons of Winchester in the tenth century had wives whom they treated with gross indecency,[1] and Archbishop Aelfric of Canterbury, in his *Life of Aethelwold, Bishop of Winchester*, records even a worse state of things, for he describes the clergy of the cathedral as not only possessing wives, but as repudiating them and taking others. And generally in Saxon England we may accept the statement of Dr. Lingard (*Anglo-Saxon Church*, vol. ii., p. 254), that "married priests became sufficiently numerous to

---

[1] See Thorpe's *Diplomata Anglic. Ævi Saxon.* p. 260.

bid defiance to the laws both of the Church and the State." On the continent of Europe things were no better. Helyot, with special reference to the eleventh century, declares that discipline among the canons was relaxed to such a point that they were simply "overwhelmed in the sink of universal incontinence."[1] There is no reason whatever for supposing that the possessing wives on the part of the Scottish Culdees, if such be the case, was anything different from such connections in England and abroad. It was not, as Mylne would suggest, an approved survival of the Eastern discipline which permitted marriage to the secular clergy, but simply an outcome of the general decay of ecclesiastical discipline in the West.[2]

Even after the thorough investigation made by Reeves, the question of the origin of the Culdees remains obscure. The researches of this scholar point to the fact, which is abundantly evident in the Irish Church and the Columban Church of Scotland, that the busy life of the monastic communities came by some to be regarded as a state less perfect than the life of retired devotion which might be found in a "desert," a name sometimes, as we have seen, applied to a cell removed only a short way from the general buildings of the monastery. At first, retirement to such place was only for a time, but afterwards there were those who sought a life-long seclusion in these or in remoter solitudes. Absolute solitude seems to

---

[1] *Histoire des Ordres Monast.* vol. i., col. 774, edit. Migne.
[2] We have no *contemporary* evidence, however, for the marriage of the Scottish Culdees.

have proved, as time went on, too trying for human nature, and, by and by, groups of cells were formed, and "anchorites," "hermits," and "Cele De" (in Scotland "Keledei") were names bestowed upon their occupants.

The *name*, as well as the office and position, of the Keledei, has been much discussed. The notion of the historians of a later time connecting the word with the Latin *Cultores Dei* has given rise to the popular form "Culdees." But this has found less general acceptance among recent historians. Reeves and Skene concur in deriving the word from the Irish Celé Dé, which the former would render as "Servants of God," while the latter would take Celé in its sense of "companion" or "friend." On behalf of Skene's view, it may be remarked that "servant of God" (*servus Dei*) was a common designation of any one who had adopted the monastic life; while in the case before us a very distinct and special class of devotees is intended. Again, Colgan, whom Reeves describes as "a master of the Irish language," declares that the word should be rendered in Latin *Deicola* or *Amadeus*.

Though with great diffidence, after the declarations of two such eminent authorities, I am disposed to think that more may be said than is now generally supposed for the old view that *Culdee* is a corruption of *Cultor Dei*, or connected with *colo*. *Colidei* is the form in which the word appears at York, and Dr. Lingard (*Anglo-Saxon Church*, vol. ii., p. 294) has pointed out that the prebendaries of Canterbury are in an old charter styled *Cultores Clerici*. I would venture to suggest that in Saxon England *Colidei* was formed from *cultor Dei*, but that a word not unlike in sound in the Celtic tongue (though philologically distinct and originally of a somewhat different sense) was used to designate the same class of persons.

Whatever obscurities still surround both the name and the office of the Culdees, of one thing we may be certain—there is not the smallest shred of evidence for the notion that the Culdees differed from the rest of Christendom at the period either in regard to faith or in their views of Church government.[1] They probably originated in an attempt to aim at the higher perfections of an ascetic life. They next were united in small corporations, resembling Canons Regular elsewhere, and were occupied mainly in maintaining the round of Divine service, together with certain duties connected, in some places, with the exercise of

---

[1] The notion is not yet wholly exploded, but it is no longer entertained by the better informed among Presbyterian writers. Thus, in the first volume of a recent history, entitled *The Church of Scotland, Past and Present*, edited by Dr. R. H. Story, Professor of Ecclesiastical History in the University of Glasgow, Dr. James Campbell writes (p. 216), "Some have maintained that they [the Culdees] had an Eastern origin, and were our earliest evangelists. It has been more generally believed that Columba was their founder ; that their form of Church government was characterized by the exclusion of bishops and adherence to primitive Presbyterian parity; that they rejected transubstantiation and other errors of later ages ; and preserved their purity of doctrine and worship till swept away by the advancing tide of Romanism. In the light of recent inquiries these opinions are seen to be erroneous."

hospitality to strangers. In the widespread decay of Church discipline in the ninth, tenth, and eleventh centuries, the Culdees fell away, and at the time of the great revival of Church life under St. Margaret, their name is associated not with rigour but with laxity.

CHAPTER XIII.

THE FAITH AND RITUAL OF THE CELTIC CHURCH—
THE TONSURE AND EASTER COMPUTATION.

WHEN we come to deal with the religious beliefs and practices of the Celtic Church in Scotland, we are met at the outset by the fact that extremely few literary remains of the Celtic period have in the long lapse of years come down to us in safety. The writings of Adamnan, abbat of Iona (679-704), are almost the only documents that supply information on these subjects from what we may perhaps venture to call a Scottish source; while the *Book of Deer* (which will be described hereafter[1]) is the solitary liturgical relic of the Celtic Church in Scotland. But happily it is made plain on investigation that we are entitled to rely with confidence on documents of distinctively Irish origin as expressing a faith and describing ritual and disciplinary observances which are substantially—indeed, perhaps we might say absolutely—identical with what was professed and what was practised in the Celtic churches of northern

---

[1] See p. 248.

Britain. It is in respect to the religious beliefs and usages of the people as with Celtic art and Celtic architecture. Scotland cannot be studied apart from Ireland. Just as the copious riches of Irish archæology constantly help us to supply with confidence what is insufficiently expressed, or only hinted at obscurely in the comparatively scanty relics of Celtic civilization in Scotland, so the more abundant literary remains of Irish Christianity help us to understand what is vague or uncertain in the few written documents that can claim a Scottish birthplace. The literary documents of the Celtic Church in Ireland may be as reasonably appealed to for the illustration of the faith and religious ceremonial of the Celtic Church in Scotland, as the writings of English Churchmen might in an after age be cited to illustrate the faith and usages of any of the daughter churches of the colonies. Indeed, none of our colonial churches, even with the facilities of communication afforded by modern civilization, is able to maintain such constant and such close intercourse with home as did the Church of the west coast of Scotland with the neighbouring shores of Ireland.

On the great fundamental doctrines of the Christian creed there is no reason to suppose that any of the Celtic churches varied from the faith of the Church catholic. We learn indeed on respectable authority,[1] that in the year 429 the errors on the subject of Original Sin, Free Will, Grace, and Predestination, which are designated by the name "Pelagianism," were

[1] Prosper of Aquitaine.

introduced, if they had not already made way, among the British Christians. But the heresy was not allowed to spread itself unchecked. The British ecclesiastics sought aid from the neighbouring Church of Gaul, and St. Loup, bishop of Troyes, with St. German, bishop of Auxerre—the latter, perhaps, as deputed by the bishop of Rome, were sent to controvert the heretical teachers. Yet, though in a remarkable public discussion the assertors of the catholic doctrine obtained, amid general applause, a triumphant victory, the erroneous views seem to have spread. In 447 St. German is again besought by orthodox Britons to come to their aid, and on this occasion he is said not only to have vanquished his Pelagian antagonists in argument, but to have caused them to be banished from Britain. Whether the trouble caused by Pelagianism extended to the British Church in the north, it is impossible to say; but the hold of this error in any part of Britain was brief, and on its extinction no further complaints are made as to doctrinal errors of a grave kind existing in any of the Celtic churches of the islands.

No documents of the ancient Celtic Church surpass in interest the writings of St. Patrick, the apostle of Ireland. At the present day there is probably no competent scholar who doubts the genuineness of the *Confession* and the *Epistle to the Subjects of Coroticus*. Both the external and internal evidence in favour of the prevailing belief is overwhelming.[1]

[1] Those who desire to see the subject ably discussed should consult Todd's *St. Patrick* and Stokes' *Ireland and the Celtic*

For myself I can say that no literary monuments of antiquity have ever impressed me with a more satisfying sense of their genuineness. Dealing with a country and period, the study of which has been rendered highly embarrassing by the imaginative combinations, inventions, cross-lights, and fanciful colouring of subsequent hagiologists and historians, we eagerly seize upon these authentic relics. The view of religion and of society which they present may, it is true, be rather narrowly restricted, still we have the happiness of being assured of the truth and reality of what little is told us.

In the early part of the *Confession*, Patrick makes a profession of his faith in respect to the doctrine of the Holy Trinity, which, though not in express terms "homoöusian," leaves us no reason to question that as regards the central doctrines of the Christian Creed, the faith received by the Irish Scots was that of the Catholics as distinguished from the Arians. And indeed, at the date when the *Confession* was written—that is, in St. Patrick's old age—and for those for whom he wrote, there was probably no need to be more precise. Patrick, acknowledging God's wonderful goodness towards him, signifies that no other recompense (*retributio*) can be made to God than to

---

Church, pp. 25 *sq.;* also the article "Patrick" by the same writer in Smith and Wace's *Dictionary of Christian Biography*, where the more curious student will find abundant references to earlier writings on the subject. Dr. Skene, referring to the *Confession* and the *Epistle to Coroticus*, writes: "These documents we accept as undoubtedly genuine" (*Celtic Scotland*, vol. ii., p. 20). See *ante* p. 33.

exalt Him and declare Him before every nation under heaven, and so he proceeds to state "that there is none other God, nor ever was, nor shall be hereafter, save only the Lord, the Father unbegotten, without beginning, from whom is all beginning, upholding all things:

"And His Son Jesus Christ, whom we acknowledge to have been always spiritually with the Father, before the beginning of the world; begotten in an ineffable manner before all beginning. And by Him were made things visible and invisible. And being made man, and having overcome death, He was received into heaven unto the Father. And He [the Father] hath given to Him all power, above every name, of things in heaven, and things in earth, and things under the earth, that every tongue should confess that Jesus Christ is Lord and God. Whom we believe, and we look for His coming, who is ere long to be Judge of quick and dead, who will render to every man according to his works.

"Who hath shed forth in us abundantly the gift of the Holy Ghost, the pledge of immortality, who maketh the faithful and obedient to become the sons of God the Father, and joint-heirs with Christ, whom we confess and worship one God in the Trinity of the most holy Name."

There is now preserved in the Ambrosian Library of Milan an Irish MS., written some two hundred years after the death of St. Patrick. It formerly belonged to the great monastery of Bangor, in the county Down. It is known as the *Antiphonary of Bangor*, and contains, beside hymns and prayers, etc., a Creed which, though declaring the same great truths, uses language differing in a remarkable way from the Niceno-Constantinopolitan symbol, and, indeed, I may add, from all other known forms of the Creed.[1] It deserves a place here, and runs as follows:—

"I believe in God the Father, Almighty, Invisible, Maker of all created things visible and invisible.

"I believe also in Jesus Christ, His only Son, our Lord, God Almighty, conceived of the Holy Ghost, born of the Virgin Mary; He suffered under Pontius Pilate; Who, having been crucified and buried, descended into hell; on the third day He rose again from the dead, ascended into heaven, and sat on the right hand of God the Father Almighty; from thence He shall come to judge the quick and the dead.

"I believe also in the Holy Ghost, God Almighty, having one substance (*unam habentem substantiam*) with the Father and the Son. [I believe] that there is a holy Catholic Church, remission of sins, communion of saints, resurrection of the flesh. I believe [that there is] life after death, and eternal life in the glory of Christ. I believe all these things in God.[2] Amen."

There is something very striking in the emphatic assertions with the recurrent phrases, "I believe in Jesus Christ ... *God Almighty*." "I believe in the

---

[1] The text of this MS. has been recently (1893) produced in photographic fac-simile, and edited by the Rev. F. E. Warren for the *Henry Bradshaw Society*.

[2] "Hæc omnia credo in Deum." The sense of this last clause is not free from ambiguity.

Holy Ghost, *God Almighty*." While the phrase "of one substance," ordinarily applied to the Second Person of the Blessed Trinity, is here applied to the Third Person, and in the form "having one substance with the Father and the Son." There is no faltering in this Creed's assertion of catholic theology. The declaration, too, that God is Himself "invisible," though the Creator of all things visible and invisible, may have been found desirable in a country where, as it would seem, the worship of the powers of nature (*e.g.* of the sun) [1] at one time had place.

The two unquestionably genuine writings of St. Patrick are documents of no great length; and the special objects with which each was written have nothing to do with dogmatic controversy. Accordingly, it is not to be wondered at if from them we are able to derive but little information as to many topics on which we would now gladly have some guidance. But the fact of their undoubted genuineness makes us eagerly prize every smallest gleam of light they throw on a period so deeply enveloped in gloom. On the doctrine of the Trinity in Unity, we have seen there is a full and express testimony, and we have no reason to question that, on the other fundamental doctrines of the Faith, St. Patrick did not differ from the general belief of his time.

The *Confession* was written when the author was well advanced in years (cap. i., sec. 3), and its main object

[1] See *Confession*, cap. v., sec. 25. "That sun which we behold, at God's command rises daily for us,—but it shall never reign, nor shall its splendour continue; but all even that worship it, miserable beings, shall wretchedly come to punishment."

seems to have been to vindicate himself for having undertaken the missionary episcopate of Ireland. It is the utterance of an humble, earnest Christian, whose heart was aflame with the love of souls. The writer is painfully alive to his deficiencies in literary culture, and the barbarous and ungrammatical Latin of his writings justifies his self-abasement in this respect. The *Epistle to the Christian Subjects of Coroticus* consists of an indignant protest against the greed and cruelty of that prince,[1] who harried the Irish coast, slaughtered many, and carried off into slavery great numbers of Christian men and women.

The personal portrait, which the unconscious touches of the writer bring out stroke by stroke before our eyes, constitutes the main charm of both writings. But their extreme preciousness as genuine productions of their age (being, as Sir Samuel Ferguson (*Patrician Documents*), has pointed out, "the oldest documents in British history") has caused them to be subjected to a minute and even microscopic scrutiny. For our present purpose there is not much to be gathered; but we learn the following particulars :—(1) We find Patrick claiming to be constituted "bishop in Ireland" (*Corot.*, cap. i., sec. 2). (2) He personally ordains clergy, as we learn in more passages than one, but nowhere more clearly than when, asserting that all he had done for Ireland he had done without reward, he declares, "When the Lord ordained everywhere clergy through my humble ministry, I dispensed the rite gratuitously" (*Confess.* cap. v., sec.

---

[1] See p. 34.

22). It would seem from other authorities that the practice of the Presbyters present laying on hands together with the bishop at the ordination of a Presbyter, was not perhaps in early times the practice of the Celtic Church.[1] (3) The rite of Confirmation was administered by St. Patrick. This, too, he would have his readers understand, was done gratuitously (*Ibid.*). (4) Both the *Confession* and *Epistle to Coroticus* abound in quotations from the Scriptures of the Old and New Testaments, and, apart from direct quotations, the texture of his diction is in a large measure woven out of biblical language; but, like most contemporary writers, he quotes somewhat loosely. (5) Like many contemporary writers, he cites, as divinely-inspired Scripture, passages from the Apocrypha or deutero-canonical books. (6) He quotes from an earlier Latin version or versions, not from the revised version of St. Jerome. (7) He testifies to the attraction and rapid spread of the monastic system. Both men and women (some of the latter being of high rank) eagerly sought to devote themselves, under conventual rule, to the service of God (*Confess.*, cap. iv., sec. 18, etc.). Here are the beginnings in Ireland (Ninian had already introduced the system into northern Britain) of what was, during the whole of the Celtic period of our Church's history, its dominating characteristic. The monastery was everywhere the home and seminary of Christian learning, the centre of Christian work, and everywhere, as it were, the military base of operations against the powers of heathendom. There is not one

---

[1] See Adamnan, *Vita Columb.*, lib. i., c. xxix. But see p. 255.

name of eminence in the history of Celtic Christianity that is not closely connected with the monastic life. (8) Though baptism is frequently referred to in the writings of St. Patrick, it is curious that there is no direct reference to the Eucharist. We find, however, the statement made (*Confess.*, cap. v., sec. 21), that St. Patrick was careful, despite the offence he gave, to return to their owners certain personal ornaments cast upon "the *altar*" by "religious women and virgins of Christ."

It is to the more abundant writings of Adamnan that we turn for the fullest information as to the ecclesiastical usages of the ancient Scottish Church. These writings, however, it must be remembered, picture to us the state of things at a period removed by a hundred years from that of St. Patrick. Dr. Reeves, late bishop of Down and Connor, in his edition of Adamnan's *Life of St. Columba*, has, by his splendid wealth of learned illustration, made comparatively easy the task of subsequent inquirers; and in what follows I have, like every recent historian, made free use of his labours.[1]

It is well first to reiterate that, speaking generally, there is no evidence of the Celtic Church entertaining in a definite manner any doctrine differing from the prevailing faith of the rest of Western Christendom at the time. More especial prominence may be found given to certain notions, but substantially the faith of

[1] I would also express my indebtedness to the very valuable work of the Rev. F. E. Warren, entitled *The Liturgy and Ritual of the Celtic Church*, Oxford, 1881.

Christendom was one. There would be no necessity to emphasize what might be naturally expected, were it not that the early Scottish and Irish Church has been sometimes represented as possessing a doctrinally purer and more primitive Christianity than was to be found at the time elsewhere. Take, for example, the Eucharist. Nowhere in Christendom in the sixth century do we find the formulated doctrine that afterwards came to be known as Transubstantiation. But in the Church of St. Columba the opinion and sentiment in regard to the Eucharist, so far as we can gather them, were substantially the same as may be found elsewhere at the same period. The notices in Adamnan are doubtless historical, not dogmatic, but the language used by him is just what might be expected from contemporary writers on the Continent. Thus the priest "stood before the *altar*," to "consecrate the sacred *oblation*" (lib. iii., c. 18). Elsewhere the "sacred *mysteries*," "the *mysteries* of the sacred *oblation*," "the sacred *mysteries* of the Eucharist," are terms employed. And the priest who consecrates is said *Christi corpus conficere* (lib. i., c. 35). These expressions were the common language of Western Christendom at the time of Adamnan, and indeed at an earlier time than his. It is worth observing, however, that so far as the notices in Adamnan throw light on the subject, we have no reason to suppose that there were, ordinarily, any celebrations of the Eucharist except on the Lord's Day and festivals. A daily celebration had been established in many parts of Christendom long before this date; and it is remarkable that in a monastery where there were several priests a daily mass does not appear to have been said.

As might be expected from the character of the narrative of the missionary labours of the community, the notices we have of Baptism are in connection with converts from heathenism. The importance attached to the administration of the rite may be gathered from the following narrative (which is interesting also in other respects), recorded in the *Life* (lib. iii., c. 15). "At another time, when the holy man was journeying beyond the dorsum of Britain, near the lake of the river Nisa (Loch Ness), he was suddenly inspired by the Holy Spirit, and said to the brethren who accompanied him, 'Let us hasten to meet the holy angels who have come from the highest regions of heaven to bear away the soul of a heathen, and are waiting there for our coming that we may baptize him before he dies, who has preserved his natural virtue (*naturale bonum*) through a long life even to extreme old age.' And, when he had said this, the aged saint hurried on in front of his companions as fast as he could till he came to the district called Airchart-dan [? Glen Urquhart], where he found an old man, Emchat, who, hearing the word of God preached by the saint, believed, and was baptized, and immediately in joy and confidence passed to the Lord, with the angels who had come to meet him. His son, Virolec, also believed, and was baptized with his whole house." The recognition by Columba of the preservation of his "natural goodness" by the old heathen man is a very interesting feature.

With this passage may be compared a very remarkable utterance to be found in the *Senchus Mor* ("Great Antiquity"), a very remarkable compilation professing to embody St. Patrick's reform and ratification of the Brehon Laws: "Now *the judgments of true nature which the Holy Ghost had spoken* through the mouths of the Brehons and just poets of the men of Erin, from the first occupation of this island down to the reception of the faith, were all exhibited by Dubhthach (Chief Bard of Ireland) to Patrick. Whatever did not clash with the Word of God, in the written Law, and in the New Testament, and with the consciences of the believers, was confirmed in the laws of the Brehons by Patrick."[1] There is in this something that reminds one of the large views and spiritual insight of Justin Martyr and Clement of Alexandria, with respect to God's revelation of His will to the pagan philosophers.

Let us now consider some of the more peculiar, or, at least, more markedly emphasized, features in the current religious belief of the days of St. Columba.

Prominence given to the agency of Demons and good Angels.—The extraordinary prominence given to the agency of good and evil angels in the Christian thought of the time cannot fail to strike the modern reader of Adamnan. And the same feature appears also in the lives of others of the Celtic saints. We are not here concerned with the question of the reasonableness of such prominence; but we observe, as an interesting phenomenon, that particular aspects

---

[1] Healy's *Insula Sanctorum et Doctorum*, p. 53.

of truth and particular phases of belief assume at some periods a magnitude and a proportion that at other periods would, to say the least, seem to have an air of exaggeration, if not of caricature. For Adamnan the evil spirits are not only tempters offering their seductions to the human heart, but they possess power of a physical kind over other creatures of God. Thus demons, by their art, can raise tempests and agitate the sea. Indeed, legions of demons are described in one place as raising a violent tempest and causing a great darkness, while it was yet day (lib. ii., c. 35). They can take possession of a well, and render its water noxious (lib. ii., c. 10). They can make blood have all the appearance of milk; and so, on one occasion, they enabled a sorcerer, till detected by the saint, to pass himself off as one who would perform the miracle of drawing milk from a bull (lib. ii., c. 16). They at times are visible to the bodily eyes (lib. i., c. 1). They are "very black" in colour (lib. ii., c. 9). They on one occasion made an assault in great numbers upon the saint and the monastery with "iron spits." The saint fought against the countless hordes single-handed for the greater part of the day, and finally, with the help of the good angels, expelled them from the island. But perhaps the most entertaining and instructive of these stories is found in the chapter (lib. ii., c. 15) entitled, "Concerning the expulsion of a devil who was lying hidden in a milk-pail"; and to taste the genuine flavour of the story, we must hear it as it is told us by Adamnan. "At another time, a certain youth, Columbanus by name, grandson of

Briun, coming suddenly, stopped at the door of the little hut in which the blessed man was engaged in writing. This same youth, returning from the milking of the cows and carrying on his back a vessel full of new milk, asked the saint to bless his load, as he was wont. Then the saint, being at some distance away, raised his hand and made the saving sign (*i. e.* of the Cross) in the air, which thereupon was moved by a violent concussion, the bar which fastened the lid was thrust back out of the two holes in the sides of the pail and shot away to a distance, the lid fell to the ground, and the greater part of the milk was spilled. The young lad lays down the pail, with the little milk that remained, on the ground, and falls as a suppliant on his knees. But the saint, addressing him, said, 'Rise up, Columbanus; thou hast acted negligently in thy work to-day, for thou didst not put to flight the devil that was lurking in the bottom of the empty pail before the milk was poured in, by marking it with the sign of the Cross of our Lord. And now, as thou seest, being unable to endure the virtue of that sign, he has been made to tremble, the whole pail being shaken, and has spilled the milk in his hasty flight. Bring, then, the pail nearer to me, that I may bless it.' And this being done, the half-empty vessel which the saint had blessed was at the same moment found miraculously filled; and the little that had remained at the bottom had quickly increased under the benediction of his holy hand till it reached the brim."

This story has not been recounted with a view to

raise a smile, but to illustrate the beliefs of the period with which we are dealing.[1] Again, on more than one occasion St. Columba sees demons contending in the air with the angels for the souls of persons recently deceased (lib. iii., cc. 7, 11, 12, 14, etc.). And our views of the spirit world are enlarged by the story of an affectionate wife, who, having died a year before, joined in mid-air with the holy angels in a fight with demons for the soul of her husband who had just died. This conception, no doubt, would have been less startling at a time when women were not unknown to engage in military service.

If evil angels figure largely in the narrative, so also do the good angels. They appear to Columba again and again; and, though ordinarily invisible to others, they were on one occasion detected in numbers by a prying monk, who had acted the spy upon the saint's privacy (lib. iii., c. 17). On another occasion, while Columba was writing in his little cell in Iona, he was heard to cry suddenly, "Help! help!" The two brothers who were in attendance at the door at once inquired what was wanted, and were told that it was only that he had ordered the angel of the Lord, who was standing among them, to save a brother monk who was at that moment falling from the roof of a great house at Derry in Ireland, and who, by the aid of the angel "flying with the speed of lightning," was caught before he reached the ground (lib. iii., c. 16).

[1] In a *Manuale Exorcismorum* (Antuerpiæ 1626), issued with the approbation of the bishop of Antwerp, which lies before me, there is to be found an "Exorcismus pro lacte," and an "Exorcismus pro butyro."

At another time, when, contrary to his wish, the saint's life was prolonged in answer to the prayers of the churches, the angels who had come for his soul were stopped on the other side of the sound, and stood there upon a rock, anxious to fulfil their mission.

In an atmosphere of this kind the whole *Life* is bathed. It may be that in our day we make too little of angelic ministrations, and too little of the power of evil spirits. I shall not discuss the question. I only note that we live in a world of religious thought very different from that of St. Columba. And I am convinced that it is quite as important to understanding the time that we should know the truth on this subject, as that we should know it upon questions concerning the archæology of tonsures and canonical hours.

Illustrations of the current belief of the early Celtic Church could be supplied in abundance from the records of Irish hagiology. It may suffice to notice the parallel to the memorable combat in which, after a long struggle, St. Columba expelled the demons from Iona, that is afforded in the story of St. Patrick as recorded in the *Tripartite Life*, when "on Cruachan-aichle, the modern Croagh Patrick, he had his last encounter with the demons of Ireland. When to the violent ringing of his bell, accompanied by the recital of psalms, and the invocation of the sacred Name, his adversaries were unwilling to yield, he flung the bell with all his might into the thickest of their ranks, and thereby spread such consternation among them, that they all fled with precipitation into the sea, and left the island free from their spiritual aggressions for seven years, seven months, and seven days."[1] Whether the demons were ever so long absent from Ireland, may indeed be questioned; but we need feel little hesitation in believing that they have been very active at various times since then in that "most distressful country."

As for Scotland, it is sad to remember that the terror which darkened life during the witch-finding and witch-burning post-Reformation times shows us the vigorous survival of the belief in the powerful agency of demons, while the counterbalancing faith in the constant ministry of the heavenly angels was an inappreciable factor in popular thought.

Invocation of Saints.—Adamnan leaves us in no doubt as to the fact that in his time the aid of the prayers of departed saints was sought in the Scottish Church. In Columba's lifetime we have evidence to show that his prayers were believed to be especially efficacious. Persons at a great distance were convinced in their distress that if St. Columba's prayers could be had, Heaven might be more successfully approached (lib. ii., cc. 5, 41). Similarly, St. Columba, in peril at sea, called on St. Canice, then in Ireland, to aid him by his prayers (lib. ii., c. 12). Columba himself, on the memorable evening preceding his death, declared: "These, O my children, are the last words I address to you, that ye be at peace and have unfeigned charity among yourselves; and if you follow the example of the

[1] Dr. Reeves' *St. Patrick's Bell and Shrine.*

holy fathers, God the Comforter of the good will be your helper, and *I, abiding with Him, will intercede for you*" (lib. iii., c. 24). It was not unnatural then that, after his death, they would remind him of his promise. This they seem to have done by the somewhat remarkable plan of placing, on a special occasion, some of his books and garments upon the altar, and by the invocation of his name. And God granted to the holy man, we are told, an answer to their requests (lib. ii., c. 46). Again, a plague is stopped in answer to the prayers of St. Columba, now departed (lib. ii., c. 47). We have instances of even reproaches directed against St. Columba, when he seemed slow to answer the supplications addressed to him (*et quodammodo quasi accusare nostrum Columbam cœpimus*, lib. ii., c. 46).

Prayers for the Dead.—"If there is one practice in the Christian Church," wrote the late Dean Plumptre, "not specifically recognized in the New Testament, which can claim the sanction of primitive antiquity, it is that of praying for the souls of the faithful departed." And there is no reason to suppose that the Celtic Church differed from the rest of Christendom in this particular. But, while the evidence is clear for later dates, what the reader is most struck with in the account of St. Columba's life is silence where we should have expected references to the practice. It was not, as I think, till the notion of Purgatory had been given definiteness and importance by Pope Gregory the Great (590—604), that the somewhat vague and general prayers for the "rest and refreshment" of the faithful dead, which had been given a place in the Liturgies, developed into the expression of desire for the relief of souls suffering pains in the other world. Columba's labours were all but concluded before the writings of Gregory could possibly have made their influence felt in Ireland and Scotland. Notions which St. Augustine had thought permissible to be entertained as a private opinion became consolidated and given a precision and definiteness unknown before the time of Gregory. It may be somewhat of an over-statement to say, with Shröckh and Hagenbach,[1] that Gregory was "the inventor of Purgatory," but it was his writings, and more especially the *Dialogues*, with their visions exhibiting the state of the departed, that gave the main impetus to the belief that souls could be relieved from purgatorial pains by the prayers of the faithful.

Now, with one exception (if indeed it can be regarded as an exception), we find, so far as I can recollect, not a single example of prayers for the dead in Adamnan's *Life of St. Columba*. We are here considering the question merely from the historical standpoint; and it is of interest to notice the general view that is presented throughout the book. In one place a soul is represented as being carried off to "the place of suffering" (*ad loca pœnarum*), but it will perhaps be thought that a sufficiently clear interpretation of the expression is to be found by observing that it is *demons* who carry off this soul, and that it is the soul

[1] *History of Christian Doctrines*, vol. ii., p. 97.

of one who is suddenly slain in the midst of his guilt (lib. i., c. 30). In another place (lib. i., c. 1), Adamnan speaks of the saint seeing the souls of the righteous being carried to the highest heaven (*ad summa cœlorum*). Accounts of deaths are frequent, and it is certainly noteworthy that there does not seem to be any expression that would lead us to suppose that Columba had before his mind a place of purgatorial pains. The argument from silence is doubtless always hazardous, but the hazard diminishes in proportion with the likelihood that the belief, if it existed, would have expressed itself.

The one possible exception is found in book iii., chap. 13, which is entitled, "Of the vision of holy angels who carried to heaven the soul of the bishop, St. Columban Mocu Loigse." The title is contemporary, be it observed, with the text, which on account of its importance may be transcribed.

"One morning, while the brethren were putting on their sandals and preparing to go to the different duties of the monastery, the saint, on the contrary, bade them rest that day and prepare for the holy oblation, ordering also that some addition should be made to their repast, such as was given on the Lord's Day. 'It behoves me to-day,' said he, 'although I be unworthy, to celebrate the holy mysteries of the Eucharist out of veneration for that soul which this last night ascended to paradise beyond the starry spaces of the heavens, borne amid choirs of holy angels.' And when he had spoken the brethren did as they were bid, and rested that day according to the commandment of the saint; and the sacred mysteries [1] having been prepared, they accompany the saint to the church in their white robes (*albati*) as on festivals (*quasi die solenni*). But it came to pass that when in the course of chanting the offices that customary prayer was being sung in which the name of St. Martin is commemorated, the saint said suddenly to the chanters, when they came to the place where the name occurs, 'To-day ye must chant for St. Columban, the bishop.' Then all the brethren who were there understood that Columban, the bishop in Leinster, the dear friend of Columba, had passed to the Lord."

Let us see now what is to be learned from this story. First, we may notice, in passing, that it is suggested by the narrative that the Eucharist was not celebrated daily. Secondly, if "*paradise*" stood by itself, we might be the more ready to understand it of the intermediate state of the blessed dead, but the heading of the chapter, which is of the same date as the text of the earliest manuscript of the *Life*, interprets it as "*heaven.*" Thirdly, it would seem as if the saint desired that the name of Columban should be substituted for that of St. Martin, or, more probably, placed before it in the prayer. Now, if we could be sure what this prayer was, all would be clear. But, so far as I know, it was not the practice in the West at this period, in those prayers of the mass in which the names of acknowledged saints occur, to

[1] I read with the thirteenth-century manuscript, in Archbishop Marsh's library, *misteriis* for *ministeriis*.

pray for them, but rather to pray to God that we might be aided by their intercessions. Dr. Bernard MacCarthy, in his learned discussion on the Stowe Missal, in the *Transactions of the Royal Irish Academy*,[1] has, I think, suggested the truth when he considers that "the customary prayer" (*consueta deprecatio*) is the prayer known as *Cum omnibus*, which declares that the spiritual sacrifice was offered to God the Father, Son, and Holy Spirit by the celebrant for himself and for his people [or the monks of his monastery], for the whole body of the Church catholic, "and for *commemorating*" (*pro commemorando*) the venerable patriarchs, prophets, apostles, martyrs, and all saints, "*that they may vouchsafe to earnestly entreat our Lord God for us.*" Then follows, in this ancient Irish missal, a list of the Old Testament worthies and prophets — St. John the Baptist, St. Mary the Virgin, the Apostles, and other early saints, and "likewise," it goes on, "the bishops, Martin, Gregory, Maximus, Felix, ... etc." Observe that in this, the most ancient of all Irish missals, the name of Martin comes first among the bishops; so that I fancy we may not unreasonably picture to ourselves Columba, after the words "*Item episcoporum*," stopping the chanters, and uttering the words transcribed above.

The point of the story seems to me to be that St. Columba treated the day as the festival of the saint. He at once placed his departed friend among the glorified saints. The celebration is held "out of

[1] Vol. xxvii.; see pp. 156 and 217.

veneration" for the soul departed, and the chanting *pro Columbano episcopo* is to be understood as a chanting *pro commemorando Columbano episcopo*, his prayers being sought for the worshippers, and not the worshippers' prayers being offered for him. In a word, it was, as we would say in our present language, rather a festival-mass than a requiem-mass. This may seem a great departure from primitive usage; but I am only endeavouring to interpret historically an historical document.

What has been said gives us no warrant for supposing that there was any omission from the Liturgy of the customary prayer "for all who rest in Christ," that God would grant them "a place of refreshment, light, and peace." Indeed, in our oldest Irish missal—the Stowe Missal—which some would place as early as not very long after the death of St. Columba,[1] we find this prayer.[2] And, grammatically, it is doubtless applicable to the saints, the long lists of whom, including St. Mary the Virgin, precede it.[3] If this latter view be the true one, we have here both prayers for the departed saints, as in some of the

[1] "The second quarter of the seventh century," Dr. MacCarthy. Mr. Warren (*Liturgy and Ritual of the Celtic Church*, p. 199) believes, on liturgical grounds, that the oldest part of the manuscript cannot be placed earlier than the ninth century. So that one cannot speak with confidence as to inferences dependent on its date.
[2] Mr. Henry Bradshaw discovered that the binder of the Stowe Missal altered the true pagination, which will be found correctly in Dr. MacCarthy's paper in *The Transactions of the Royal Irish Academy*, vol. xxvii.
[3] See also in the Stowe Missal the mass *pro mortuis pluribus*.

liturgies of the early Church, and also the prayer that these saints would entreat God for the worshippers.

Mr. Warren (*Liturgy and Ritual of the Celtic Church*, p. 105) has cited from Walafrid Strabo's *Life of St. Gall*, the apostle of Switzerland, a passage which illustrates the practice of the Celtic Church less than twenty years after the death of Columba. When St. Gall was aware that St. Columbanus, of Luxeuil, "had passed from the miseries of this life to the joys of Paradise" (A.D. 615), he ordered that the sacrifice of the mass should be offered "for his rest." In the meagreness of records of Scottish origin, it may be permitted us to cite the scribe's colophon in the Reichenau codex of Adamnan's *Life of St. Columba*, "an early eighth century MS.": "Whoever reads these little books of the virtues (? miraculous powers) of Columba, let him entreat the Lord for me, Dorbbene, that I may possess eternal life after death." Similarly, Adamnan himself added to the end of his book, *Concerning the Holy Places*, an entreaty for the readers' prayers for the "Divine clemency" on behalf of the "holy priest Arculf," who dictated it; and that for himself, "the wretched sinner who wrote it," they would entreat "Christ, the Judge of the world." This last phrase reminds one of the request of St. Paul on behalf of Onesiphorus, that he might "find mercy of the Lord *in that day*" (2 Tim. i. 18). Again, some of the early Irish monumental epigraphs request prayers for the departed.[1]

---

[1] See Warren, *loc. cit.*, where other illustrations will be found. The colophons of the scribes, though suggestive of the belief in

As regards direct invocation of the saints, it seems to me that Mr. Warren (*Liturgy and Ritual*, etc., p. 108) has somewhat overstated the case in alleging that "there are no instances recorded of the modern practice of praying to departed saints." Confining ourselves to Adamnan's *Life of St. Columba*, we are told that it was "with psalms and fasting and the invocation of his [Columba's] name" that the monks of Adamnan's time besought on one occasion a favourable wind for their voyage; and on another, when the wind was adverse, the words of a direct address to him are recorded thus: "Does our injurious delay please thee, O saint? Hitherto we hoped that some comfort and help in our labours would have been afforded by thee, through God's favour, since we thought that thou wert held in great honour by God." The Litany of Saints in the Stowe Missal may date from the eighth century. From the evidence adduced, it would seem probable that at the time of Adamnan the transition to direct prayers addressed to the saints had begun in the Columban Church.

Features of interest in the Ritual of the Celtic Church.—We may now turn to notice some of the more remarkable features of the ritual of the Celtic Church.[1] The bread used in the Eucharist was, contrary to the prevailing practice in the West at the time, sometimes,

---

the efficacy of prayers for the dead, cannot ordinarily be cited as conclusive proofs.

[1] For other examples, fuller details, and authorities, see Mr. Warren's valuable work.

if not generally, unleavened. St. Gall, according to his biographer, Walafrid Strabo, was accustomed to use unleavened bread. But instances of a similar variation from the prevailing practice are also to be found in the history of the Anglo-Saxon Church. I am not satisfied that this usage prevailed generally in the Celtic Church.

The mixed chalice, we may say with much confidence, was universal in the Celtic Church. Our earliest Irish missal, already referred to, supplies (in an appended tract in the Irish tongue) ritual directions for the mixture, which was to be accompanied with certain prayers. It is worth noticing the peculiarity that the water was first placed in the chalice.[1] The same tract supplies mystical interpretations of the symbolism of the water and of the wine added to it. As regards the mixed chalice, the universal practice of the early Church was naturally adhered to.

In the Irish tract in the Stowe Missal we find most elaborate directions for the fraction, and the placing of the particles in a cruciform shape upon the paten, together with explanations of the symbolism. We find nothing exactly like it in any known missal, but features resembling it may be found in the Eastern and the Spanish liturgies. It would seem that the cross thus made was to be surrounded at Easter with a circle—"circuit wheel"—of other portions, and Dr. MacCarthy reminds us in this connection of the familiar form of Celtic monumental crosses. And it is minutely prescribed from which portions of this figure

---

[1] MacCarthy, in the *Transact. Royal Irish Acad.*, vol. xxvii., p. 245.

various classes of persons were to be communicated. Thus, if we may follow the guidance of Dr. MacCarthy, the celebrant communicated himself with the portion in the centre of the cross; bishops were communicated with portions from the upper part of the shaft; priests from the left arm of the cross; the clergy below the rank of priests from the right arm; anchorites from the lower part of the shaft; "clerical students" from the upper left quadrant of the surrounding circle; "innocent youths"[1] from the upper right quadrant; "penitents" from the lower left quadrant; married persons and first communicants from the lower right quadrant.

Not less artificial is the regulation of the various numbers of the portions which, according to this Irish tract, were to be consecrated on various occasions; and not less fanciful the reasons assigned for these numbers. Thus, five for ordinary days, "in figure of the five senses"; seven on the festivals of saints and virgins (except the chief), "in figure of the seven gifts of the Holy Spirit"; eight for martyrs, "in figure of the octonary of the New Testament" (*i. e.* the four Gospels, Acts, Pauline Epistles, Catholic Epistles, and Apocalypse); nine on the Lord's Day, "in figure of the nine folks of Heaven, and of the nine grades of the Church";[2] eleven for the Apostles, "in figure of

---

[1] Does this phrase point to the practice of communicating infants?

[2] The commonly-received grades of the Heavenly Hierarchy need not be recounted. In "the nine grades of the Church," perhaps the writer concurred with Isidore in adding *bishops* and *clerks* to the seven now reckoned in the Roman Church.

the imperfect number of the Apostles after the scandal of Judas"; twelve on the day of the commemoration of the Last Supper, "in remembrance of the perfect number of the Apostles"; thirteen on little Easter [Low Sunday] and on the Feast of the Ascension, in figure of Christ with the Twelve, and (as is worth observing in explanation of how an uncertain number of communicants was to be dealt with) this is added, " at first. They are to be distributed more minutely in going to Communion." " The five, and the seven, and the eight and the nine, and the eleven, and the twelve, and the thirteen—they are five [and] sixty together, and that is the number of parts which is wont to be in the Host of Easter and of the Nativity, and of Pentecost; for all that is contained in Christ."[1] How far this complex, highly artificial, and, as most persons will think, unedifying ritual prevailed, we are unable to say, and when it made its appearance it is impossible to judge till some definite pronouncement has been generally accepted by palæographers upon the date of this portion of the volume known as the Stowe Missal. As it stands, however, it will serve to disabuse the minds of those who would regard the Celtic Church as characteristically marked by a simple and primitive plainness of ceremonial. The reader must not suppose that the ritual directions here transcribed are the mere outcome of the wanton fancy of the Celts of Ireland. In a tract attributed to Ildefonsus, who was bishop of Toledo from 657 to 667, we find

---

[1] MacCarthy, *loc. cit.*, p. 253.

some curious resemblance to the practices enjoined in Ireland. We find that the "breads" were to be arranged in certain forms and their number was to vary with the festival. Thus, on Christmas Day, at each of the three masses, five portions were to be arranged in the form of a cross, and twelve others in a circle around it, the five to signify Christ and the four evangelists, and the surrounding circle the choir of angels. At Easter, at each of three masses, five and forty in the shape of a cross. At Pentecost, also five and forty arranged as a cross in the middle of a square (symbolizing the heavenly Jerusalem). On the feasts of the Ascension and Transfiguration, the same number and form as at Christmas. On Sundays and festivals of the saints only five, in the form of a cross. The centre "bread" was to be somewhat larger than the rest as signifying "the Lamb in the midst." The resemblance between these regulations and those of the Irish tract are obvious, and one may reasonably suspect a more than accidental connection between the two.

The Greek Church at the present day, in the office of the Prothesis (or preparation of the elements before the celebration of the Liturgy), has an elaborate arrangement, on the "disk" or paten, of portions of the bread. With some few modern additions the rite is ancient. These portions are meant to symbolize "The Holy Lamb" in the midst, St. Mary the Virgin, the prophets, the Apostles, Basil and the great œcumenical doctors, Stephen and other martyrs, Antony and other ascetics, Cosmas and Damian and other unmercenary saints (*i. e.* those who took no reward for their miracles of healing, etc.), Joachim and Anna, and all saints, the Emperor of Russia, the Holy Synod, living bishops, etc., private persons of the living whom it is desired to remember, private persons of the dead whom it is desired to remember.[1] While another symbolical arrangement devised on a different principle exists in the Mozarabic Missal.[2]

Joint Consecration of the Eucharist by Presbyters.— A custom which, it would seem, is absolutely unique is brought to our notice by an incident in the life of Columba, as related by Adamnan (lib. 1., c. 35). The story is related by us in full in another place (p. 252) for another purpose, and the reader is referred to it. A second priest was invited by the celebrant, if only of the rank of a priest, to join in the consecration, at least as regards the manual acts (*panem frangere*). But a bishop, when celebrating, took the service alone. This practice seems to be the exact reverse of a usage known elsewhere in the West, that presbyters should join both in the words and manual acts with a bishop when celebrating the Eucharist. In the present Roman service for the ordination of priests, the rubric directs the bishop at the celebration to raise his voice somewhat, so that the priests who

---

[1] The existing rite is exhibited in Rajewsky's *Euchologion der Orthodox-Katholischen Kirche*, Wien, 1861. The reader may also consult Neale and Littedale's translations of the *Liturgies of S.S. Mark, James, etc.*, p. 179.

[2] The Mozarabic arrangement may conveniently be found pictured in Mr. Hammond's *Liturgies, Eastern and Western*, p. 341.

have been just ordained may be able to repeat all the words with him, and especially the words of consecration, which should be said at the same moment by the ordained priests and the bishop. And as late as the fifteenth century, on Holy Thursday at Chartres, six priests, standing in line at the altar with the bishop, three on his right and three on his left, sang the mass together with him, and also with him performed all the enjoined ceremonies.[1]

Communion in both kinds.—Had we no specific evidence as to the practice of the Celtic Church, we might reasonably believe that it did not differ from that of the rest of Christendom. And there is no question that down to the twelfth century the Communion was administered in both kinds to the laity. But we possess in the documents of the Celtic Church which have come down to us, definite and independent evidence establishing the fact. Thus, to take first our solitary Scottish liturgical fragment, the Book of Deer, from an office for the Communion of the Sick, we read first the notice, "Here give the sacrifice to him," then the benediction, or words of delivery, "The body with the blood of our Lord Jesus Christ be health to thee for eternal life and salvation"; then immediately follow the words, "Refreshed with the body and blood of Christ let us ever say to Thee, O Lord, Alleluia, Alleluia. . . . I will take the cup of salvation and call upon the name of the Lord. Alleluia, Alleluia." Both

[1] Warren (*Liturg. and Rit. of Celtic Church*, p. 129), who gives his authorities.

elements, as Mr. Warren remarks, "seem to have been administered at once," the bread having been dipped in the wine. This method, technically known as "intinction," had obvious advantages in communicating the sick. It prevails at the present day in the Greek Church for the general communicating of the laity, a spoon being used for conveying the sacrament to the mouth of the recipient. In the West, in 675, the practice was condemned at the Council of Braga, because our Lord had delivered to His Apostles the bread and the wine separately, but notwithstanding the practice spread. The later history of the usage does not concern us.

In the Irish *Antiphonary of Bangor* we meet the following Communion formulæ: "We have received the body of the Lord, and we have drunk His blood; we will fear no evil, for the Lord is with us. . . . Take ye this sacred body of the Lord and the blood of the Saviour, unto life everlasting. Alleluia."[1] And "Refreshed," etc., as in the Book of Deer. In the Book of Mulling (eighth century?) the rubric for the administration runs: "Then he is refreshed with the body and blood." In a ninth-century Irish MS. at St. Gall,[2] we have the Communion anthem, "Come ye, eat My bread and drink My wine which I have mixed for you"; and the post-communion, "We give Thee thanks, O Lord, Holy Father, Almighty, Everlasting God, who hast satiated us with the communion of the body and the blood of Christ." In the Stowe

---
[1] Compare Hymn 313 (from *Antiphonary of Bangor*) in *Hymns Ancient and Modern*.   [2] See Warren, *loc. cit.*, p. 179.

Missal the Communion anthem appears, "Eat, O My friends; alleluia; and drink ye abundantly (*inebriamini*), O most beloved; alleluia." All these fall in with, if they do not absolutely demonstrate, the existence of the Communion in both kinds.

The study of the Irish liturgical remains and of our solitary Scottish liturgical relic of the Celtic period, the Book of Deer (see p. 248), leaves no doubt that it was from Gallican, not Roman sources, the liturgical worship of the Celtic Church had its origin. A thorough treatment of the subject would involve us in liturgical technicalities unsuitable to a work such as this. But ample proof will be found adduced by Mr. Warren in his *Liturgy and Ritual of the Celtic Church*.

This may not be an inconvenient place for saying something of two of the more important subjects of controversy between the Irish and the Roman parties.

The Tonsure.—Among the subjects of lively controversy between those who represented the Roman mission in Britain and the adherents of the Celtic Church, was the form of the ecclesiastical tonsure. The question does not appear to have been raised by the wise Augustine of Canterbury; but subsequently it roused the most violent animosities between the two parties. The Roman tonsure consisted in a circle, more or less wide, on the top of the head being made bare with the razor, while a fringe of hair surrounded it like a crown, which was mystically regarded as symbolizing the Saviour's crown of thorns.

The Celtic tonsure, as I understand it, like the Roman tonsure, showed a fringe of hair in front, but the top of the head was not shaved beyond a line drawn from ear to ear, so that, viewed from behind, there was nothing that marked the ecclesiastic or monk from the ordinary layman. Recent writers seem to concur generally in thinking that the Celtic tonsure showed the whole of the front of the head as clean shaved; but the original authorities do not seem to me to bear this out. The passage in the Abbat Ceolfrid's Letter to Naiton, king of the Picts (A.D. 710), preserved by Bede,[1] seems very distinctly to say that, viewed in front, there seemed to be a crown, but that when you looked at the back of the head you discovered that the "crown," which you thought you saw, was cut short, was not a real and complete "crown." It is plain that if the whole of the hair on the front of the head was shaved off, there would not be anything resembling a *corona* of hair. The shorn part of the head seems to have had no special significance for most of the old writers, except as being essential to bring out the significant part—the surrounding fringe of hair, which symbolized the sufferings of our Lord.[2]

The Celtic tonsure seemed to the Roman party to be a maimed piece of symbolism; it exhibited

---

[1] *Hist. Eccl.*, lib. v., c. 22.
[2] If this view is correct, the figure of St. Columba depicted in the St. Gall manuscript of Adamnan's *Life* of the saint, with a frontal fringe of hair, may possibly not be, as Bishop Reeves supposes, a mistake into which a ninth-century copyist might fall. See *Historians of Scotland*, vol. vi., p. cxiv.

only a truncated "crown" to those who could look all round.

The words of Ceolfrid are so precise and vivid that they seem to me to quite outweigh what some would infer, perhaps too hastily, from a passage in an epistle attributed to the writer known as Gildas (570?),[1] who says that the Romans asserted that the Celtic tonsure had its origin in that of Simon Magus, whose tonsure extended *only* to all the anterior part of the head from ear to ear.[2]

The matter is of little moment; but if we try to picture to ourselves the ancient Irish and Scottish monks, it of course makes a difference in the image we create before the mind's eye.

It is a question of more interest how the difference between the two tonsures originated. If monasticism was introduced into Ireland from the "great monastery" of Whithorn in the north, there can be little doubt that a tonsure of the Roman shape came with it.—The Greek tonsure, or shaving the whole head, called "the tonsure of St. Paul," if once introduced and prevailing, could never, I imagine, have become transformed into the Celtic tonsure, while it is not difficult for any one who is familiar with the gradual transformations of ecclesiastical vestures to under-

---

[1] The section of the second epistle which refers to the tonsure is corrupt in its text, and is regarded by Haddan and Stubbs (*Councils*, vol. i., pp. 108 *sq.*) as of a later date than Gildas, though prior to the general adoption of the Roman tonsure.

[2] The text of the same passage which Archbishop Usher cites from a different MS. omits the mention of "all the anterior part of the head." *Antiq. Brit. Eccl.*, p. 479, edit. 1687.

stand how the Roman tonsure may have been in the course of years curtailed at the back of the head, and so changed into what I take to be the Celtic form. I cannot think that there is the slightest evidence for supposing, with Prof. Rhys (*Celtic Britain*, p. 72), that the Celtic tonsure was a revival of the practice of the Druids.[1]

At the time when the controversy between the Roman and Celtic ecclesiastics on the subject of the shape of the tonsure began to wax warm, the Roman party declared that the tonsure of their opponents was derived from Simon Magus, while their own was that of Simon Peter, the chief of the Apostles. But this opprobrious language had, so far as we know, no historical foundation, and was, no doubt, only one of the amenities so common in excited religious debate. The Celtic tonsure was sometimes further reviled by attributing its origin to the swineherd of the Irish king, Laoghaire.[2] But this story is as valueless as the former.

When we remember the bitterness of controversy between the Church party and the Puritans in the sixteenth and seventeenth centuries, about the use of

[1] As I differ from the weight of recent authority on the form of the Celtic tonsure, I think the passage of Ceolfrid on which I have laid stress should here be given. "Quæ [tonsura] aspectu, in frontis quidem superficie, coronæ videtur speciem præferre; sed ubi ad cervicem considerando perveneris, decurtatam eam quam te videre putabas invenies coronam." In *Bede*, lib. v., c. 22.

[2] This name is pronounced *Leary*. Todd's *Life of St. Patrick*, p. 150, note. The story which may account for the statement as to the tonsure is given by Rhys (*Celtic Britain*, p. 73), from Stokes' *Goidelica*.

the " corner-cap," or when we recall more recent heated discussions (sometimes attended by mob violence) on the wearing of the black gown or surplice in the pulpit, we may perhaps be more inclined to extend our charity to those who found " a principle at stake " in a matter apparently so trivial as hair-cutting. On the part of the Irish and Scotch, there was a natural attachment to a practice which they had derived from their predecessors in the faith, holy men whose memories were held in the most profound veneration. And further, it might not unreasonably rouse the indignation of the Celtic party if it were sought arbitrarily to impose upon them an observance, the acceptance of which might be construed into a badge of subjection to a foreign authority. Their own mode of hair-cutting had been handed down to them from the past ; why, they might reasonably ask, should they give it up ? Why should they submit to the requirements of those who possessed no right to command ? We can easily understand how good and independent-minded men might argue thus. The student of English history knows well it was not for a matter of twenty shillings that John Hampden resisted the imposition of the ship-money.

The Easter Controversy.—The same spirit of loyalty to their forefathers in the faith entered largely into the firmness with which the members of the Celtic Church resisted the pressure exerted by the Roman party that they should adopt the mode of calculating the fall of Easter which prevailed in other parts of Western Christendom. In this controversy, however, the strangers had more reason on their side than in the matter of the tonsure.

In past times there were mistakes among students as to the nature of the difference on this subject between the Celtic and the Roman Churches. Some erroneously imagined that the Scottish Church followed the practice of the "Quartodecimans" in the second century. But this is now known to be an entirely incorrect view. It is enough for our purpose to state that while the "Quartodecimans" celebrated Easter on the fourteenth day of the first Jewish month, without regard to what day of the week their Easter-day, thus calculated, might happen to be, the Irish or Scottish Church always observed Easter upon a Sunday. The difference between the Celtic churchmen and the rest of the West at the time of the controversy arose out of the fact that the Celtic Church calculated Easter by the aid of a cycle which, while retained by them, had been abandoned elsewhere as being less astronomically correct. An explanation in detail would involve many elaborate astronomical considerations that would be out of place here.[1]

"The important facts," as Mr. F. E. Warren says, "are these—that before the Council of Nice the practice of the British harmonized with that of the Roman

---

[1] The curious may consult Prof. Stokes' *Ireland and the Celtic Church*, pp. 149—155; Haddan and Stubbs' *Councils*, vol. i., p. 152, Appendix; the article "Easter" in Smith and Cheetham's *Dictionary of Christian Antiquities;* Usher's *Brit. Eccles. Antiq.*, cap. xvii.; Skene, *Celtic Scotland*, vol. ii., pp. 7—10.

Church, the most ancient Roman table for Easter agreeing with that of the British Church; but that, owing to its [subsequent] isolation from the rest of Western Christendom, the Celtic Church had never adopted the various alterations and improvements which, on astronomical and not on theological grounds, had been from time to time accepted by the Continental Church" (*Liturgy and Ritual of the Celtic Church*, p. 64). It was not till A. D. 463 that the Roman Church adopted the cycle in the form which Augustine of Canterbury and his followers desired to press upon their Celtic brethren. Both Scotland and Ireland had received Christianity at an earlier date, and the old method of calculating Easter had had in these countries many long years of possession when it was first sought to oust it in favour of the more accurate system. It is not improbable that if the Roman missionaries had confined themselves to methods of calm exposition and reasoning, the British Churches would on this point have given way long before they did so in fact. But violent invective did not lead to the result desired. As the Celtic tonsure was styled by the opprobrious name of "the tonsure of Simon Magus," so the offensive and utterly inapplicable title of "Quartodecimans" was affixed to the supporters of the Celtic Easter. The evils of protracted and embittered controversy must in justice be laid chiefly at the door of the Roman party. Men of the Celtic race are certainly not slow in resenting anything that savours of assumption; yet we need not seek to offer excuses for the uncharitableness of such Celtic ecclesiastics as would refuse to eat, not only at the same table, but even under the same roof with their brethren of the Roman party.[1]

ADDITIONAL NOTE.

'THE BOOK OF DEER.'

The solitary liturgical relic of the Celtic Church in Scotland is to be found in the Book of Deer, now deposited in the University Library at Cambridge. As described by Dr. John Stuart, in his admirable edition printed for the Spalding Club (1869), it consists of eighty-six folios, of small but rather wide 8vo. form, and contains the Gospel of St. John and portions of the other three Gospels; a fragment of an Office for the Visitation of the Sick; the Apostles' Creed; and a charter of King David I. to the clerics of Deer, which is situated in almost the centre of the district of Buchan, in the north-east of Aberdeenshire. The character of the handwriting has led palæographers, like Professor Westwood, to assign the part of earliest date to the ninth century. Its illuminations and ornaments are quite of the same kind as those of many Irish Books of the Gospels. Its connection with the Columban monastery at Deer is unquestionable, but we have no materials to help us to determine whether it was the work of an Irish or native (*i. e.*

---

[1] As was alleged of the Irish bishop, Dagam. Bede, *Eccles. Hist.*, lib. ii., c. 4.

Pictish) scribe. The Creed is of the same date as the Gospels, but the fragment of the Visitation of the Sick " is in a considerably later hand," while certain entries of grants of land, written in the vernacular Gaelic, appear to have been inserted in the eleventh and twelfth centuries. The liturgical portion of the Book of Deer, which is very brief, may be found in Mr. Warren's *Liturgy and Ritual of the Celtic Church*, a volume more easily accessible than Dr. Stuart's. The full-page representations of the Evangelists are of the usual ostentatiously grotesque kind, which leave little doubt that the artists deliberately avoided any attempt at realistic portraiture. Three of the four figures show a curious square ornament upon the breast, apparently suspended by straps from the neck. This ornament may not improbably represent a case in which the book of each Evangelist's Gospel is preserved (see p. 319). The figure prefixed to the Gospel of St. Luke is represented in the frontispiece of this volume.

CHAPTER XIV.

THE EPISCOPATE IN THE CELTIC CHURCH.

It may seem to us, with the enlarged range of early documentary evidence of late years opened up or made more generally available, that it would be impossible for any candid inquirer to entertain the view long prevalent in this country, that the ancient Church in Scotland was "Presbyterian" in its organization. But even apart from the misleading influence of party sentiment, it was in fact not difficult for writers in the sixteenth, the seventeenth, and indeed, as one may add, the eighteenth century, to misunderstand, or to draw unwarrantable inferences from the documents that were most ready at hand. Such Scottish writers as John of Fordun (see p. 43) and the very able and distinguished John Major (1469—1550)[1] were ecclesiastics of the Roman Church. It was not unnaturally supposed that their statements might on such a subject be accepted without question. These statements were

[1] See the *Life of Major*, by Mr. Æ. J. G. Mackay, prefixed to Major's *History of Greater Britain* (1892), among the publications of the *Scottish History Society*.

repeated by George Buchanan, and by many subsequent historians, almost to our own day. The notions so long prevailing popularly in Scotland were thus very natural, more especially as they fell in with Presbyterian opinion and sentiment.

When we come to examine the primary evidence for ourselves we find that the very first authentic testimony to Christian missionary efforts in Scotland, that of Bede (*Eccles. Hist.*, lib. iii., c. 4), represents Ninian as a bishop. The authority of the *Life of St. Kentigern* is, as we have seen, of comparatively little value; but such as it is, it declares Kentigern to have been a bishop. But it is to that store-house of authentic facts, the *Life* of his contemporary, Columba, that we turn for the most trustworthy information on the subject. And as to the existence of the Episcopate, as distinct from the Presbyterate, in the time of Columba, there can be no possible doubt. In his time, and in the missionary Church founded by him, it is absolutely certain that bishops existed as a distinct order, possessing powers and privileges which were not shared in by presbyters.

It has been already pointed out that, as the more abundant remains of ancient Irish architecture and Irish art should be utilized for the true understanding of the ancient architecture and art of Celtic Scotland, so the copious ecclesiastical documents of Ireland cannot with reason be overlooked in any attempt to gain a correct view of the condition of the contemporary Church in Scotland, which was its offshoot. But I prefer, as sufficient for our purpose, confining ourselves, at the outset, to an examination of the invaluable work, Adamnan's *Life* of the great Scottish missionary, with a view to see what may be learned from that source alone on the question before us.

Two incidents recorded by Adamnan are deserving of careful examination. The first story runs as follows: "Concerning Cronan the Bishop.[1] At another time a certain pilgrim from the province of Munster came to the saint (*i. e.* Columba). This man in his humility did all that he could to disguise himself, so that no one might know that he was a bishop; but this could not be hidden from the saint, for on the next Lord's Day, having been commanded by the saint to consecrate the Body of Christ, as the custom was, he calls to him, the saint, that they might together, as two Presbyters, break the bread of the Lord.[2] Thereupon the saint went to the altar, and suddenly looking into his face, thus addresses him: 'Christ bless thee, brother; do thou break this bread alone, according to the rite of bishops. Now we know that thou art a bishop. Why hast thou so long endeavoured to disguise thyself so that the reverence (*veneratio*) due to thee from us might not be rendered?' On hearing the saint's words, the humble pilgrim was greatly astonished, and reverenced (*veneratus est*) Christ in the saint. And those who were present in much amazement gave glory to the Lord" (lib. i., cap. 35).

Here, then, we see a bishop; we see that his passing

[1] This title, which is wanting from some of the later MSS., is found in the earliest, the Reichenau, text (known as Cod. A), attributed by Reeves to the beginning of the eighth century. It may have been transcribed during the life of the author.

[2] On joint consecration by Presbyters, see p. 238.

himself off as a presbyter was regarded as a proof of his *humility;* we see that a special reverence was held to be due to bishops; we see that bishops celebrated the Eucharist with a peculiar rite without associating a presbyter in the act. We see the great abbat, the founder of the monastery, a man of royal blood, as being merely a presbyter, giving place to the unknown stranger from Munster because he was a bishop.

The second passage from the *Life of St. Columba* which calls for special notice in this connection may now be cited. "The prophecy of the blessed man concerning Findchan the presbyter, founder of that monastery in the Ethican land (Tiree), which in the Scotic tongue is called Artchain. At another time, Findchan, the presbyter and soldier of Christ (*i. e.* a monk), brought with him, in the dress of a cleric, from Scotia (*i.e.* Ireland) to Britain, Aid, surnamed the Black (Aid Dubh, of the Irish records), who was sprung from a royal stock, and of the race of the Picts; and this with a view to his spending some years with him in his monastery. Now this Aid the Black had been a man stained with much blood and had slaughtered many. It was he, too, who had slain Diarmit, son of Cerbul, by the appointment of God, King of all Scotia (Ireland). This same Aid then, after some time was spent in retirement, was, a bishop having been summoned, ordained a presbyter, although not rightly (*non recte*), in the house of the aforesaid Findchan. Yet the bishop did not dare to place a hand upon his head unless the same Findchan, who loved Aid after the flesh (*carnaliter amans*), would first place his right hand on his head, in token of concurrence and approval (*pro confirmatione*). When such an ordination as this was afterwards made known to the saint, he was sore displeased; and then forthwith he pronounces this terrible sentence upon that Findchan and Aid who had been ordained: 'That right hand which Findchan, contrary to the law of God and the rule of the Church (*contra fas et jus ecclesiasticum*), placed upon the head of the son of perdition, shall presently rot, and, after great pain and torture, shall be interred in the earth before himself; and he shall survive his buried hand many years. But Aid, who was unwarrantably (*indebite*) ordained, shall return as a dog to his vomit, and become again a bloody murderer,'" etc. We need not, for our purpose, relate how the prophecies were fulfilled.

In this story we learn that when it was sought to ordain Aid, a bishop had to be sent for. We learn that the ordination was by the laying on of the bishop's hand. We learn that, probably knowing the infamous repute of Aid, the bishop would not venture to ordain him till Findchan, head of the monastery, had committed himself to formal approval by laying on his hand. If Findchan believed that he could by his own act have ordained his friend of ill-repute, there would have been no need of calling in an unwilling bishop.[1] We may add that it appears that

---

[1] It may be worth mentioning that the name of this Findchan is, according to Reeves, preserved in *Kilfinichen*, a parish in the island of Mull.

ordination to the Presbyterate was by the laying on of hands, and that perhaps here, as elsewhere in the West at this time, and as still preserved in the ordinal of the Church of England, presbyters joined with the bishop in the act. The bishop's insisting on Findchan's first placing his hand on the head of Aid may perhaps be expressed in words: "Let me see that you, the head of this monastery, are going to take your share in the ordination of this man, so that I shall not have to bear the blame alone."

It will be observed that no punishment is recorded to have been inflicted on the ordaining bishop. And the explanation may probably be found if we assume that the bishop was a member of the community in Tiree, and would have been under the pressure of monastic obedience to the head of the house. This leads us on to notice the fact that it was the general rule that the heads of Columban monasteries should not have higher rank than the great founder, the presbyter Columba. But the episcopal offices belonging to ordination had to be performed, and so we very commonly find a bishop among the members of the community. The Scottish Church of the Columban period was mainly, if not universally, monastic; and these two facts brought about the unusual arrangement that bishops (as members of the community) were subject to the jurisdiction of the abbat, or head of their house.

In any country ministered to in things spiritual by secular clergy, the position of the bishop is one of superiority, both as regards the "right of order" and the "right of jurisdiction." In a country where religion is represented by the monastic system, while the bishop's "right of order" remains untouched, his "right of jurisdiction" is affected, unless it happened that the head of the monastery (as was not unfrequent in Ireland, and not unknown in Scotland) was himself of episcopal rank. Bede took note of the anomaly in the Scottish Church. Writing of Hii (Iona), he says, "It was the usage that that island should always have for its ruler (*rectorem*) an abbat who was a presbyter, to whose rule both the whole province and even the bishops themselves, by an unusual arrangement, should be subjected, in accordance with the example of their first teacher, who was not a bishop, but a presbyter and monk" (*Eccles. Hist.*, lib. iii., c. 4).

A very striking characteristic of the Celtic Church, whether in Scotland or Ireland, was its monastic form. The land was held for Christ by a number of fortresses or garrisons, of which metaphor we are reminded by the rampart-circled monasteries.[1] The commandants of these fortresses, more especially in Scotland (as generally established by Columban monks), were more frequently presbyters than bishops. In a wild, unsettled, and uncivilized country, a diocesan organization can never be much more than a paper organization—a scheme, it may be, beautifully designed, but incapable of being fully realized for many long years. The wonderful successes of the Irish missions may well suggest the query whether the planting down

---

[1] See p. 124.

in a heathen country of communities of ardent workers under the guidance of a capable head, possessing large powers of action and control, who might be (in accordance with what is at once the primitive and the prevailing and general order of the Church) a bishop, would not, even now, be more likely to be effective than the methods generally followed in our modern missions.

The position so commonly occupied by the bishop in relation to the abbat of the Columban monasteries, though differing from the prevailing usage of the Christian Church, and to a large extent contrary to the design for which episcopacy was primarily established, does not stand in history wholly without parallel. The practice of raising priests to the episcopal order though they possessed no sees, was not peculiar to the Celts. As early as the fourth century, as we learn from the historian Sozomen, two of the monks of Edessa, whose names he records, were raised to the episcopate, not as having jurisdiction, but "for the sake of honourable distinction." He adds that they were consecrated in their own monasteries (*Eccles. Hist.*, lib. vi., c. 34). In the monastery of Mount Sinai we learn that in the eleventh century there were five hundred monks subject to an abbat, and having their own bishop. In the West the great Italian monastery of Monte Cassino, and the monasteries of St. Martin at Tours, and of St. Denys at Paris, possessed an arrangement by which one of the monks was consecrated bishop and was ready to perform any episcopal act required, though possessing

R

no jurisdiction.[1] In the great abbey of Fulda, the most important and influential monastery in mid-Germany—indeed perhaps one might say in the whole land of German-speaking people—ecclesiastical jurisdiction was, up to 1752, exercised over the wide extent of territory attached to the abbey by the presbyter abbat, but one of his subject monks was invested with the episcopal character, and performed such offices as the discipline of the Church confines to the episcopate.[2]

An English churchman is in our day further helped to understand the subordination of the bishop to the abbat by recalling the not unfrequent practice of appointing bishops who have retired from their sees in the colonies to offices in English cathedral establishments. Such a bishop holding an archdeaconry or canonry is subject to the dean in his cathedral, but he is still a bishop. In respect to the organization of the early Irish Church, of which the Scottish Church of Columba was only a colonial offshoot, Dr. Todd[3] seems to have correctly stated the case that the most remarkable feature was the extraordinary multiplication of bishops. "There was no restraint upon their being consecrated. Every man of eminence for piety or learning was advanced to the order of bishop, as a sort of *degree*, or mark of distinction. Many of them lived as solitaries or in monasteries. Many of them established

---

[1] The authorities for these statements will be found in Dr. Todd's *St. Patrick*, pp. 55—57.

[2] Benedict XIV. erected the territory of Fulda into a bishopric in the year 1752. *Acta SS.*, Octob. viii., p. 165.

[3] *St. Patrick, Apostle of Ireland*, p. 27.

schools for the practice of the religious life and the cultivation of sacred learning, having no diocese or fixed episcopal duties; and many of them, influenced by missionary zeal, went forth to the Continent, to Great Britain, or to other then heathen lands, to preach the Gospel of Christ to the Gentiles." Having no sees and no endowments, it was easy for every considerable monastery to possess a bishop for the performance of such ecclesiastical offices as were confined to the highest order of the ministry. The famous double monastery of Kildare, with communities of both monks and nuns under the headship of St. Brigid, possessed a bishop. An early biographer [1] of the great abbess declares how that when the monastery had been founded she came on consideration to the conclusion "that she could not be without a high priest to consecrate churches and to settle the ecclesiastical degrees in them" (*i. e.* to ordain presbyters and other clergy). She selected for this purpose a solitary of high repute for piety, and arranged that he should "govern the Church with her in episcopal dignity, that nothing of sacerdotal order should be wanting in her churches." There may be here somewhat of the colouring of a later age, but there is no reason to question the fact that the monastery of Kildare possessed a bishop, subject, in his monastic relations, to the abbess.

In Ireland, bishops not unfrequently were heads of monastic houses, and in Scotland there seem to be at

---

[1] Cogitosus, whom Dr. Graves (Bishop of Limerick) places in the seventh, but Petrie and Todd in the ninth, century.

least two instances, Lismore and Kingarth, where a bishop was chief of the monastic establishment; but, as we have seen, it became a rule of the Columban monks that the ecclesiastical rank attained by the founder should not be surpassed by his successors. It may be really true (see p. 89) that it was by what some would call an *accident* that Columba had not been made a bishop. The devout minds of his followers may rather have regarded the occurrence as revealing the Divine will. The superior dignity of the episcopal rank may also have been one of the reasons why those who aimed at perfecting the virtue of humility would shun the dignity. But however this may be, that bishops as distinguished from presbyters were well known in the Columban monasteries there cannot be the slightest doubt.

Among the verses of the bard Dallan Forgaill, Columba's contemporary, may be found lines describing the company that attended on the saint when he went to the Council of Drumceatt (see p. 103).

> "Forty Priests was their number:
> Twenty Bishops noble, worthy.
> For singing psalms, a practice without blame,
> Fifty Deacons, thirty Students."

I see no reason to question this statement. It shows us the three orders of the Christian ministry. The bishops are numerous; and, without laying much stress on the poetic effusion, the epithets of honour are applied to the bishops. One may notice in passing that the Diaconate seems to have been something more than, with ourselves in modern times, a mere short probationary period before the priesthood.

To sum up, then, what may be inferred from the sources of information at our disposal. The Bishop in the Columban Church, as a member of the monastic house, was subject to his abbat. But he possessed certain rights and prerogatives that were never infringed by presbyters. There is not a particle of evidence that any but a bishop was ever permitted, or ever attempted, to confer holy orders.[1]

The straits to which the exigence of their position has driven some controversialists, may be sufficiently illustrated by citing a case which has been much relied upon to show that the power of ordination was exercised by presbyters in the Columban Church. The story of Aidan's mission to Northumbria has been already told (p. 159); but it is necessary, in order to appreciate the supposed force of the argument formerly alleged by Presbyterian writers, to have before us the exact words of Bede (*Eccles. Hist.*, lib. iii., c. 5). The historian, after relating how King Oswald had requested that a bishop (*antistes*) should be sent to his kingdom from the province of the Scots, tells how the story ran that the first person sent in response to the request had returned to Iona, and declared in an assembly of the elders (*in conventu seniorum*) his

---

[1] Even in the mediæval Church of Scotland (and the practice is known elsewhere), a bishop was sometimes a canon in his own cathedral, and in that capacity subordinate to the dean. Thus, at Aberdeen, according to the Cathedral Statutes of 1256, the bishop was one of the thirteen canons. See Grub, *Eccles. Hist. of Scot.*, vol. i., p. 334.

hopelessness of effecting the conversion of such a barbarous and intractable people as the Angles, and that Aidan was chosen to undertake the work; "and so ordaining him, they sent him to preach" (*sicque illum ordinantes ad prædicandum miserunt.*) Now, in discussing this passage, it was pointed out, first, that Bede says "ordaining," not "consecrating."[1] But while it is true that in modern times it is customary to use the word "consecrate" when speaking of bishops, and "ordain" when speaking of priests, it is well known to students of ecclesiastical antiquities that "ordain" was in former days constantly used of bishops as well as of the lower orders of the ministry. It would be easy to fill page after page with examples from the Latin Fathers and Western Councils of examples of this use of the word "ordain"; while, on the other hand, the word "consecrate" is frequently used of priests and deacons. It may suffice to quote the very first words cited by John Morinus in his well-known work,[2] as the very earliest account of Latin ordinations, "Let the bishop who is about to be *ordained* be first examined"; while successive Pontificals and other ritual books give us such expressions as "Prayer for bishops about to be *ordained*," "When a bishop is *ordained*," "The *ordination* of a bishop begins thus," "Exhortation to the people when a bishop is *ordained*," etc. But what is more pertinent to our purpose, Bede himself uses the word "ordain"

---

[1] See *A Vindication of the Ecclesiastical Part of Sir James Dalrymple's Historical Collections*, p. 10 sq.
[2] *Commentarius de sacris ecclesiæ ordinationibus*, p. 259 sq.

in his accounts of the consecrations of bishops and archbishops of the Roman communion, of whose episcopal character, as distinguished from presbyters, there has been no question. Thus, speaking of St. Augustine of Canterbury, he writes (lib. i., c. 27), "By the archbishop of the same city [Arles] he [Augustine] was ordained archbishop for the nation of the Angles." Augustine, in turn, "*ordained* two bishops, namely, Mellitus and Justus," for London and Rochester (lib. ii., c. 3). His own successor, Laurence, he also "ordained" for Canterbury, "lest, upon his death, the Church, as yet unsettled, might begin to falter, if it should be destitute of a pastor, though but for one hour" (lib. ii., c. 4). In a later part of his work (lib. iii., c. 28) Bede uses the words "consecrate" and "ordain" without distinction, though employing "ordain" more frequently.[1]

But passing from this point in regard to the word "ordaining," to which perhaps it may be thought more consideration has been given than it deserves, we have to examine the second point, viz., that Bede's account represents those who formed the assembly of seniors (*conventus seniorum*) as discussing the discourse of Aidan, and judging him to be "worthy

---

[1] Bishop Gillan, a learned non-juring divine of the Scottish Church, who acted as Bishop of Dunblane (1731—1735), has given the illustrations of the use of the word from Bede, in his able anonymous pamphlet, *Some Remarks upon Sir James Dalrymple's Historical Collections, with an Answer to the Vindication of the Ecclesiastical part of them.* Gillan falls into some errors of his own, but he gives, on the whole, a very effective reply to Sir James Dalrymple.

of the episcopate," and as "ordaining" him and sending him to King Oswald. The question which arises is—Can we reasonably, with our knowledge of the existence of bishops, properly so called, in the Columban monasteries, and of how the laying on of a bishop's hands was regarded as necessary for ordination to the priesthood (see p. 253), fairly interpret the words, "and so ordaining him," in any other way than as equivalent to "and so causing him to be ordained"? The Roman missionaries were ready enough to dwell on differences, even mere ritual differences, between the British and Scottish Churches on the one hand, and their own on the other; but no complaint was ever made that the Churches of our islands had ventured on such a departure from the universal practice of Christendom as to allow presbyters to ordain a bishop. Indeed, the argument that the "seniors" themselves performed the rite might prove too much even for Presbyterian controversialists; for how do we know that the *seniors* were not most of them, or all of them, merely lay monks? This mode of interpretation of the phrase reminds us of Bishop Colenso's method, who, from the direction in Leviticus (iv. 11, 12), that "the skin of the bullock, and all his flesh, with his head, and with his legs, and his inwards, and his dung, even the whole bullock, shall he (the Priest) carry forth without the camp," etc., seriously constructs the picture of "the Priest having himself to carry on his back on foot [for a distance equal to] from St. Paul's to the outskirts of the Metropolis, the skin, and flesh, and head, and legs, and inwards, and dung, even the whole bullock."[1] Such are the absurdities to which men are driven by a resolution to hold by a pre-assumed conclusion.

As the question has, however, been raised, it may be mentioned that Dr. Bright has collected some passages where it is beyond doubt that the person said to *ordain*, in reality only *caused to be ordained*. Thus the Emperor Otho III., in his decree, writes: " We have elected and ordained Sylvester as Pope." Gregory of Tours also uses the word "ordain" of the action of a king. And it would seem to be similarly used of Kenwalch, king of the West Saxons.[2] Much more important than any elaborate consideration of such a familiar figure of speech, is a recognition of the particular circumstances of the case before us. Oswald, as is probable, after the death of his father, had been hospitably received at Iona, had been there instructed in the Christian faith, and had there been baptized. When he ascended the throne, and asked that a bishop (*antistes*) should be sent him by the Scots, it may surely be presumed that he had learned at Iona what a bishop was, and how much such was needed in a missionary Church. If there were no bishops in the Church where he had received his religious education, it may be well inquired, how came he to esteem them of importance? But Aidan was not sent till he had first received "the grade of the Episcopate" (*Eccles. Hist.*, lib. iii., c. 5). Can we

---

[1] *The Pentateuch and Book of Joshua Critically Examined*, p. 40.
[2] See *Chapters of Early English Church History*, p. 134.

doubt that Bede, who does not scruple to tell us of an "unusual" subjection of the bishops to the Abbat of Hy, would have told us of the incomparably more "unusual" (because absolutely unique) custom of the Scottish presbyters dispensing with the services of the bishops who, as he mentions, were among them, and taking on themselves to ordain a bishop for King Oswald?

More space has been given to the consideration of this incident than it intrinsically deserves. But controversialists had, contrary to the whole drift of the context, pressed a familiar *usus loquendi* into a literalness that gives the lie to history and to commonsense.

The character and the extent of episcopal jurisdiction has varied in different countries and at different times. It has been affected by the canons of Councils, by civil enactments, by the encroachments of monarchs, by Papal usurpations; but "the right of order" has never varied. The question of real importance is, not whether the Scottish bishops of the Columban period possessed such diocesan jurisdiction as was known in later times, but whether they possessed the exclusive power to confer Holy Orders and convey the apostolic commission, and were thus essentially distinguished as a different grade from the presbyters. History leaves no reasonable doubt as to the answer.

CHAPTER XV.

ST. MARGARET OF SCOTLAND.

FOR those who have made no special study in the obscure and confused period of Scottish civil history before the close of the eleventh century, some few historic names have been rescued from oblivion, and made commonly familiar by the genius of Shakespeare. Without considering the accuracy of his presentment of the story, the master's great tragedy has made every one familiar with the figures of Macbeth, of King Duncan, and of Malcolm, the son of the murdered king.

The death of Duncan has been assigned to the year 1040. Malcolm, still in early youth, fled south, and in his exile attained the power of speaking the language of his future English wife. "He grew up into manhood under [Edward] the Confessor's benign protection . . . standing before the Confessor's throne, consorting with the Confessor's knights, sitting at the Confessor's table."[1]

Macbeth (Macbeda) is remarkable as having been

---

[1] Palgrave's *History of England and Normandy*, vol. iv., p. 311.

the only Scottish king who visited Rome. His pilgrimage thither, and the lavish bounty bestowed by him there upon the poor, has been, conjecturally, connected by some modern historians with remorse for his treacherous slaughter of King Duncan. Benefactions to his native church are also recorded. The Register of St. Andrews includes a notice of grants made by him and his queen, Gruoch—the "Lady Macbeth" of Shakespeare—to the Culdee hermits of St. Serf's Inch in Lochleven.

The Malcolm of Shakespeare is Malcolm III., or Malcolm Canmore[1] of history. In 1057 he successfully avenged his father's death, and seated himself upon the throne of Scotland; and some ten years later the record of his life brings before us an interesting and important point of contact between the histories of Scotland and England.

The Battle of Hastings (1066) and its outcome, the establishment of the Norman dynasty, which was the beginning of a new era for England, exercised also important influences, direct and indirect, upon the fortunes of Scotland and the Scottish Church. On the death of Harold, the leading English nobles, with the concurrence of the citizens of London and the Archbishop of York, resolved to raise to the throne Edgar the Ætheling, grandson of Edmund Ironside. The further military successes of William of Normandy induced the temporary submission of Edgar and his adherents. But in 1068 a league was formed for the restoration of Edgar; and to this end the Earl of

---

[1] That is, "of the Great Head," *Ceann-mor*.

Northumberland and Malcolm, king of Scotland, agreed to afford military aid. But William was again triumphant, and Edgar Ætheling, accompanied by his mother and his sisters Margaret and Christina, fled for safety to the court of Malcolm. Soon after their arrival the hand of Margaret was sought by Malcolm, who was then (as some think) a widower, and after much reluctance on her brother's part, and also on her own, due to her desire to devote herself to a life of virginity in a convent, the marriage was celebrated.[1]

Previous to this date the Celtic Church in Scotland had fallen into degenerate ways, when compared with the days of its early fame. Intestine wars and the ravages of the Northmen had destroyed all sense of security, and checked the growth of those Christian labours that demand such sense of security. The early fervour of religion had waxed cold; discipline had relaxed; the civil power had largely encroached on the rights of the Church; lay usurpations of Church property were frequent; the marriage or concubinage of the clergy was not uncommon;[2] and laymen assumed not only the possessions, but dignities and titles properly belonging to churchmen. Thus King Malcolm's father, Duncan, is represented as the son of the "Abbat of Dunkeld," who was, in truth, a powerful military chief, with wide possessions, and who

---

[1] Skene (*Celtic Scotland*, vol. i., p. 422) places the marriage in 1068. Freeman (*Norman Conquest*, vol. iv., p. 782) argues for 1070.

[2] The common surnames, Mactaggart "son of the priest," Macpherson "son of the parson," Macnab "son of the abbat," MacPrior, and MacVicar have been pointed to in this connection.

had married a daughter of Malcolm II. Even St. Margaret's own son, Ethelred, was as a youth lay "Abbat of Dunkeld."

The disregard of the sanctity of the Lord's Day was widespread; certain near degrees of affinity were regarded as no bar to marriage; and there were several strange usages in ecclesiastical order and ceremonial that naturally surprised and offended the Saxon princess.

We are so fortunate as to possess a contemporary account of Queen Margaret's mode of life at her husband's court.[1] The title—the *Life of St. Margaret* —is misleading, for it supplies us with no consecutive biography or connected history of events, but only with some interesting and graphic pictures, helping us to conceive with clearness her daily round of duties and devotions, together with some notices of her last hours. This account was written at the request of Matilda ("the good Queen Maude"), daughter of Malcolm and Margaret, and wife of Henry I., king of England,[2] by whose marriage the blood of the old Saxon kings was united with that of the Norman sovereigns. The writer of the *Life* was an ecclesiastic who was on terms

---

[1] The *Life of St. Margaret* is printed by the Bollandists in the *Acta Sanctorum* (June 10). This text was reprinted by Pinkerton (1789) in his *Vitæ Antiquæ Sanctorum, etc.*, of which, after a century, a new edition appeared, *Lives of the Scottish Saints*, edited by Metcalf (1889). The Surtees Society have printed the *Life* (in vol. 51 of their publications) from a different text from that published by the Bollandists.

[2] Thus Queen Victoria is a lineal descendant of St. Margaret of Scotland. The Stuart line enters our Queen's genealogy through the marriage from another English princess, Margaret Tudor, sister of Henry VIII., with James IV.

of very close intimacy with Queen Margaret, and had been, apparently, her confessor, and who, with the almost universal concurrence of scholars,[1] is identified with Turgot, at one time Prior of Durham, and who subsequently was made Bishop of St. Andrews (Aug. 1, 1109—Aug. 31, 1115).

When at the request of a queen the biography of her mother was undertaken by a mediæval ecclesiastic, it was scarcely possible but that the result should be a highly laudatory *éloge*. But making the allowances needful under the circumstances, one cannot read the *Life of Queen Margaret* without being convinced that it gives us a substantially true account of a good and pious woman, of much intellectual capacity and force of character.

From the history of Simeon of Durham,[2] we learn something of the ruthless and ferocious character of the man who was to be Margaret's future husband. Just at the time of the arrival in Scotland of Edgar with his mother and sisters, Malcolm's army was returning from a terrible inroad into the English possessions. The sacred territory of St. Cuthbert was ravaged. The order went forth that none were to be spared. The old, both men and women, were slaughtered, in the language of Simeon, "like swine." Infants snatched from the breast were flung up by the

---

[1] The Bollandist editor, Papebroch, on the authority of the MS. which supplied his text, assigns the *Life* to a contemporary monk of Durham, named Theodoric. But Fordun cites the book as Turgot's, and it is assigned to him in the British Museum text.

[2] *Simeonis Dunelm. Opp.* (Surtees Society, vol. 51).

Scottish soldiers "in sport" into the air, and caught upon the points of their lances. Churches and those who sought refuge in them were given to the flames. The young of both sexes were dragged in bonds to Scotland.[1] There was no Scottish household so poor that it might not possess an English slave. Allowance no doubt must be made for the hideously cruel character of warfare at the time; William of Normandy had set a fearful example. Margaret had certainly no easy task before her in her efforts to soften and mould the disposition of this fierce soldier.

The king's devoted affection to his queen is exhibited by Turgot in one of the most beautiful passages in the story. "I was astonished, I confess," he writes, "at this great miracle of God's mercy, when I perceived in the king at times such earnestness in prayer, and, in the heart of a man living in the world, such compunction for sin." "She taught him by her exhortation and by her example to pray to God with heartfelt groanings and tears." "*There was in him a sort of dread of offending one whose life was so worthy of veneration*, for he saw that Christ in very deed dwelt within her; yea, he hastened to obey in all things her wishes and wise counsels." "With God's help, she made him most ready to concur in works of justice, mercy, almsgiving, and other virtues." But more valuable than these general statements is the

---

[1] Hill Burton writes: "The Scots king swept Northumberland with a ferocity and cruelty which, beyond all the other bloody raids of the period, have left this one as a memorable story of calamity in the English chronicles" (*History of Scotland*, vol. i., p. 375).

vivid picture presented to us in the following words: "Although he was ignorant of letters, he would turn over and examine the books which she used either for prayer or study; and whenever he heard her express especial affection for a particular book, he too would regard it with special affection, kissing it and often touching it with his hands. Sometimes he sent for a goldsmith whom he would command to ornament the volume handsomely with gold and gems. And when the work was finished the king himself would carry the book back to the queen as a loving proof of his devotion" (cap. ii., sec. 11).

In this connection may be mentioned the only incident related by Turgot which savours of the miraculous; for it is remarkable, and adds to our respect for the general trustworthiness of the narrative, that it is singularly free from the supernatural marvels which corruscate with such brilliance and frequency in hagiological literature. Among St. Margaret's treasures was a beautifully-illuminated Book of the Gospels, adorned with gold and gems. The figures of the four Evangelists were painted and gilt, and all the capital letters throughout the volume were brilliant with gold. One day, through the carelessness of the bearer in crossing a ford, it fell into the water. It was long sought, and at last discovered lying open in the depth of the stream! The current had carried away the slips of silk which were inserted to protect the illuminated capitals. Yet, strange to say, it was quite uninjured, except for some very slight stains of damp on the last leaves. "Whatever others may think," says Turgot, "I believe that this wonder was wrought by our Lord out of His love for this venerated queen." I see no reason whatever for supposing, as Hill Burton (*Hist. of Scotland*, vol. i., p. 382) imagines, that Turgot's *Life* of the queen was written with the object of obtaining for her an authoritative recognition "in the calendar of saints." It is substantially a truthful portraiture, singularly free from vulgar marvels. The recovery and identification a few years ago of what seems certainly to be the very volume referred to, in the story above related, is one of the most curious of the surprises that meet us from time to time in bibliographical history. Queen Margaret's precious "Book of the Gospels" is now one of the treasures of the Bodleian Library.[1]

In connection with the credibility of this story, which Turgot, it will be observed, relates at second-hand, it may be well to recall a remark previously made on the importance of a study of what we may call "comparative hagiology." It was the correct thing for a saint's books not to be injured by water. Thus, in Adamnan's *Life of St. Columba* (lib. ii., c. 8), we find how a volume written by the saint after being for twenty days in the river Boyne was dry and wholly uninjured. Again, a book of hymns in the saint's handwriting, after lying in a river from Christmas to Whitsuntide, was similarly protected. And in an ancient Irish life of St. Columba, contained in the manuscript known as *Leabhar Breac*,

[1] See Appendix III.

now in the library of the Royal Irish Academy, we read—

> "Three hundred splendid, lasting books
> Noble-bright he wrote.

Whatever book, moreover, his hand would write, how long soever it would be under water, not even one letter in it would be obliterated." Again, Simeon of Durham (*Hist. Eccl. Dunelm*, lib. ii., c. 12) relates, with reference to the Lindisfarne Gospels (see p. 183), that on an occasion of the monk's attempting to cross to Ireland in the ninth century, the precious volume fell into the sea, but after three days it was discovered on the coast of Whithorn, with only a few stains of water, which it still exhibits. Here, in this last case, we have the same careful qualification, which might seem to give an air of truthfulness to the miracle of St. Margaret's book.[1]

Margaret was a good mother no less than a good

---

[1] To the remarks here made the following interesting passage may be added: "In the Annals of Clonmacnois the translator, Connell Macgeoghegan, has alluded to the belief in Ireland respecting the peculiar property of St. Columba's MSS. in resisting the influence of moisture, in which he refers to the Book of Durrow. 'He, *i. e.* Columba, wrote 300 books with his own hand. They were all New Testaments; he left a book to each of his churches in the kingdom, which books have a strange property, which is, that if they, or any of them, had sunk to the bottom of the deepest waters, they would not lose one letter, or sign, or character of them, which I have seen tried partly by myself on that book of them which is at Dorowe (Durrow) in the King's Co., for I saw the ignorant man that had the same in his custody, when sickness came on cattle, for their remedy put water on the book and suffer it to rest therein, and saw also cattle return thereby to their former state, and the book receive no loss.'"—Miss Stokes' *Early Christian Art in Ireland*, p. 20

wife. The member of the household entrusted with the charge of her children was authorized and enjoined to use strictness and even corporal chastisement whenever it was necessary, and in the result we know that the pains bestowed on "the godly upbringing" of her sons and daughters were not in vain. During the reigns of three of her six sons—Edgar, Alexander, and David—much was done in many directions under their favouring care for the well-being of the Scottish people and the advancement of religion; and in the purity of their lives these monarchs contrast in a favourable way with the prevailing licentiousness of too many of their contemporaries elsewhere. Edmund is the only one of her children who is said to have fallen away for a time from the religious standard set by their mother's example; but repentance marked his after life, and its sincerity was testified by his abandoning a life of pleasure in the world for the seclusion of the cloister.[1] Her two daughters, Matilda and Mary, were educated in the convent of Romsey, under their mother's sister Christina, who was abbess. A question afterwards arose as to the lawfulness of the projected marriage of Matilda with the King of England. The archbishop, Anselm, and a council of prelates at Lambeth examined into the case, and it was proved that Matilda, though wearing the religious habit as a protection from the licentious violence of the Normans, had never taken the vows; and, to the joy of the English people, she became "the good Queen Maude" of history.

[1] Edmund became a monk at Montacute, in Somersetshire.

The court of Scotland during Margaret's life was marked by the rare combination of much splendour and much strictness of manners. The increase of material prosperity showed itself in the abundance of rich plate, mostly of gold and silver, that now adorned the king's table. At the instance of the queen, foreign merchants brought their wares, hitherto unknown, to Scotland; fabrics of divers colours were now purchased by the people for their dress, and new fashions in costume made their way.[1] She insisted on a larger and more dignified retinue attending upon the king in all his public appearances, and the palace and court exhibited a magnificence entirely new to Scotland. Margaret herself thought it her duty to maintain in all outward forms the state and dignity of the Queen of Scotland; but her life was, nevertheless, one of extraordinary religious severity. Turgot declares that in his experience he had never known any one, of whatever rank or position, so given to prayer, fasting, and works of mercy. More especially did she mark the forty days before Christmas and the forty days of Lent. We may notice, in passing, that as early as the seventh century, as we find from Bede (*Eccles. Hist.*, lib. iii., c. 27 ; lib. iv., c. 30), the forty days' fast before the feast of the Nativity was practised, at least by the more devout, in England. At

---

[1] Margaret's father, Edward, had been brought up in Hungary, and there she herself had been born, and there had spent her early years, before her father and his family were invited back to England (1057) by Edward the Confessor. Her notions of the world and its commerce must have been wider than those which would naturally belong to a native-born Scottish lady.

these seasons, the queen, after taking some rest in the beginning of the night, went to the church, and there said, first, the "Matins of the Holy Trinity," then, the "Matins of the Holy Cross," and then, the "Matins of the Blessed Virgin." Then she began the "Office of the Dead"; and after that the Psalter, which, according to Turgot, she would sometimes on holy days recite completely even twice or thrice. And before the celebration of the public mass on holy days she would have five or six masses sung in her presence. The maintenance of an intelligent attention throughout such prolonged services we may with confidence declare to be impossible; and the belief in the efficacy of a mechanical repetition of words could not fail to be fostered by the laudations freely bestowed upon such practices as those of St. Margaret. But for us it is of interest to know what were esteemed in the eleventh century as the marks and tokens of an especially devout mind.[1]

After matins and lauds were finished, St. Margaret, together with the king, washed the feet of six poor persons, and gave them alms. She then went to take some sleep. When it was day she rose and again

---

[1] It may, perhaps, be worth observing that "Hours of the Holy Cross" was certainly, at a later period, a favourite form of devotion. At matins, the betrayal of our Lord was commemorated; at prime, His mocking; at tierce, His scourging; at sext, His crucifixion; at nones, His death; at evensong, His descent from the Cross; at compline, His burial. An early translation, in north-country English, of the York "Hours of the Cross" will be found in Canon Simmons' *Lay Folks Mass Book* (p. 82, *sq.*). See, too, Maskell's *Monumenta Ritualia*, vol. iii., p. 10 *sq.*

devoted herself to prayers and reading the Psalter, intermingled with such works of charity as the tending of little orphan children, whom she took—says her biographer—on her knee, and fed "with her own spoon." Three hundred poor people were then brought into the great hall, and having been seated in order, the king and queen entered, and in the presence of only the chaplains and a few others, served the tables, the king on one side and the queen on the other, and "waited upon Christ in His poor." The queen then returned to the church. Then, when it was time for the queen's own repast, she first waited upon twenty-four poor persons, who were by her orders especially attached to the court, and accompanied her in her various progresses. She was at all times very sparing in her own food; but during the fasts of Lent and Advent her severity with herself was so great that she brought on a painful ailment, from which she suffered till the day of her death.

In her manners the queen was bright and animated, but her mirth never descended to loud laughter. She could be severe when severity was needed, as the Psalmist counsels when he says, "Be ye angry and sin not." [1]

The queen's gifts to the Church were many and splendid. The church dedicated to the Holy Trinity [2]

---

[1] The editor of the Surtees edition of the *Life of St. Margaret* tells us this verse is to be found in Ephesians iv. 26, and *not* in the Psalms. He was evidently not as familiar with the Psalter as Queen Margaret or her biographer, or he would have found *Irascimini et nolite peccare* at Psalm iv. 5.

[2] The interesting Abbey Church at Dunfermline, which in several of its features reminds one of Durham Cathedral, was completed by Margaret's son, David I., and dedicated in 1150.

at Dunfermline, the principal royal residence, was erected by her, and she bestowed upon it many gifts, such as vessels of pure and solid gold for the service of the altar, and a superb cross covered with gold, silver, and precious stones. Another magnificent cross was given to St. Andrews, and her ladies of rank were constantly engaged in the embroidery of "copes for the cantors, chasubles, stoles, altar-cloths, and other ecclesiastical vestments and ornaments." It may be noticed that the embroidery with gold wire or thread of gold attained such excellence in England that it was known as *Opus Anglicum*, and doubtless the Saxon princess saw very quickly the poverty and meagreness of the Scottish ecclesiastical ornaments as compared with those with which she had been familiar in earlier days. Ladies of royal blood like St. Etheldreda, the four daughters of Edward the Elder, and Emma, the wife of King Canute, had long before made themselves famous for their skill in such labours as these. From another source, the Norman chronicler Ordericus Vitalis (lib. viii., c. 22), we learn that Margaret rebuilt the ruined monastery of Iona.

The queen was, we are told, much addicted to visiting the anchorites, who were to be found in many parts of Scotland. She entreated their prayers, and, not being able to induce them to accept any gift, she begged them to enjoin upon her some act of charity or mercy, which she punctually fulfilled. It will be remembered that Lochleven (see p. 202) was only a few miles from Dunfermline; and the Chartulary of St. Andrews (p. 202) records a grant of land from

Malcolm and Margaret to God Almighty and the Keledei of Lochleven. In the reign of Alexander, Margaret's son, we know there was an anchorite living in the island of Inchcolm in the Forth, a short distance from the village of Aberdour. This island would also have been of easy access from Dunfermline.

St. Andrews was at that time much frequented by pilgrims from all quarters; to be of service to those coming from the south, the queen ordered the erection of houses on both sides of the Firth of Forth, where the travellers could be sheltered and entertained till they could be ferried over. In stormy weather these pilgrims might be detained on either shore for many days together. Ships for conveying them across were also provided, and no charge was allowed to be made.

Naturally the pitiable condition of the English slaves in Scotland roused the compassion of the good queen. She had inquiry made in all parts of Scotland for cases of special hardship or ill-usage, and none could tell the number of those whom she ransomed and restored to liberty.

The chapter of St. Margaret's *Life* which has excited most interest among ecclesiastical antiquarians is that in which is related her efforts to bring the native Church into conformity with the discipline and usages of the Church in which she had been brought up. We are told that at her instance frequent "councils" were held to effect her object. But the most remarkable of these was one in which she herself, attended by a very few of her own way of thinking (perhaps the three English brethren, who, as we learn from a letter of her early instructor, Lanfranc, he had at her request despatched to the Scottish Court), debated for three days the points at issue between her and the native ecclesiastics. It would appear that, while the queen conversed in the English tongue, the Scottish representatives carried on the debate in Gaelic, for Malcolm—who, we are told, spoke English as well as his own tongue—is represented as acting the part of interpreter on both sides.

The first point discussed was what the queen, with pardonable ignorance, regarded as a novel and foreign usage, viz., beginning Lent, not on Ash Wednesday, but on the Monday following. As is now well known, the practice to which Margaret objected was simply a survival of ancient usage, at one time common in Western Christendom. Gregory the Great is generally credited, though perhaps on insufficient grounds, with having added Ash Wednesday and the three following days to the Lenten fast in the Church of Rome, but the ordinance was not everywhere followed; and even to this day the great Church of St. Ambrose at Milan, following in this, as in several other particulars, its own rite, observes Lent in conformity with the usage which St. Margaret regarded with such distress.[1]

[1] See Bingham's *Antiquities*, book xxi., chap. i., and the article "Lent" in Smith and Cheetham's *Dict. of Chr. Antiq.*. The remarkable variety as to the length of time observed for the Lent fast, particularly in the East, is brought out clearly by the historian Socrates (v. 22). Mr. Warren (*Liturgy and Ritual of the Celtic Church*, p. 7) is disposed to see a trace of the more ancient practice in the Sarum direction to cover up all crosses, etc. on *the first Monday* in Lent.

The second point at issue was the non-reception of the Eucharist on Easter Day. This most extraordinary practice was certainly no relic of ancient Columban Christianity, as it appears in Adamnan (*Vita Columbæ*, lib. ii., c. 39) we have express reference to reception at the Paschal solemnity. The Scottish opponents of the queen cited the warning of St. Paul against "eating and drinking unworthily." The queen promptly replied, "Shall then none who are sinners taste of the sacred mysteries? None, not even the infant of a day old, is without the stain of sin.[1] If none ought to receive, why does the Lord say in the Gospel, 'Unless ye shall eat the flesh of the Son of Man, and drink His blood, ye shall have no life in you'?" She then explained the words of St. Paul in their true sense; and the overwhelming force of her argument was admitted. Lord Hailes (*Ann. of Scot.*, vol. i., p. 42) is doubtless quite mistaken in inferring from this passage that "the clergy of Scotland had ceased to celebrate the communion of the Lord's Supper," if he means that they had ceased to celebrate mass. But it seems to me that the argument adduced by the supporters of the Scottish practice indicates that reception beyond that of the celebrant had generally ceased. There is no hint (as Mr. Joseph Robertson (*Stat. Eccl. Scot.*, I. xxiii.) would suggest) that the objection was based on

[1] This argument may perhaps point to a continuance of the universal practice in the ancient Church of communicating infants. Some years after Queen Margaret's death, we have a notice of the usage at Poictiers, and traces of the practice lingered in France for centuries after that time. See Scudamore's *Notitia Eucharistica*, 2nd edit., p. 55.

a regard for the special *sanctity of Easter*. The conclusion that I regard as most probable is, that the laity never communicated except at the hour of death. The Book of Deer (see p. 239) contains the formula for communicating the sick, and hence I make the exception. It has been remarked that at the present day, in some parts of the Scottish Highlands, among the more rigid Presbyterians to avoid reception is considered the mark of a scrupulous piety.

The third point had reference to the ritual of the mass. Turgot tells us that "in some places there were some of the Scots who, contrary to the usage of the whole Church, had been accustomed to celebrate mass with some barbarous rite or other (*nescio quo ritu barbaro*)." The queen was much scandalized, and so exerted herself that henceforth there was not one in the whole nation of the Scots that would presume to follow the objectionable practices. I am quite unable to accept Skene's view that the barbarous rite consisted in the Scottish vernacular being used instead of Latin. There is, so far as I know, not a particle of evidence in support of this contention; and one can hardly doubt that such a startling deviation from general practice would have been expressly noticed and commented on by the queen's biographer. Much more likely, as I take it, is the supposition that some varieties of ceremonial (see p. 238) and, perhaps, of the language of the missal, would have grievously offended the queen. Any practice with which she was not familiar in her much-loved English Church would easily enough be reckoned as "barbarous" by her.[1]

The fourth question in debate was the general disregard of the sanctity of the Lord's Day, so that ordinary labour was carried on as on other days. The queen contended for the veneration due to the Lord's Day on account of the Lord's resurrection, and Pope Gregory was cited by her in support of her view. In this matter also she was completely successful, so that no one would even carry a burden on the sacred day or require any other person to do so.[2]

The last point pressed by St. Margaret at this council belonged rather to the region of morals than of mere ecclesiastical order. Marriage with a stepmother, and of a woman with her deceased husband's brother, had been customs in Scotland. These customs were henceforth in Scotland rigidly suppressed. From Augustine of Canterbury's question to Pope Gregory whether men might marry their step-mothers, we learn that this practice existed in southern Britain in the sixth century (Bede, *Eccles. Hist.*, lib. i., c. 27); and nearly a century after St. Margaret's time this offensive custom was still common among the Irish. In Ireland also marriage with a brother's widow was frequent.

Turgot adds that the queen succeeded in expelling

---

[1] Such extraordinary regulations, for instance, as those described at p. 235, if they came to the knowledge of the queen, might not unnaturally have been reckoned by her as constituting a "barbarous rite."

[2] Skene's notion that Saturday was observed as a day of rest in the Columban Church seems wholly without foundation. See *Celtic Scotland*, vol. ii., p. 350.

many other abuses; but these he does not specify. Apart from the interest that attaches to the picture presented of the personal character of the good queen, this section dealing with the differences between the practices of Scottish and English Christianity at the close of the eleventh century is the most important part of the *Life*. It is to be regretted that Turgot did not enter into particulars more fully.

Margaret's success as a controversialist may have been, we may suspect, in large measure due to the fact, related by Turgot, that Malcolm was prepared both to say and *do* whatever she might direct as to the questions at issue. He was not a man to be trifled with.

In 1093, Malcolm and his eldest son Edward advanced with an army into Northumberland. He was entrapped, as it would seem, by the Earl, Robert of Mowbray, into an ambush, and fell by the sword, together with the prince and heir to the throne, not far from the town of Alnwick. His troops were wholly dispersed—some fled, some were slain in battle, and others were swept away in trying to cross the swollen river Alne. Two of the country people placed the king's forsaken body on a cart, and conveyed it to Tynemouth, where it was buried.

While Malcolm was absent on this expedition, his wife was lying afflicted with sore sickness in the Castle of Edinburgh. At an interview with Turgot, some considerable time before, she had anticipated that she was not destined for a long life. Bidding him farewell, she made two solemn requests—first that he would remember her in his prayers, and, secondly, that he would watch over the spiritual welfare of her dear sons and daughters, above all begging him to warn any of them whom he saw in danger of being puffed up by the dignity of earthly state, not to neglect the happiness of the life which is eternal. Her last sickness was tedious and painful. For more than half a year she was seldom able to rise from her bed. She was attended by a priest, who afterwards became a monk of Durham, and who related the closing incidents of her life to Turgot. She was naturally full of anxiety about the king, whom she had entreated not to go with the army; and the expression of her apprehensions, upon a day which afterwards proved to be the day of the king's death, was regarded as something very remarkable. On the fourth day after the king's death, and while yet in ignorance of the event, feeling a little stronger, she rose and went to the oratory [1] to hear mass, and to partake of "the holy viaticum of the body and blood of the Lord." She returned to her bed much worse, and she begged the priest and other ministers of the altar to stand near and recite the psalms for the commendation of a departing soul. She also asked that the Black Cross of Scotland should

---

[1] The oratory here spoken of may be the little chapel of St. Margaret on the summit of the Castle Rock. This chapel is the oldest building in Edinburgh. In estimating the age of buildings of this period, it is too often forgotten that the Norman style had made itself sensibly felt in Britain before the Norman Conquest. In 1845 this building was used as a powder magazine for firing occasional salutes from the neighbouring battery.

be brought her,[1] and, holding it before her eyes with both her hands, she repeated the whole of the Fiftieth Psalm (*i. e.* the Fifty-first, according to the numbering followed in our Bible and Prayer-book). At this point her son Edgar, who had escaped from the fatal expedition, entered the room. The queen at once inquired about his father and brother. Fearing to make known the terrible truth, he replied that they were well. She, with a deep sigh, cried, "I know it, my son, I know it. By this Holy Cross, by the tie of our blood, I adjure thee to tell me the truth." Under this pressure Edgar related the facts. Then, raising both her eyes and her hands to heaven, she exclaimed, "All praise to Thee, Almighty God, who hast been pleased that I should suffer this deep sorrow at my departing, and I trust that by this suffering it is Thy pleasure that I should be purified from some of the stains of my sins." Then she prayed in words taken from the service of the mass, "Lord Jesus Christ,

---

[1] The Black Rood was a gold cross set with diamonds, containing, as in a reliquary which opened and shut, "a portion of the true Cross." The figure of the Saviour, which ornamented it, was carved out of massive ivory. The queen had brought it with her to Scotland, and it is generally said to have received its name from the black case in which it was preserved. The queen's youngest son, David, afterwards built the abbey-church of Holy Rood, outside the city of Edinburgh, perhaps in its honour. The Black Rood was carried off to England by Edward I.; but it was restored, to the indignation of the English, by Queen Isabella in 1327, on the demand of Robert Bruce. In 1346 David II. took the precious relic with the army into England, and on his defeat at the battle of Neville's Cross, near Durham, the Black Rood fell into the hands of the victors, and was deposited in Durham Cathedral, where up to the Reformation it was exposed for veneration in the south aisle.

who according to the Father's will, by the operation of the Holy Spirit, hast by Thy death given life to the world, deliver me." As she uttered the words "deliver me," her soul departed to Christ. Her body was removed to Dunfermline, and deposited in the church which she had built, and, as she directed, opposite the altar. The remains of her husband were afterwards removed from his English grave, and buried by the body of his queen.[1]

It is a noteworthy and significant fact that shortly before his death Malcolm Canmore had ceased to hold, as part of the kingdom of Scotland, Iona, the sacred burying-place of Scottish kings, the birthplace, and for so many long years the fostering home, of Celtic Christianity. In the same year Fothad, the last of the Celtic bishops of St. Andrews, died.

With St. Margaret one great chapter of Scottish Church history closes and another is begun. The peculiar characteristics of Celtic Christianity rapidly

[1] The general sentiment of the Scottish people is commonly thought to have been formally sanctioned in 1250 or 1251 by Pope Innocent IV., when, according to Papebroch (followed by Alban Butler), St. Margaret was canonized. But the publication in 1864 of Theiner's *Vetera Monumenta Hibernorum et Scotorum historiam illustrantia*, has raised a serious doubt on this question, for we find in a document there printed (p. 499), Innocent VIII. in 1487 addressing a letter to the Archbishop of St. Andrews, the Bishop of Glasgow, and others, in reference to a petition of King James for the canonization of Margaret, formerly Queen of Scotland. It seems to me that no other Margaret than the wife of Malcolm Canmore answers satisfactorily the conditions of the case. At all events, long before this time the Saxon Margaret, if not formally canonized at Rome, was regarded by the Scottish people as a saint, and her cultus was well established.

T

disappear and the mediæval Church in Scotland in its faith, discipline, ritual, and organization is entirely akin to the mediæval Church in the kingdom of England. "The old Celtic Church," in the words of Skene (*Celtic Scotland*, vol. ii., p. 417), "came to an end, leaving no vestiges behind it, save here and there the roofless walls of what had once been a church, and the numerous old burying-grounds, to which the people still cling with tenacity, and where occasionally an ancient Celtic cross tells of its former state. All else has disappeared; and the only records we have of their history are the names of the saints by whom they were founded, preserved in old calendars, the fountains [wells] near the old churches bearing their name, the village fairs of immemorial antiquity held on their day, and here and there a few lay families holding a small portion of land, as hereditary custodiers of the pastoral staff or other relic of the reputed founder of the Church, with some small remains of its jurisdiction."

Turgot records neither the day nor the year of St. Margaret's death. But we learn from Simeon of Durham and other English chroniclers that Malcolm's defeat and death took place on "St. Brice's Day" (*i. e.* 13 Nov.) 1093; and so in accordance with Turgot's narrative the death of St. Margaret is placed on November 16. At this date St. Margaret is placed by the *Aberdeen Breviary;* and at this date "Margaret Queen" is entered correctly in the Kalendar of the Book of Common Prayer, prepared for Scotland under Laud's sanction, and published in 1637. It is somewhat amusing to find Pope Innocent XII. in 1693 removing the Feast of St. Margaret to June 10, at the instance of King James II. of England, that being the birthday of his son, "the old Chevalier." This was a rather singular mode of paying a compliment.

CHAPTER XVI.

THE ARCHÆOLOGY OF THE CELTIC CHURCH IN SCOTLAND IN ITS HISTORICAL RELATIONS.

We have seen that the documentary remains of Celtic Christianity in Scotland are few, and, with the exception of the invaluable work of Adamnan, meagre and unsatisfying. The remains of a material kind are more numerous, though they are scanty, compared with similar productions in Ireland.[1]

Buildings.—The architectural relics of the ancient Scottish Christianity consist of a few small and ruined churches, chiefly in the Western Highlands, and here and there the remains of bee-hive cells of stone, which gave shelter to monks or to the solitary anchorite, together with a number of high-crosses and monumental stones.

The remains of Celtic Christianity in Scotland and Ireland ought properly to be studied together. Just

---

[1] A very thorough treatment of the Christian archæology of Scotland will be found in Dr. Joseph Anderson's masterly work, entitled *Scotland in Early Christian Times*, in two series, to which I am deeply indebted throughout this chapter. Dr. Anderson is chiefly concerned, however, with archæology proper, and not with archæology in its relation to history.

as Roman remains at Treves, or at Lincoln and York, find their proper illustrations in Italy, so the scanty relics of early Scottish art and architecture are to be rightly understood by a reference to Ireland. The same types recur in both countries, but in number and excellence the Irish work far surpasses all that has survived to our time in Scotland.

We have already noticed that the remains of early Celtic Christianity at its Scottish centre, Iona, have perished. The visitor to the island may perhaps be persuaded that he sees in an elevated ridge with flattened top the remains of the *cashel*, or *vallum*, which protected the ancient monastery, and a pile of stones to the west of the island, to be found with difficulty, may possibly be the remains of a cell. It is impossible to fix the date of the two high-crosses that alone remain, though they are certainly both very distinctly of the Celtic type. Everything else represents the work of the mediæval Church.

Not far from Iona to the south, between Mull and Scarba, is Eilean-na-Naoimh, one of the Garveloch islands, or "Isles of the Sea." Reeves and Skene concur in identifying it with the Hinba of the *Life of St. Columba*. Here we find a small church, twenty-one feet in length, dry-built of undressed stones. It has in the east end one small square-headed window, widely splayed both inside and outside, and a square-headed doorway in the west end, the jambs of the door being inclined so that the entrance is narrower at the top than at the bottom. Close to the shore is a bee-hive cell, the roof of which has fallen in. If the identification with Hinba is correct, the humble church of this island held at the same time within its sacred walls five men, each one of whom made his lasting mark upon the history of the Gospel in our islands; and close beneath that little window St. Columba celebrated the Holy Mysteries in the presence of St. Brendan, St. Cainnech, St. Comgall, and St. Cormac (see p. 113).

The remains of similar cells, but in this instance surrounded by a *cashel*, or rampart, may be seen on what was formerly an island in Loch Columcille in Skye. The little church of Columcille close by is just the same length as that at Eilean-na-Naoimh.

Close by the great cliff of the promontory of

Deerness, in Orkney, is a little island on which are the ruins of a group of eighteen cells of uncemented stone, together with a little church, of dimensions similar to those described above. Whatever doubts may exist as to the dates of these structures, " they reveal to us," as Dr. Anderson remarks, "a typical form, of which it can be said with truth that no earlier is known to exist, or is likely now to be discovered." [1]

Though, as was natural to expect, no remains of them have survived, documentary evidence makes it certain that churches in the early part of the Celtic period were not unfrequently constructed of timber, which churches were perhaps contemporaneous in some instances with the small structures of stone already described. Thus there is some reason to believe that the church erected by St. Columba at Iona was of wood. Indeed Bede (*Eccl. Hist.*, lib. iii., c. 25) speaks of churches of wood as characteristic of the northern builders, when he tells us that the Scottish Finan (see p. 177) built his cathedral at Lindisfarne "not of stone, but wholly of hewn timber after the manner of the Scots, and he roofed it with a thatch of reeds." Again, in 710, Naiton, king of the Picts (see p. 146), whose sympathies were not with the Columban monks in their adherence to their distinctive Easter computation and their characteristic tonsure, asks Ceolfrid to send him architects "who would make in his nation a church *of stone* after the manner of the Romans" (*Eccl. Hist.*, lib. v., c. 21). The wooden structure of Iona apparently gave

---

[1] *Scotland in Early Christian Times.* First Series, p. 106.

place to a stone building after the incursions of the Northmen had shown what an easy prey to fire the wooden buildings had been (see p. 195).

Chancelled churches, with some few doubtful exceptions, belong to the period when Norman influence made itself felt. One chamber, one door, one window characterize the earliest work in stone. In such primitive erections, or in wooden structures, the great missionary saints celebrated the worship of God.

Round Towers.—One of the most curious and interesting features of the ecclesiastical architecture of Ireland is exhibited in the Round Towers, of which no less than one hundred and eighteen specimens, either perfect or fragmentary, were known to exist at the beginning of the century.[1] In Scotland at least two[2] buildings of the same type remain, both, happily, all but perfect—one at Brechin, in Forfarshire, the other at Abernethy in Perthshire—both, it will be seen, in the eastern part of Scotland. The former is 86 feet 9 inches high (omitting the height of the later octagonal cap), the latter (which has no cap) is 72 feet. As in the prevailing Irish type, they stand free of any other buildings. The doors are at some distance from the ground, and must originally have been

---

[1] See Miss Stokes' *Early Christian Art in Ireland*, p. 164. Lord Dunraven, *Notes on Irish Architecture*, places the number at present in Ireland as seventy-six.

[2] The round tower, structurally connected with the church, in Egilsay (a small island of the Orkneys) presents more perplexing problems than could be discussed here with advantage. The reader is referred to Dr. Anderson's work already referred to.

entered with the help of a ladder. The purpose of these buildings was long doubtful, but is now generally agreed upon by archæologists. Everything points to their having been used as places of security for the ecclesiastics with their treasure of sacred bells, croziers, shrines, and other relics, against the raids of pillagers. Their Irish name *cloictheach* (bell-house) may be simply the translation of the name *campanile*, that was given to the buildings on the Continent which suggested this form, and which were really used as bell-towers. But whatever difficulty is suggested by the *name*, we possess no bells of the Celtic period of any considerable size (see p. 304), or such as would make it an object to build towers of this kind in which they might be hung; and the Irish annalists leave us in no doubt that the Towers were used as places of refuge in sudden emergency. They were certainly well fitted to afford a valuable protection, if their occupants were likely to be before long relieved by a friendly force. Such emergency might at any time arise, not only from the incursions of the Northmen, but from intestine feuds and tribal wars. The following passages cited in Petrie's *Essay on the Origin and Use of the Round Towers of Ireland* make clear, what indeed we might ourselves have concluded from an inspection of the buildings, that while highly serviceable as a protection in sudden raids, they were not fitted to sustain any lengthened and organized attack from a powerful enemy.

"A.D. 948. The *cloictheach* of Slane was burned by the Danes, with its full of reliques, with

Caoinechair, Reader of Slane, and the crozier of the patron saint, and a bell—the best of bells."—*Annals of the Four Masters.*

"A.D. 1097. The *cloictheach* of the Monastery, *i. e.* of Monasterboice, with many books and treasures, was burnt."—*Annals of the Four Masters.*

Architectural reasons induce Dr. Anderson to believe that the Brechin Tower must be referred to a period at least later than the first half of the tenth century. More than this cannot be said with certainty. Boece tells us that the Danes assailed Brechin and its church in the reign of Malcolm II. (1001-1031), and burned it. This only shows that the place, easily approached from the sea at Montrose, was such as might well warrant the construction of a place of defence and refuge. But the evidence goes no further.

Dr. Petrie is confident that the age of the Abernethy Tower is "much greater than that of Brechin," and places it in the early part of the eighth century. To this conclusion, however, Dr. Anderson gives reason for demurring. And at present we can say no more with absolute confidence. But if the two Scottish Round Towers were suggested by those in Ireland, we are led to believe that Dr. Petrie has very unduly antedated the structure at Abernethy. "The annalists of Ireland do not refer to such buildings till the year 950; and in the entries regarding the attacks of the Northmen from 789 to 845 it is recorded that the clergy fled for safety into the woods, where they celebrated the divine mysteries, and spent their days in prayer and fasting; but in the year 950, and for two centuries later, we read of the 'cloiccthech,' house of a bell, as a special object of attack to the Northmen."[1]

I would only add that the entire absence of such buildings from the west of Scotland seems to me also to point to the late date of the Brechin and Abernethy Towers, as suggesting the time when the centre of the Scottish ecclesiastical system had passed from the west and been well established in the east of Scotland. It was to Ireland the monks of Iona would naturally carry off their sacred treasure in the case of a threatened raid of the Northmen. And in a spot so isolated as Iona, the defence afforded by a Round Tower, useful as it would have been for a temporary asylum, would be of little lasting value, as the chance of the relief of the occupants from outside would be comparatively small.

Sculptured Stone Crosses.—We have notices in Adamnan's work of the erection of crosses in Iona, before the writer's time, to mark the place of some notable occurrence. Thus on the spot where the aged St. Columba rested on his way from the barn to the monastery, upon the last day of his life, a cross was erected and fixed in a mill-stone (*Vita S. Col.*, lib. iii., c. 24). Another cross was raised at the spot, "before the door of the kiln," where Ernan, the uncle of the saint, suddenly died (lib. i., c. 35); and, if I am correct in my understanding of the passage, a third at the spot, twenty-four paces off, where the

---

[1] Stokes, *Early Christian Art in Ireland*, p. 173.

saint, who was approaching to meet his guest, was standing when Ernan fell.[1] But of the material or character of these crosses we know nothing.

In later days there were certainly several crosses in Iona, of which only two—St. Martin's, and the cross commonly called Maclean's—now remain perfect. These, together with fragments of others, and the names given to places in the local topography of the island, suggest that perhaps there once existed some fifteen or twenty of these striking monuments.

It is a curious fact that it is in the east of Scotland, north of the Forth, we find what appear to be the earliest of the Celtic crosses. These are not free-standing crosses, exhibiting at a distance the cruciform shape, but are sculptured upon great erect oblong slabs of stone. The noble free-standing crosses, such as the dignified and imposing cross of St. Martin at Iona, are regarded by archæologists as of a later date.

One noticeable feature will be found in all the crosses of Celtic origin. They are recessed or ornamented at the intersections of the arms with the shaft. A very common, but not universal, feature is the circle which surrounds the crossing, and connects the transverse and vertical limbs. A certain sign of a late date is the presence of foliageous ornament, the earlier specimens being adorned with one or more of such forms as interlacing ribbon-work, fret-work, bosses, twistings of serpentine forms, or

---

[1] The translator in the *Historians of Scotland* (vol. vi., p. 33) renders "restitit" *resided*, as I think, quite incorrectly.

other zoomorphic decoration, and what is known as "the escaping spiral" and "trumpet" ornament. A certain sign of a still later date than the earlier specimens of foliage is the presence of the figure of the Crucified upon the Cross. The earlier crosses, and the crosses which exhibited the purest and finest specimens of Celtic art, are symbolical, or merely decorative in their ornament.

If one may venture on a conjecture as to why it is the east of Scotland that has preserved the earliest type of Celtic cross, it may be suggested that after the expulsion of the Columban monks by King Naiton from the kingdom of the Picts, Irish influences were less likely to possess extensive power in that part of the country. The connection was in a measure interrupted. In the west the marked artistic superiority, which at a later period characterized Irish art, would, as I imagine, have more readily effected a substitution of better work for the rude crosses of an earlier time. Irish art in its decay, perhaps for the same reason, affected the west rather than the east of Scotland. Along the east of Scotland then, in the Pictish kingdom, we find the most primitive type; in the west the type both in its perfection and in its decline.[1]

The period to which the several groups of monumental crosses are to be assigned is still open to

---

[1] Beside Dr. Anderson's work, the student should consult Dr. John Stuart's superb volumes, the *Sculptured Stones of Scotland*, which exhibit with great beauty the elaboration and intricacies of the artistic designs.

much question. The best specimens of the decorated crosses we are led to believe are not to be connected with the period of early Celtic Christianity, and very competent authorities would place them not earlier at least than the beginning of the tenth century. More uncertainty attaches to the dates of the ruder examples and to the incised crosses. But Stuart gives weighty reasons for supposing that some of the crosses in the Pictish district of Scotland date from the early part of the eighth century,[1] that is, from the time of Adamnan and Cuthbert.

Christian Symbols in Caves.—We have already called attention to instances of the practice of the early Celtic monks retiring for a time to some place of solitude for the purposes of greater seclusion from the busy world of monastic life, and the exercise of a less interrupted devotion. Such a place of retirement was styled, in the ecclesiastical language of the day, a "Desert." The caves along the Scottish sea-coast would obviously afford many places not unsuited for this purpose, and in many instances local tradition is strong in connecting the names of eminent ecclesiastics with caves. Careful examination of these caves has in several cases discovered sculptures of Christian origin upon their rocky walls. To take the earliest instances, a cave about three miles from Whithorn has from time immemorial borne the name of "St. Ninian's Cave." Only a few years ago Sir Herbert Maxwell undertook the investigation of this cave, and after a large quantity of gravel and rubbish had been removed,

---

[1] *Sculptured Stones of Scotland*, vol. ii., preface, p. xvii.

he was rewarded by finding several well-defined specimens of sculptured crosses, in their character of an early date.

What is now the town of Dysart, on the coast of Fife, is believed to owe its name to the neighbourhood having once afforded a "Desert" to St. Serf. I do not know whether the cave has been examined with such thoroughness as that displayed by Sir Herbert Maxwell, but when Dr. Stuart published the second volume of the *Sculptured Stones* (1865) no distinctively Christian markings were found. The rock, however, it should be remarked, is of a soft sandstone, from which carvings would be easily removed by natural causes. According to the legend, read as the Third Lesson on St. Serf's Day (July 1st) in the *Aberdeen Breviary*, it was in the cave of Dysart that the devil engaged the saint in a theological discussion upon various knotty questions which are given at length in Wyntoun's *Cronykil* (book v., ch. xii.).[1] Finally the devil acknowledged himself beaten, and told the saint "he kend hym for a wys man," and so departed, never again to return.

At St. Andrews there is a cave that bears the name of St. Regulus; but Dr. Stuart observes, "The crumbling surface of the sandstone shows no remains of sculpture."[2] A few miles to the south, however, at Kinkell, the walls of a cave show sculptured crosses; and rounding Fifeness at a few miles to the south the

---

[1] Wyntoun was Prior of the monastery of St. Serf's, Inch, Lochleven, towards the end of the fourteenth century.
[2] *Sculptured Stones*, vol. ii., preface, p. lxxxviii.

caves of Caiplie show many crosses, some of them executed with an eye to artistic effect. There are other caves associated with the names of Scottish saints, such as St. Kiaran's, near Campbelton, St. Medan's on the Bay of Luce, and St. Monan's, near the village of that name in Fife. These "Deserts" of the early saints deserve a more thorough and systematic investigation than has yet been bestowed upon them.[1]

Bells.—Associations of much interest gather round the ancient bells of the Celtic Church. From the view-point of the student of art the earliest and most highly honoured of these relics are wholly devoid of merit. They are of the rudest construction, and entirely wanting in decoration. They are simply sheets of iron hammered into an oblong quadrilateral shape, and kept in position by rivets, a flattened loop of the same metal being attached to the crown of the bell as a handle.[2] Sometimes these iron bells were given a coating, inside and out, by being dipped into molten bronze. Some of the bells of a later date are cast in bronze, and assume some elegance of form; and occasionally the handle is slightly decorated. All the bells that have survived are small; and are in fact hand-bells. Not a single specimen of what could now be reckoned a church-bell has come down to us, and we have no reason to suppose that any such were hung in Scottish churches during the period with

[1] Many town-lands in Ireland, and at least six parishes, have names of which "Desert" forms a part.
[2] The ancient bell of the Irish missionary, St. Gall, in Switzerland, is of this type.

which we are dealing.¹ Yet, of little interest as are these bells considered merely as works of art, they have in many instances been regarded by the Celtic people of the country with profound reverence and even awe. It was doubtless mainly as personal relics of the ancient saints that they assumed this importance. If we did not know that the use of the " sacring-bell," with the elevation of the consecrated elements of the Eucharist, did not come into use till the twelfth century, we might be led perhaps to fancy that at least the smaller bells might have had in popular esteem some special sacredness attached to them as connected with this rite. But, so far as we know, these bells could have no ordinary sacred use, except

[1] The following are measurements of some interesting bells—

Bell	Height in inches	Breadth at the mouth in inches
Bell of Kilmichael Glassary, Argyleshire (Iron)	$3\frac{1}{4}$	$2\frac{1}{4} \times 1\frac{1}{2}$
Bell of Guthrie, Forfarshire (Iron)	7	$5\frac{1}{2} \times 4\frac{1}{2}$
Bell of Struan, Perthshire (Iron)	11	$7 \times 5\frac{1}{4}$
Bell of Birnie, Morayshire (Hammered Iron)	18	6×4
Bell of Birsay, Orkney (Iron)	12	9×7
Bell from the Broch of Burrian, North Ronaldshay	$2\frac{1}{4}$	2×1
St. Ringan's (*i.e.* Ninian's) Bell (Iron), in National Museum, Scotland	$6\frac{1}{2}$	$4\frac{1}{4} \times 4$
St. Columkill's Bell (Iron), in National Museum, Scotland	$10\frac{3}{4}$	8 imperfect
St. Fillan's Bell (Cast Bronze), in National Museum, Scotland	12	9×6
Bell of Insh, Inverness-shire (Cast Bronze)	10	$9 \times 7\frac{1}{4}$

To which for purposes of comparison may be added similar measurements of the famous *Bell of St. Patrick's Will*, composed of two pieces of sheet-iron, which is 6 inches high, and $5 \times 3\frac{3}{4}$ inches at the mouth.

that of calling the monastic brethren to prayer at the regular hours and in sudden emergencies.[1]

However the belief arose, supernatural powers and miraculous occurrences are often connected in the ancient legends with these bells. The Pope of Rome gave St. Ternan (see p. 46) a present of a bell when he visited that city, but the Scottish saint, thinking it too troublesome to take it with him, left it behind. The bell, however, followed him in his journey, day by day, all the way till he reached Scotland. Such, at least, is the tale read for edification in the churches of Scotland up to the time of the Reformation.[2]

St. Mungo's bell was reckoned of such importance that it figures to this day, with his salmon, his bird, and his tree, in the arms of the city of Glasgow, as it had done previously in the seals of some mediæval bishops of that diocese. In St. Patrick's legendary history, his bell—indeed more than one bell—plays an important part (see p. 224). In the equipment he provides for a missionary priest a bell figures together with a chalice; and it was thought worth recording the name of the attendant, Sinell of Cell Dareis, whose duty it was to carry the saint's hand-bell. When St. Patrick ordained Fiech to be bishop, he gave him a crozier and a bell, as badges of his office.[3] According to the legend of St. Kiaran, who is repre-

---

[1] See Adamnan's *Life of St. Columba*, lib. ii., c. 43; lib. iii., c. 14; lib. i., c. 7; lib. iii., c. 24.
[2] See *Aberdeen Breviary*, Feast of St. Ternan.
[3] See Dr. Reeves' *St. Patrick's Bell and Shrine*, prefixed to Marcus Ward's fine chromo-lithographic plates representing these relics (Belfast, 1850).

sented as the first bishop of Ossory, St. Patrick, meeting the saint in Italy, told him to go and build a monastery in the centre of Ireland. Kiaran, complaining that the direction as to the locality was vague, St. Patrick gave him a bell, which would be mute till he came to the right spot, but would then ring out, and so it came to pass St. Patrick's own bell was enshrined (between A.D. 1091—1105) in a case ornamented with gold, silver, and gems; and the practice of thus honouring and protecting ancient bells was common in Ireland. In Scotland we still possess two enshrined bells. One of these is the Bell of Kilmichael Glassary (in Argyleshire), the highly ornamental shrine of brass being regarded by experts as in the style of the twelfth century. Dr. Anderson (*ut supr.*, p. 208) suggests the possibility that the bell thus honoured is no other than the bell made for St. Columba's contemporary, St. Moluag, bishop of Lismore. The memory of this saint was much honoured in the mediæval Church, his festival (June 25) appearing in the Kalendar of the *Aberdeen Breviary* as (in technical language) a "double major." Now the Second Lesson appointed for that day relates that at one time the saint wanted a neighbouring smith to make for him a square iron bell (*ferream campanam et quadratam*) which he much needed. The smith pleaded in excuse that he had no coals, whereupon St. Moluag, "trusting the very great goodness of God Almighty," left the smithy, and soon returned with a bundle of reeds, which he asked the smith to substitute for coals. The smith was an angry man, and threw the bundle and the iron together into the furnace to convince the saint of his folly; but, to the astonishment of all, the iron was soon fit for the hammer, and the bell was made, which was ever after held in great honour in the Church of Lismore, even "to this day" (*i. e.* 1510). The Kilmichael Glassary Bell and its shrine are now preserved in the National Museum of Antiquities, Edinburgh.

The other enshrined bell that remains in Scotland is the Guthrie Bell, preserved at Guthrie Castle in Forfarshire. It is of hammered iron, and the shrine (perhaps fourteenth-century work) is of bronze decorated originally with silver, gilding, and precious stones. So far as I know, outside the Celtic Church the shrining of bells is unknown.

The religious awe with which these ancient relics were regarded has its curious exemplification in the statement of Giraldus Cambrensis, that the people of Scotland, Ireland, and Wales considered an oath made upon one of the ancient bells or croziers as much more binding than an oath made upon the Gospels. In Ireland the Bell of St. Columkille went under the native name of "God's Vengeance," in reference to the awful consequences of perjury that were to be apprehended by those who had falsely sworn upon this sacred object. Among another Celtic people, the peasants of Brittany, the Bell of St. Winwaloe, who is believed to have flourished in the fifth century, was held in great veneration in modern times.[1]

---

[1] *Acta Sanctorum* of the Bollandists, March 3.

In many cases, as in Scotland, a special custodian was appointed for the safe guardianship of a bell or of a crozier, and his office was endowed by the great and wealthy with grants of land. The honourable office of warden of the bell, as with other similar offices, sometimes became hereditary. And it is in a measure, perhaps, due to the connection between the tenure of the land and the possession of the bell that we owe the preservation of some of these interesting relics. The history of these hereditary offices belongs, however, to a period later than that with which we are dealing.

However largely superstitious fears entered into the feelings associated with these ancient bells, something may, surely, be credited to the sentiment of personal reverence for the memory of the great servants of God, who laboured so devotedly for the Christianizing of Scotland.

It is a very interesting fact that in more than one instance bells of the quadrate shape and obviously of the ancient type have been preserved by the country people of Scottish parishes in the Highlands without any other protection than that afforded by the prevailing sentiment of the neighbourhood. In the upper part of Glenlyon, in an old graveyard, an ancient bell, of hammered iron, shaped quadrangularly, and fastened with rivets, has stood, it is believed for centuries, in the open air. The Bell of St. Finan (bronze) lies on a flat stone in the graveyard of Eilean Finan, in Loch Shiel, in Inverness-shire. The Bell of Insh-on-the-Spey is of cast bronze. It used to stand a few years ago (I do not know whether it still so stands) on the sill of one of the church windows. An interesting local tradition, the more valuable, perhaps, because its real historical significance is quite unperceived by the people of the district, declares that it was once removed, but kept crying perpetually, "Tom Eunan, Tom Eunan" (*i.e.* "the hill or mount of Eunan"), till it made its way back to the hill of that name on which the church is erected. Now Eunan, as we have seen (p. 147), was one of the curious phonetic transformations of Adamnan. It may well be, as Dr. Anderson thinks, that this bell was in some very real way connected with the ninth abbat of Iona and biographer of St. Columba. Another bell that formerly had the reputation of always returning to its own place is the Bell of St. Fillan, from Strathfillan, a fine bronze bell, now deposited in the National Museum of Antiquities, Edinburgh. As late as the end of the last century, when the bell was most culpably removed by an English tourist and conveyed to his home in England, St. Fillan's bell was believed to possess supernatural powers, more particularly in cases of lunacy.[1]

The Pastoral Staff.—Among other personal relics of the Celtic saints, the staff, or crozier, was held in great veneration. Like the bell, it possessed not only personal associations, but also the associations which connect themselves with an ecclesiastical office of high dignity. Again, as in the case of the bell, the rude original was by and by protected by a handsome

---

[1] Anderson, *Scotland in Early Christian Times*, p. 192.

covering of metal, highly decorated and gemmed. And, as with the bells, in process of time an hereditary keeper of the relic is often found, honoured by an endowment in land attached to his office.

Scotland still possesses some remains of the croziers of the Celtic Church. While to the art student the decorated crook of St. Fillan's crozier, presently to be described, is valued as a beautiful specimen of ornamentation, to the student of ecclesiastical antiquity incomparably the most interesting of these remains is the "Bachul More" ("the great *baculus*," or staff), now in the possession of the Duke of Argyll at Inverary Castle. This is, with reason, believed to be the staff of St. Moluag, bishop of Lismore, whose death is placed five years before that of St. Columba, and the story of whose miraculous bell (see p. 307) formed part of the lectionary of the mediæval Church. The metal covering has almost wholly disappeared, and we see a plain rude staff of wood, but two feet ten inches in length, with a slightly-curved head, probably the actual blackthorn stick carried by the bishop thirteen hundred years ago.[1] If the staff, as it now exists, gives us the original size, it will not be unique. One of the figures at the door of the Round Tower at Brechin holds a short staff with a crook; and one of the illustrations of the Gospels of MacDurnan (about A.D. 925), now in Lambeth Library, represents St.

---

[1] The name Moluag deserves a word of comment. "The original name is Lugaidh, pronounced Lua, with the endearing suffix *oc*, Luoc or Luoch, and the honorific *mo*, Molua, Moluoc, Moloch." (Bishop Forbes, *Kalendars of Scottish Saints*, p. 409.)

Luke with a crooked stick about the same size as St. Moluag's.[1] It may be added that the hereditary keeper of the crozier of St. Moluag possessed a small freehold of land in virtue of his office.

Another example of an ancient Scottish crozier is that of St. Fillan, whose memory still survives in the name of the village of St. Fillans, beautifully situated at the east end of Loch Earn, and well known to summer tourists in Perthshire. The lovely valley of Strathfillan, in the west of Perthshire, also owes its name to this saint. Bishop Forbes would place his life in the second half of the eighth century. The account given of his history in the Lessons of the *Aberdeen Breviary* surpasses the histories of most Celtic saints in the extravagance of its absurdities. The saint was born with a stone in his mouth, which phenomenon so annoyed his father that he had the infant thrown into a lake. After a year he was recovered by good Bishop Ybar, who found him playing with the angels. In after years he was seen through a chink in his cell, by a prying servant of the monastery, engaged in writing in the dark by the light which flowed from his left hand, which served as a candle. "By divine permission" a tame crane in the monastery pecked out the spying eye of the servant; but St. Fillan, on the supplication of the brethren, restored its power of sight. A wolf killed one of a yoke of oxen employed by the saint, but on the prayers of the saint the wolf came back, submitted

[1] This figure is given in Stuart's *Sculptured Stones*, vol. ii., p. 78.

himself to harness, and supplied the place of his victim. After these and other such marvels, it was no wonder that the saint's fame was great and widespread. It is a fact in history that what was believed to be his arm enshrined in silver played an important part at the battle of Bannockburn. The head of his crozier, which had been carried from Scotland by a member of the family of the hereditary keeper, who emigrated to Canada, was recently recovered, and is now deposited in the National Museum of Antiquities in Edinburgh. With its exquisite character as a work of art we are not here concerned; but a careful examination of the relic has revealed an inner metal crook, which would seem to show that the original staff had been twice enshrined in a decorated covering.[1] This crozier-head very well exhibits an interesting peculiarity in the form assumed by the Celtic croziers. The curve of the crook, having made about the third of a circle outward, drops suddenly into a short rectilineal, or almost rectilineal, pendant. This feature, which also appears in the illuminated representations of saints in the Irish manuscripts, is regarded by archæologists as a characteristic mark of the Celtic crozier.[2]

The staff of St. Columba, given by him to St. Mungo, was preserved, enshrined in gold and precious stones, at Ripon. And we possess historical evidence

[1] See Anderson, *Scotland in Early Christian Times*, pp. 219—224.
[2] The name *Quigrich*, applied to St. Fillan's crozier, is of uncertain meaning, and a discussion of the speculations that have been made on the subject would be out of place here,

that the croziers of St. Donnan, St. Fergus, and St. Munn were preserved and regarded with veneration in different parts of Scotland; but they are now unfortunately lost or in concealment. Here, as elsewhere, Irish hagiology and Irish art is much richer than the colonial Church in Scotland. From St. Patrick's famous crozier—"the staff of Jesus"—downwards, illustrations of our subject are abundant in Ireland.[1]

Books and Book-Covers.—Our solitary relic, the Book of Deer,[2] suffices to show that the same spirit of loving reverence for the sacred Scriptures that manifests itself so abundantly in the decoration bestowed upon the Irish manuscripts was not absent from Scotland. The artistic ornament of this book is indeed much inferior to many of the splendid specimens in the sister island, but there is enough to show us something of the care and patience of those who were perhaps native scribes. The text is written with elegance, and the decorated capitals and borders exhibit much artistic skill. The human figures indeed are rude and even grotesque; but this is a feature in more or less degree exhibited in most of the best Irish manuscripts. There is no attempt at realistic representation; and one cannot doubt, however we

---

[1] The story of the exchange of staffs made by St. Columba and St. Mungo has been already related (p. 57). So, too, the story of the marvel of St. Ninian's staff. A miracle connected with the staff of St. Cainnech is related by Adamnan (*Vita S. Columbæ*, lib. ii., c. 13). This saint is known as Canice in Ireland, and Kenneth in Scotland.

[2] See p. 248.

may account for it, that the avoidance of verisimilitude is deliberate and designed.[1]

We have seen how devoted St. Columba was to the transcription of the sacred writings, and certainly before the close of the seventh century the scribe (*Scribhnidh* or *Schribhneoir*) appears as a recognized member of the Irish monasteries. The high esteem in which he was held may be inferred from an Irish canon of the eighth century, which makes the mulct for the blood of a scribe equal to that for the blood of an abbat or bishop. Again, it was ordained that stealing from "a king, a bishop, or a scribe" should receive the same penalty. "Sometimes in Scotland," writes Mr. Warren,[2] "in the seventh to tenth centuries, a scribe was elected to be an abbat or a bishop, and the head of a diocese or monastery thought that it added to the dignity of his position to be able to append the title of 'scriba' to his name... The eighteenth and thirtieth Abbats of Iona, in 797 and 978, and the Bishop of the Isles of Alba in 961, are also recorded to have been scribes."

Some of the manuscripts written, or supposed to have been written, by eminent saints were naturally objects deeply venerated, and they were honoured by being enclosed in decorated cases of bronze or silver, beautifully ornamented and adorned with gold and valuable stones. A case of this kind was known as a *cumdach*. Some fine examples of these book-shrines

---

[1] A striking example from an Irish Psalter in St. John's College, Oxford, is given in the article "Miniature" in Smith and Cheetham's *Dictionary of Christian Antiquities.*
[2] *Liturgy and Ritual of the Celtic Church*, p. 18.

are preserved in Ireland. None of those that have come down to us can be assigned to a date earlier than the tenth century. The books which they contained were doubtless in many instances much earlier. Historically one of the most interesting is the case that enshrines a Psalter ascribed, not without some probability, to the penmanship of St. Columba, which was believed to carry with it victory in battle. Hence this Psalter was known as the *Cathach* or "Battler."[1] Fifty leaves and the silver *cumdach* of this precious relic still remain, and are deposited by the chief of the O'Donnells in the Museum of the Royal Irish Academy. The old order for its use in war was that it should be "sent thrice right-wise around the army of the Cinel Conaill (one of the northern branches of the Hy Neill to which St. Columba belonged) when they are going to battle. . . . And it is on the breast of a co-arb or a cleric, who to the best of his power is free from mortal sin, that the Cathach should be, when it is brought round the army."[2]

No specimen of a Scottish *cumdach* has been preserved, so far as we know. But we possess a notice[3] of a silver *cumdach* made by Fothad, the first of that name, Bishop of St. Andrews about 950, for a copy of the Gospels, which was to be seen, as we learn

---

[1] Another relic of St. Columba used as a "Battler" was a crozier of his carried as a standard into battle and called *Cath-bhuaidh*, that is *Battle-victory*. See Reeves, *Historians of Scotland*, vol. vi., p. xcix.

[2] See Reeves' *Life of St. Columba* (*Historians of Scotland*, vol. vi. p. xlii).

[3] In Bower's continuation of Fordun's history, *Scotichronicon*.

elsewhere, on the high altar at St. Andrews in the middle of the fourteenth century. The case was inscribed with a Latin elegiac couplet setting forth that "Fothad, who is chief bishop (*summus episcopus Scottis*) for the Scots constructed this case (*thecam*) of an ancient Gospel."

Another notice of a Scottish *cumdach* informs us that St. Ternan's copy of St. Matthew's Gospel was preserved at Banchory Ternan "enclosed in a metal case covered with silver and gold."[1]

There is reason also for thinking that the large square case-like ornament which is pictured as suspended from the neck of three of the four Evangelists in the illustrations of the Book of Deer represents a *cumdach*. It is not uncommon in similar illustrations to find each of the Evangelists carrying a book, doubtless meant for his own Gospel, in his hand; and it is not improbable that in the Book of Deer the figures are represented as carrying each his own Gospel suspended in its case by straps round his neck. It is certain[2] that leather satchels for carrying books were so suspended on the breast by straps, and in an Irish *Life of St. Columba*[3] that saint is recorded to have made a hundred such satchels.[4] Lastly, the pillar-stones of Scotland afford,

---

[1] *Martyrology of Aberdeen.*
[2] See Adamnan's *Life of St. Columba*, lib. ii., c. 8.
[3] Translated by Mr. Hennessey, and appended to the second volume of Skene's *Celtic Scotland.*
[4] Whatever a *polaire*, by some taken to mean a satchel, may have been, it is certainly, in the passage referred to, spoken of as distinct from satchels. "A hundred fine artistic *polaires;* with a hundred croziers, with a hundred satchels."

according to Dr. Stuart,[1] some examples of *cumdachs* represented in the sculptures.

Not only did Ireland, the mother-church of the Scotland colony, construct book-shrines, but we know that in the daughter-church of Northumbria a similar practice existed. Eadfrid, bishop of Lindisfarne (698—721), wrote and illuminated the famous "Lindisfarne Gospels," one of the most beautiful manuscripts of its kind. His successor, Bishop Ethelwold, caused a case to be made for it by "Bilfrith the anchorite," a skilful worker in metals, who adorned it with pure silver, gold, and gems.

[1] *Sculptured Stones*, vol. ii., p. 25.

APPENDICES.

I. THE *ALTUS* OF ST. COLUMBA.

AMONG the writings attributed to St. Columba is a very remarkable Latin poem, commonly known as the *Altus*, from the first words of its opening lines—

> Altus Prosator Vetustus
> Dierum et Ingenitus.

The verses were first printed by Colgan, and in our own time by Dr. Todd in the second Fasciculus of his *Liber Hymnorum*. A fresh interest has been awakened in this ancient sacred poem by its recent publication under the editorship of the Marquis of Bute.[1]

The poem consists of twenty-two stanzas (or *capitula*) of twelve lines each (with the exception of the first, which consists of fourteen lines), the initial letters of the stanzas exhibiting an alphabetical arrangement, which would, doubtless, serve as a help to memory. The Latinity is rude, and the text, perhaps, corrupt; certainly in more than one place the sense is very obscure. But Lord Bute's estimate is hardly exaggerated when he writes—"The intrinsic merits of the composition are undoubtedly very great, especially in the latter *capitula*, some of which the

---

[1] *The Altus of St. Columba*, edited, with a prose paraphrase and notes, by John, Marquess of Bute, 1882.

editor thinks would not suffer by comparison with the *Dies Iræ.*" The ancient belief of the people attached many benefits, temporal and spiritual, to those who recited these verses. The devil would not know their path to waylay them; their enemies would fail to find them; angels would attend them as they sung the poem; it was a protection against sudden death; peace would reign in the house where it was chanted, and plenty and prosperity would wait upon the singers. Pope Gregory the Great, as legend relates, was pleased with the poem which had been sent to him by St. Columba, and was granted to perceive the angels listening as it was recited in his presence. The Pope saw but one fault in it—it was a mistake to confine the praises of the Blessed Trinity to only one stanza.

Through the kindness of the Rev. Anthony Mitchell, whose poetic gifts are well known to his friends, I am permitted to print here his very able and spirited rendering of the *Altus*—a task which, when the many difficulties attendant upon it are considered, seems to me to have been accomplished with singular skill. We are given a glimpse, in the stanza commencing with the letter I, of the writer's strange conceptions of the physical causes of clouds and rain. The obscure and difficult stanza commencing with U baffles interpreters. Orion is probably to be understood in a mystical sense, as signifying some evil spiritual power or anti-Christian system. The other parts of the poem, however, are intelligible, and several of the stanzas are marked by a high degree of imaginative power. The prominence given to the conceptions of good and evil angels falls in with striking features in Adamnan's story of St. Columba's life; and the tendency shown to dwell upon what is dark and terrible will seem natural to those who have justly apprehended the character of the reputed author of the poem.

THE *ALTUS* OF ST. COLUMBA.

ANCIENT of days, enthroned on high!
    The Father unbegotten He,
Whom space containeth not, nor time,
    Who was and is and aye shall be:
And one-born Son, and Holy Ghost,
    Who co-eternal glory share,
One only God, of Persons Three,
    We praise, acknowledge, and declare.

BEINGS celestial first He made;
    Angels and archangels of light,
In Principalities and Thrones,
    And mystic rank of Power and Might:
That Love and Majesty Divine
    Not aimlessly alone might dwell,
But vessels have, wherein to pour
    Full wealth of gifts ineffable.

CAST from the highest heights of heaven,
    Far from the Angels' shining state,
Fadeth from glory Lucifer
    Falling in scorn infatuate.
Angels apostate share his fall,
    Steeled with his hate, and fired with pride,
Banishèd from their fellows bright
    Who in the heavenly seats abide.

DIREFUL and foul, the Dragon great,
    Whose deadly rage was known of old,
The slippery serpent, wilier
    Than living thing that earth doth hold:

From the bright realm of heaven he could
    A third part of the stars entice,
In Hell's abyss to quench their light,
    In headlong fall from Paradise.

EARTH next and heaven, sea and sky,
    Found shape within the Eternal mind,
And stood created. Next appeared
    The fruitful herb, and tree in kind:
Sun, moon, and stars that climb the heavens,
    And birds and fishes, great and small,
And beasts and herds and living things,
    And man to be the king of all.

FROM every glad Angelic tongue
    Soon as the stars sprang into light,
Burst forth the wondering shout that praised
    The heavenly Creator's might.
And as His handiwork they viewed
    Arose from loving hearts and free,
The tribute due of wondrous song
    Swelling in sweetest harmony.

'GAINST Satan's wiles and Hell's assault
    Our primal parents could not stand:
And into new abysses fell
    The leader and his horrid band;
Fierce forms, with noise of beating wings,
    Too dread for sight of mortal eye,
Who fettered, far from human ken,
    Within their prison houses lie.

HIM, banished from his first estate,
    The Lord cast out for evermore;
And now his wild and rebel crew
    In upper air together soar;

Invisible, lest men should gaze
   On wickedness without a name,
And, breaking every barrier down,
   Defile themselves in open shame.

IN the three quarters of the sea
   Three mighty fountains hidden lie,
Whence rise through whirling waterspouts
   Rich-laden clouds that clothe the sky:
On winds from out his treasure-house
   They speed to swell bud, vine, and grain;
While the sea-shallows emptied wait
   Until the tides return again.

KINGS' earthly glory fleeteth fast,
   And for a moment is its stay:
God hath all might: and at a nod
   The giants fall beneath His sway;
Neath waters deep, with mighty pangs,
   In fires and torments dread they rave,
Choked in the whirlpool's angry surge,
   Dashed on the rocks by every wave.

LIKE one that through a sparing sieve
   The precious grain doth slowly pour,
God sendeth down upon the earth
   The cloud-bound waters evermore:
And from the fruitful breasts of heaven,
   While changing seasons wax and wane,
The welcome streams that never fail
   Pour forth in rich supplies of rain.

MARK how the power of God supreme
   Hath hung aloft earth's giant ball,
And fixed the great encircling deep,
   His mighty hand supporting all

Upon the pillars which He made,
    The solid rocks, and cliffs that soar,
And on the sure foundations rest,
    That stand unmoved for evermore.

None doubteth that within the earth
    Glow the devouring flames of hell,
Wherein is prisoned darkest night
    Where noisome beasts and serpents dwell,
Gehenna's old and awful moan,
    And cries of men in anguish dire,
And falling tears, and gnashing teeth,
    And thirst, and hunger's burning fire.

Of realms we read beneath the world
    Where the departed spirits wait,
Who never cease to bend the knee,
    To Christ, the only Potentate.
They could not ope the written Book,
    Whose seven seals none but He might break,
Fulfilling thus the Prophet's word,
    That He should come, and victory make.

Paradise and its pleasant glades
    From the beginning God did make;
Out of whose fountain-head there flow
    Four rivers sweet, earth's thirst to slake.
And midmost stands the tree of life,
    With leaves that neither fade nor fall,
With healing to the nations fraught,
    Whose joys abundant never pall.

Questions the Singer,—"Who hath climbed
    Sinai the mountain of the Lord?
The echoing thunders who hath heard,
    And ringing trumpet-blast outpoured?

Who saw the lightning's dazzle whirl,
  And heaving rocks that crashed and fell,
Mid metors' glare and darts of flame,
  Save Moses, judge of Israel?"

RISETH the dawn;—the day is near,
  Day of the Lord, the King of kings;
A day of wrath and vengeance just,
  Of darkness, clouds, and thunderings;
A day of anguished cries and tears,
  When glow of woman's love shall pale;
When man shall cease to strive with man,
  And all the world's desire shall fail.

SOON shall all mortals trembling stand
  Before the Judge's awful throne,
And rendering the great account
  Shudder each hateful sin to own.
Horror of night! when none can work,
  Wailing of men, and flooding tears,
Opening the books by conscience writ,
  Riving of hearts with guilty fears.

THE trump of the archangel first
  Shall blare afar its summons dread;
And then shall burst earth's prison bars,
  And sepulchres give up their dead.
The ice of death shall melt away,
  Whilst dust grows flesh, and bone meets bone,
And every spirit finds again,
  The frame that was before her own.

UNLOOSED from the pole of heaven,
  Speedeth Orion's evil ray,
Far from the clustered Pleiades,
  Over the Ocean's trackless way.

Two years shall pass ere he return
   From East again with tortuous speed,
To shine instead of Hesperus.—
   Whoso hath wisdom let him read.

Xrist the Most High from heaven descends
   The Cross His sign and banner bright.
The sun in darkness shrouds his face,
   The moon no more pours forth her light.
The stars upon the earth shall fall
   As figs unripe drop from the tree,
When earth's broad space is bathed in fire,
   And men to dens and mountains flee.

Yonder in heaven the angel host
   Their ever-ringing anthems raise,
And flash in maze of holy dance,
   The Trinity Divine to praise.
The four-and-twenty elders cast
   Their crowns before the Lamb on high,
And the four Beasts all full of eyes
   Their ceaseless triple praises cry.

Zeal of the Lord, consuming fire,
   Shall whelm the foes amazed and dumb,
Whose stony hearts will not receive
   That Christ hath from the Father come.
But we shall soar our Lord to meet,
   And so with Him shall ever be,
To reap the due rewards amidst
   The glories of Eternity.

II. THE LEGEND OF ST. REGULUS.

THE city of St. Andrews owes its name to the belief that at that place in early times were deposited some of the sacred relics of the apostle St. Andrew. The legend, as believed in mediæval times in Scotland, relates that in the time of the Emperor Constantius, the son of Constantine the Great, there was at Patras, in Achaia, a holy man named Regulus, keeper of the relics of St. Andrew, who had suffered martyrdom in that town. The emperor resolved to avenge upon the people of Patras the crucifixion of the saint, to invade the town, and carry off with him the relics of the Apostle. An angel appeared by night to Regulus, and instructed him to take from the shrine three fingers of the right hand, the large arm-bone, one tooth, and a knee-cap. On the emperor carrying off the remaining relics to Constantinople, the angel appears again to Regulus, and bids him with certain companions convey what he possessed to the western parts of the world, and there found a church to the perpetual honour and glory of St. Andrew. For two years he voyages, blown about by storms of the sea, and at length lands in the country of the Scots, and comes to "Swine's wood" (Mucros), afterwards Kilrymont. The angel indicates the place where he should build a church. Regulus sends his companions to preach the word of God to the "Picts, Scots, and Britons." Innumerable multitudes are converted, and the faith is received by Hungus, king of the Picts, with his army. Such is the story as told in the *Aberdeen Breviary*. This legend, together with two somewhat earlier forms, has been examined with much care by Skene,[1] who also takes into view notices of an

---

[1] *Proceedings of Society of Antiquaries, Scotland*, vol. iv., pp. 301—307, and *Celtic Scotland*, vol. ii., pp. 261—268.

Irish Regulus or Riaghail of Muicinis (*insula porcorum*), an island in Loch Derg, whose name appears in the Irish Martyrologies at the 16th of October. Several of the Scottish Kalendars record the Scottish Regulus on the same day, and so suggest that Regulus of Muicinis and Regulus of Mucros (*promontorium porcorum*) are the same person. Hence Skene concludes, "that the historic Regulus belongs to a Columban Church founded among those which Columba established among the southern Picts during the last years of his life, and at the same time when Cainnech of Achaboe had his hermitage there" (*i. e.* in the north-eastern corner of Fife).

There can be no question that the special cultus of St. Andrew in Scotland is of very early date. But the inquiry as to how this came to be so is, I believe, wholly insoluble by the historical monuments of antiquity that are in our hands ; and I am certain I should be only wasting time in discussing here the various conjectures on the subject. The notion that the Picts were of the race of the inhabitants of Scythia, of which country St. Andrew was the reputed Apostle, may have originated the cherished belief. Or there may possibly be some foundation of truth for the supposition that the Irish St. Riaghail brought to Fife some reputed relics of the Apostle. But, after all, this is mere guess-work.[1]

Every visitor to St. Andrews is struck with the stately and beautiful tower of the little church of St. Regulus. It is by far the most interesting, as well as the most ancient, of the many ecclesiastical ruins that mark what was for many centuries a great centre of Church life and influence. But its date is certainly several centuries later than even St. Riaghail, who himself is later by two centuries than

---

[1] Some of my reasons for demurring to accept Mr. Skene's view may be found in a paper contributed to the *Proceedings of the Society of Scottish Antiquaries,* 1892-3.

the legendary monk of Patras. So high an architectural authority as Sir Gilbert Scott (*Lectures on Mediæval Architecture*, vol. ii., p. 24) is not able to speak with confidence as to the date of the building. But it may with reason be declared to be not earlier than the tenth century, and more probably belongs to the eleventh or twelfth.

III. ST. MARGARET'S GOSPEL BOOK.

THE following very interesting account of the volume is taken from Mr. Falconer Madan's *Books in Manuscript*, 1893.

"Six years ago a little octavo volume in worn brown binding stood on the shelves of a small parish library in Suffolk, but was turned out and offered at the end of a sale at Sotheby's, presumably as being unreadable to country folk, and capable of being turned into hard cash wherewith a few works of fiction might be purchased. The contempt for it thus displayed was apparently shared by the cataloguer, who described it as " Latin Gospels of the Fourteenth Century, with English Illuminations." For the sum of £6 it passed into the Bodleian Library, and came to be catalogued as an ordinary accession. It was noticed that the writing was of the eleventh century, and that the illuminations were valuable specimens of old English work of the same century, comprising figures of the four evangelists of the Byzantine type, which was common in the west of Europe; the drapery, however, colouring and accessories were purely English. The book itself was seen to be not the complete Gospels, but such portions as were used in the service of the Mass at different times of the year. Further, it was observed that a poem in Latin hexameters had been written, apparently before the end of the same century, on a fly-leaf of the volume, which began by thanking Christ for 'displaying miracles to us in our own days,' and went on to describe how this very volume had been carried in the folds of a priest's robe to a trysting-place, in order that a binding oath might be taken on it; but that unfortunately it had been dropped, without the priest observing it, into a stream, and given up for lost. But a soldier of the party at last discovered it, plunged head first into the river, and brought it up. To every one's intense surprise, the beautiful volume was entirely uninjured, 'except two leaves, which you see at each end, in which a slight contraction appears from the effect of the water, which testify the work of Christ in protecting the sacred volume. That this work might appear to us still more miraculous, the wave washed from the middle of the book a leaf of silk. May the King and pious Queen be saved for ever, whose book was but now saved from the waves!' The silk was, no doubt, pieces placed loosely in the book to preserve the illuminations from contact with the page opposite; and, sure enough, a leaf at each end of the book showed unmistakable crinkling from immersion in water. But who were the King and Queen? By a curious accident connected with the name of Margaret, a lady to whom this story was told remembered a similar incident in Forbes-Leith's *Life of St. Margaret of Scotland*, and the mystery was solved. There in the Life is a passage in prose, beginning: 'She had a book of the Gospels beautifully adorned with gold and precious stones, and ornamented with the figures of the four evangelists, painted and gilt. . . . She had always felt a particular attachment for this book, more so than for any of the others which she usually read.' Then follows a story almost identical with the one given above, with some variant but not discrepant details. It, too, mentions the pieces of silk and the contraction on certain leaves, and adds that it was found lying *open* at the bottom of the river."

The MS., of which Mr. Madan tells the story just related, is very small, consisting of only thirty-eight leaves. The size of the pages, according to measurements kindly supplied to me by the Rev. H. A. Wilson, Fellow of Magdalen College, Oxford, is $7\frac{11}{16} \times 4\frac{5}{16}$ inches. The passages from the four Evangelists which form the contents of the book correspond to certain liturgical gospels, but are arranged so as to follow one another according to their places in the four Gospels of the New Testament canon. There is no indication of the days upon which the passages were used in the service of the Church. Each series of extracts is preceded by a full-page miniature representing one of the Evangelists. Notices of this most interesting MS. by Mr. F. Madan, Prof. Westwood, and Mr. F. E. Warren may be found in the *Academy* (Aug. 6, Aug. 20, Sept. 3, 1887).

A fac-simile reproduction of the recently found manuscript is now (1893) in preparation under the editorship of Mr. Forbes-Leith.

IV. THE KIRKMADRINE EPIGRAPH.

THE following interesting note on the inscription on the monumental stone at Kirkmadrine was contributed to the writer by the Rev. Edmund McClure—

"Your Lordship's conjecture as to *Ides* being part of a proper name, and not, as is generally assumed, the remnant of *idest*, is doubtless right. An eminent Cambridge Epigraphist puts *idest* out of the question. I would venture to suggest that the name here intended was *Idesus.* *Id* is a frequent element in early Cymric names, *e. g.* Id-nert, Id-loes, &c. (*Cambro-British Saints*), Id-cant, Id-guallon (*Lib. Landav.* new edition), and *Esu-s* is the name of a Celtic Deity, and is probably cognate with Gothic *Ansi*, Anglo-Saxon *ôs*, Old Norse *áss* (cf. Oswald, Osbjorn). It appears in the Gaulish names *Esu-nertus*, *Esu-genus*. *Viventius*, though Latin in form, does not occur, as far as I can find, among Latin personal names. It may represent an early British *Vevendi*. In the 'Cartulaire de Redon,' p. 339, appears a certain *Gueguentus*, and, at p. 281, a *Gueguant*. Fick's *Vergleichendes Wörterbuch*, fourth edition, gives a stem *Veios*, as represented in Irish *Fe* = anger: this would give the *Gue* in Gueguentus, while the stem *Vindo-s*, white, would furnish the latter part; cf. *Barrivendi*, an inscription in Carmarthenshire. *Mavorius*, if, as your Lordship suggests, it may also be read *Maiorius*, is simple enough. If *Mavorius* is the right reading, it can hardly be one of the many personal names derived from *Mars*, e. g. *Marius*, *Mamercus*, *Martialis*, &c., and may be a Latinized form of some such name as *Maguor*. The *et* coupling the last two of three names is possible in late Latin.

"The meaning of Madrine, with the accent on the last syllable, as Professor Rhys has pointed out to me, is very obscure. One is tempted to regard the *Ma* as representing the endearing prefix *Mo*, and some such name as Draighen (*Martyr. of Doneg.*)."

Another stone at Kirkmadrine with a similar ☧ has still legible
SET
FLOREN
TIVS
commonly read -s et Florentius.

INDEX.

ABERCORN, 184, 189
Abernethy, 119, 202
Adamnan, St., 144—147
,, *Life of St. Columba*, 80, 135—143
,, book, *Concerning the Holy Places*, 145, 148—151
,, transformation of name, 147
Adamnan of Coldingham, 186
Adrian, St., 74, 198
Aebba, St., 170, 185, 187
Aebba, another abbess of that name, 199
Aelred, biographer of Ninian, 23
Aid the Black, 253
Aidan, King, 102
Aidan, St., 159, 177, 261
Ailbe, St., 69
Alban, term, how applied, 11
Aldfrid, King, 144
Aldhame, 72
Aldhelm, St., 71
Altus of St. Columba, 87, 321—328
Amhra Choluimchille, 104, 111
-an, as a suffix, 86
Angels, prominence given to agency of, 220
Antonine, rampart of, 12
Apurcrossan, 120, 152
Architecture, early Celtic, 293—296

Arculf, Bishop, of Gaul, 148—151
Ard-comarb, 129
Artgaile, King, 152
Bachul More, the, 312
Baithene, 116, 128, 133
Baldred, St., 71
Ballachulish, wooden figure found at, 22
Bamborough, 144, 160
Banchory-Ternan, 47
Bangor (in Down), 104
Bangor, Antiphonary of, 212, 240
Bards, Irish, 103
Bee-hive cells, 293, 294
Bells, Celtic, 304—311
Birr, Synod of, 145
Black Rood, the, 288
Blaithmac, 154
Boece, Hector, 45
Boisil, St., 168
Brechin, 202
Brigid, St., 71, 97, 171, 259
Britius, St., 71
Brude, King, 92, 96
Cainnech, St., 97
Calpornius, 35
Candida Casa, 26, 29, 30, 191
Canice, St., 97
Cathach, St. Columba's Psalter, 318
Caves, Christian symbols in, 302

INDEX.

Cenn Cruaich, the idol, 22
Ceolfrid, 145, 146
Chad, St., 160
Ciaran, St., 69
Clog Rinny, 31, 305, 309
Clonard, 87
Coinmed, meaning of word, 103
Coldingham, 170, 185, 186, 188, 199
Coleraine, battle of, 104
Colman, frequency of name, 86.
Colman, Bishop of Lindisfarne, 178—180
Columba, St., 80—121
Columban of Luxeuil, 232
Columban Mocu Loigse, 228
Columban monasteries in Scotland, 119, 120
Comarb, 128
Comgall, St., 97, 104
Communion in both kinds, 239
Consecration, by one bishop, 89
,, *per saltum*, 89
Cooldrevny, battle of, 94
Copying of books, 132
Corman, 158
Coroticus, 34
Cronan, Bishop, 252
Crosses, sculptured Celtic, 299
Croziers, Celtic, 311—316
Culdees, *see* Keledei
Culross, 47
Cumdach, a book shrine, 317—319
Cuthbert, St., 161—176

Dallan Forgaill, 103, 104, 108, 110
Dalmeny, 147
Dalriada, 91
Dalriada, British, 96, 103
David, St., of Menevia, 56
Dead, prayers for, 226

Declan, St., 69
Decurion, office of, 35
Deer, Book of, 239, 248, 249
Demons, prominence given to agency of, 220
Desert, 181, 303
Diarmit, 114, 117, 118, 133
Diarmit, King, 253
Donnan, St., 120
Dorbbene, 232
Dornoch, 202
Drumceatt, Synod of, 103, 260
Druids, 99
Dryhthelm, story of, 181
Dunbar, 189
Dunblane, 202
Duncan, King, 267
Dunfermline, 279
Dunkeld, 119, 155, 202
Dunnichen, battle of, 189

Eadfrid, Bishop of Lindisfarne, 183
Easter controversy, 245
Eata, 160, 168
Egfrid, King, 185, 188, 190
Eigg, 120
Eilean-na-Naoimh, 112, 119, 294
Enoch, St., 32, 53, 54
Episcopate in Celtic Church, 250
Ermenburga, 188
Etchen, Bishop, 88
Ethelfrid, 157
Ethelreda, Queen, 185
Ethelwold, Abbat of Melrose, 182
Eucharist, 218
,, peculiar rites, 235 238

Fasting, 131
Finan, Bishop, 177

INDEX. 337

Findchan, 253
Finnian, St., of Clonard, 87
Finnian, St., of Moville, 86
Fordun, 40
Fordun, John of, 40
Fortrenn, 155
Fothad, Bishop, 289

Gall, St., 71
Gemman, 87
German, St., Bishop of Auxerre, 210
Gildas, 243
Gruoch, 268

Hadrian, wall of, 12
Heathenism, character of Celtic, 21, 98
Hexham, see of, 191
Hilda, St., double monastery of, 171

Ibar, St., 69
Inishowen, 90
Inismurray, 95
Innisboffin, monastery on, 179
Invocation of saints, 225
Iona, physical features of, 122—125
,, origin of name, 127
,, ravaged by Danes, 153

Jocelyn, Bishop of Glasgow, 51
Jocelyn, monk of Furness, 51
,, his Life of St. Patrick, 70
,, character of his Life of Kentigern, 64—73

Keledei, 201—207
Kenneth, St., 97
Kenneth MacAlpine, King, 154
Kentigern, St., life of, 49—58
Kilfinichen, 254

Kilwinning, 88
Kingarth, 120
Kirkmadrine, monumental sculptures at, 15

Lanfranc, Archbishop, 282
Leader Water, 161
Lent, beginning of, 282
Lex Innocentium, 194
Lindisfarne, physical features of, 159
,, ravaged by Danes, 153
,, Gospels, 183
Lismore, island of, 119, 202
Lochleven, St. Serf's Isle in, 202, 280
Lochmaree, 121
Loup, St., Bishop of Troyes, 210

Macbeth, 267
Machar, St., 120
Maelrubha, St., 120
Magi, 99
Major, John, 73
Malcolm Canmore, 271
Margaret, St., 267—291
Margaret, St., Gospel book of, 273, 331
Maude, Queen, 270, 276
May, Isle of, 197
Mayo, English monastery of, 179
Melrose, 160, 180, 184, 199
Missal, the Stowe, 230, 231
Mixed chalice, 232
Mo, prefix, 69, 312
Moinen, St., 69
Molaise, St., 95
Moluag, St., 120, 312
Monan, St., 199
Monasticism, introduced by Ninian, 28
Monifieth, 202

Y

INDEX.

Monks, military service of, 105
Monnena, St., 72
Monymusk, 202
Muintir Choluimchille, 128
Mulling, Book of, 240
Mungo, St., 49—58
Mungo, meaning of name, 54
Muthill, 202
Mylne, Alexander, 203

Naiton, King, 146
Niall Frassach, King, 152
Niduari Picts, 170
Ninian, St., life and labours of, 24—28

Olave, St., 201
Olave Tryggvesen, King, 200
Opus Anglicum, 280
Ordain, use of word, 262
Oronsay, 95, 119
Oswald, King, 140, 157, 158
Oswy, King, 178

Palladius, legend of, 40—46
Patrick, St., early history of, 34, 39
  ,,   ,, bells of, 224, 305
  ,,   ,, writings of, 33, 34, 39, 211—217
Pelagianism among the Britons, 209
Picts, a Celtic race, 18
Polaire, book-cover, 319
Potitus, 35

Regulus, St., legend of, 329
Ringan, corruption of Ninian, 31

Ripon, 161, 167
Ritual of Celtic Church, 233
Ronan, 177
Ronecht, the, 46
Rosmarky, 202
Rosnat, monastery of, 32
Round Towers, 296

St. Andrews, Keledei at, 202
Sanda, 147
Scannlan Mor, 104
Scotia, a name for Ireland, 20
Scribes, honour paid to, 317
Serf, St., 47, 74
Skye, Isle of, 136

Tara, Synod of, 145
Teilo, St., 72
Ternan, St., 46
Teviot, River, 172
Thenew, Thenog, *see* Enoch, St.
Tine, River, 165
Tiree, 119, 124
Tonsure, Celtic form of, 241
Trumwin, Bishop, 189
Tuathal, Abbat, 155
Turgot, Prior of Durham, 271
Tynynghame, 72, 184

Ultan, St., 69

Valentia, Roman province of, 13
Vinnin, 88

Walafrid Strabo, 154, 232
Whithorn, ancient cross at, 18
Wilfrid, 185, 189

York, Colidei at, 205

Richard Clay & Sons, Limited, London & Bungay.

PUBLICATIONS

OF THE

Society for Promoting Christian Knowledge.

PUBLICATIONS

OF THE

Society for Promoting Christian Knowledge.

THE
FATHERS FOR ENGLISH READERS.

A Series of Monographs on the Chief Fathers of the Church.

Fcap. 8vo., cloth boards, 2s. each.

LEO THE GREAT.
By the Rev. CHARLES GORE, M.A.

GREGORY THE GREAT.
By the Rev. J. BARMBY, B.D.

SAINT AMBROSE: his Life, Times, and Teaching.
By the Ven. ARCHDEACON THORNTON, D.D.

SAINT ATHANASIUS: his Life and Times.
By the Rev. R. WHELER BUSH (2s. 6d.).

SAINT AUGUSTINE.
By the Rev. E. L. CUTTS, B.A.

SAINT BASIL THE GREAT.
By the Rev. RICHARD T. SMITH, B.D.

SAINT BERNARD: Abbot of Clairvaux, A.D. 1091—1153.
By the Rev. S. J. EALES, M.A., D.C.L. (2s. 6d.).

SAINT HILARY OF POITIERS, AND SAINT MARTIN OF TOURS.
By the Rev. J. GIBSON CAZENOVE, D.D.

SAINT JEROME.
By the Rev. EDWARD L. CUTTS, B.A.

SAINT JOHN OF DAMASCUS.
By the Rev. J. H. LUPTON, M.A.

SAINT PATRICK: his Life and Teaching.
By the Rev. E. J. NEWELL, M.A. (2s. 6d.).

SYNESIUS OF CYRENE, Philosopher and Bishop.
By ALICE GARDNER.

THE APOSTOLIC FATHERS.
By the Rev. CANON SCOTT-HOLLAND.

THE DEFENDERS OF THE FAITH; or, The Christian Apologists of the Second and Third Centuries.
By the Rev. F. WATSON, D.D.

THE VENERABLE BEDE.
By the Rev. CANON BROWNE.

PUBLICATIONS OF THE SOCIETY

Non-Christian Religious Systems.

Fcap. 8vo., cloth boards, 2s. 6d. each.

Buddhism: Being a Sketch of the Life and Teachings of Gautama, the Buddha.
By T. W. RHYS DAVIDS. With Map.

Buddhism in China.
By the Rev. S. BEAL. With Map.

Christianity and Buddhism: a Comparison and a Contrast.
By the Rev. T. STERLING BERRY, D.D.

Confucianism and Taouism.
By Professor DOUGLAS, of the British Museum. With Map.

Hinduism.
By Sir MONIER WILLIAMS. With Map.

Islam and its Founder.
By J. W. H. STOBART. With Map.

Islam as a Missionary Religion.
By CHARLES R. HAINES (2s.).

The Coran: Its Composition and Teaching, and the Testimony it bears to the Holy Scriptures.
By Sir WILLIAM MUIR, K.C.S.I.

The Heathen World and St. Paul.

This Series is intended to throw light upon the Writings and Labours of the Apostle of the Gentiles.

Fcap. 8vo., cloth boards, 2s. each.

St. Paul in Greece.
By the Rev. G. S. DAVIES. With Map.

St. Paul in Damascus and Arabia.
By the Rev. GEORGE RAWLINSON, M.A., Canon of Canterbury. With Map.

St. Paul at Rome.
By the late Very Rev. CHARLES MERIVALE, D.D., D.C.L., Dean of Ely. With Map.

St. Paul in Asia Minor and at the Syrian Antioch.
By the late Rev. E. H. PLUMPTRE, D.D. With Map.

FOR PROMOTING CHRISTIAN KNOWLEDGE.

The Home Library.

A Series of Books illustrative of Church History, &c., specially, but not exclusively, adapted for Sunday reading.

Crown 8vo., cloth boards, 3s. 6d. each.

Black and White. Mission Stories.
  By H. FORDE.

Charlemagne.
  By the Rev. E. L. CUTTS, B.A. With Map.

Constantine the Great: The Union of Church and State.
  By the Rev. EDWARD L. CUTTS.

Great English Churchmen; or, Famous Names in English Church History and Literature.
  By the late W. H. DAVENPORT ADAMS.

John Hus. The Commencement of Resistance to Papal Authority on the part of the Inferior Clergy.
  By the Rev. A. H. WRATISLAW.

Judæa and her Rulers, from Nebuchadnezzar to Vespasian.
  By M. BRAMSTON. With Map.

Mazarin.
  By the late GUSTAVE MASSON.

Military Religious Orders of the Middle Ages: the Hospitallers, the Templars, the Teutonic Knights, and others.
  By the Rev. F. C. WOODHOUSE.

Mitslav; or, the Conversion of Pomerania.
  By the late Right Rev. R. MILMAN, D.D.

Narcissus: A Tale of Early Christian Times.
  By the Right Rev. W. BOYD CARPENTER.

Richelieu.
  By the late GUSTAVE MASSON.

Sketches of the Women of Christendom.
  By MRS. RUNDLE CHARLES.

The Churchman's Life of Wesley.
  By R. DENNY URLIN, Esq.

PUBLICATIONS OF THE S.P.C.K.

ANCIENT HISTORY FROM THE MONUMENTS.

[*This series of books is chiefly intended to illustrate the Sacred Scriptures by the results of recent Monumental researches in the East.*]

Fcap. 8vo., cloth boards, price 2s. each.

ASSYRIA, FROM THE EARLIEST TIMES TO THE FALL OF NINEVEH.
By the late GEORGE SMITH, of the Department of Oriental Antiquities, British Museum.

BABYLONIA, THE HISTORY OF.
By the late GEORGE SMITH. Edited by the Rev. Professor SAYCE.

EGYPT, FROM THE EARLIEST TIMES TO B.C. 300.
By the late S. BIRCH, LL.D., &c.

PERSIA, FROM THE EARLIEST PERIOD TO THE ARAB CONQUEST.
By the late W. S. W. VAUX, M.A., F.R.S. A New and Revised Edition, by the Rev. Professor A. H. SAYCE.

SINAI, FROM THE FOURTH EGYPTIAN DYNASTY TO THE PRESENT DAY.
By the late H. SPENCER PALMER. A New Edition, revised throughout by the Rev. Professor SAYCE.

LONDON:
NORTHUMBERLAND AVENUE, CHARING CROSS, W.C.;
43, QUEEN VICTORIA STREET, E.C.
BRIGHTON: 135, NORTH STREET.

www.ingramcontent.com/pod-product-compliance
Lightning Source LLC
Chambersburg PA
CBHW030001240426
43672CB00007B/783